THROUGH THE
# Kitchen Window

# THROUGH THE
# Kitchen Window

Women Writers Explore the Intimate
Meanings of Food and Cooking

EDITED BY

## Arlene Voski Avakian

BEACON PRESS / BOSTON

Beacon Press
25 Beacon Street
Boston, Massachusetts 02108-2892

Beacon Press books
are published under the auspices of
the Unitarian Universalist Association of Congregations.

01  00  99  98      8  7  6  5  4  3  2

Text design by Iris Weinstein
Composition by Wilsted & Taylor

The Library of Congress has catalogued the hardcover edition of this work as follows:
Through the kitchen window : women writers explore the intimate meanings
of food and cooking / edited by Arlene Voski Avakian.
p.  cm.
ISBN 0-8070-6508-0 (cloth)
ISBN 0-8070-6509-9 (paper)
1. Food  2. Cookery.  3. Feminism.  I. Avakian, Arlene Voski.
TX355.5.T47    1997
641.5—dc20        96-46130

To the women in my family who served up love and art with their daily creations of *havgitov basterma*, *abour*, all the pilafs, dolmas, and kebabs, *lahmajoon*, and the special dishes taking endless hours of preparation—*enginar*, *media*, *manti*, *herissah*, *keufteh*, and *atleakmak*. My mouth waters and my heart overflows.

# Contents

## PART ONE: INHERITANCE

# PART THREE: RESOLUTIONS

⫶ ⫶ ⫶

# List of Recipes

## MEAT AND POULTRY

## SAUCES, MARINADES, AND CONDIMENTS

## BREADS

## DESSERTS

# Acknowledgments

My first heartfelt thanks goes to the authors in this volume who took time to write essays based on faith that this book would really happen, and whose wonderful pieces made the work of putting this anthology together truly joyful. They were also very patient through some of the difficulties the collection encountered on its way to becoming a book, and many were enormously supportive, encouraging, and helpful. Neeti Maden, my agent, had a deep and unwavering understanding of the concept of this book and an incredible reservoir of diplomacy when it was needed. My editor, Tisha Hooks, had continual enthusiasm for the project and worked magic with her prodigious editorial skills. My partner Martha wrote her story for me and listened to all of mine and I am, as always, thankful to her.

❑: ❑: ❑:

# Introduction

All during my teenage years at about 5:30 every weekday evening our phone rang. My mother, grandmother, and I all knew that it was my mother's sister, my Aunty Ars, calling as she did every night to ask what my mother was making for dinner. I tried to be out of the kitchen so that I would not have to answer the phone and be a party to this discussion of food and cooking. It's not that I didn't want to speak with my aunt. I was her favorite because, as she often told me, she had wanted a girl and had had only boys. Nor was I reluctant to be a part of this nightly conversation about cooking because I hated food; on the contrary I loved to eat, especially some of the Armenian foods we had regularly. My annoyance at this phone call was like the feelings I had when the women on both sides of my extended family complain about having to decide what to cook every night. Although none of the men cooked, these discussions revealed that the women cooked to please their men. While they also noted that children, particularly boys, could be finicky about what they ate, the major focus was on the men, pleasing them and how difficult that task could be.

I could not have told you then, in the 1950s, why I hated my Aunt's nightly phone call or my female relatives' discussions about cooking. We had no language for our feelings about the injustices we suffered as women in those days. I only knew then that cooking was something I would refuse to do. That refusal became public when I proclaimed to my horrified family that I hoped that by the time I got married, something I assumed I would do, "scientists" would have produced an all-purpose pill so that I could escape cooking and the daily dilemma of deciding what to make for dinner.* I described my future table; set for two with a pill in the center of each white, china plate. This rejection of cooking was a small resistance, but even this little rejection of the expectations of me as a woman nurtured a sense of self that would eventually blossom in the Women's Liberation Movement.

Why then, forty years later, have I undertaken to edit a book about women and food which is focused on cooking and even includes recipes? Unexpectedly, I became a cook. As expected, I did marry, and since "science" had not developed the breakfast, lunch, and dinner pill, there seemed no alternative to cooking. We could not afford to eat out much, and in the early 1960s "take out" generally meant deli or Chinese American food. Someone had to cook, and it never occurred to me that that someone might be my husband. I loved to eat too much to do without good food, so I learned to cook. Like other children of immigrants I wanted to become an American, but beyond an early desire for Wonder bread and Lipton Instant Soups, I didn't want to eat like an American. By the time I was in my early teens I came to agree with my family that Americans just didn't know what good food was about. During the Kraft Theater Presentation commercials, we laughed hilariously at recipes featuring marshmallows, Miracle Whip, and gelatin. Even my father, who never did anything at the stove except make his famous omelettes, shook his head and smiled at the fantastic concoctions we considered inedible. There was never any question whatsoever in my family about the superiority of our food. Always after we stopped laughing someone would describe the American palate

*Marjorie De Vault in her book *Feeding the Family: The Social Organization of Caring Work* (Chicago: University of Chicago Press, 1991) reports that the women she interviewed for her study have the same complaints about having to negotiate children's and husbands' preferences while creating meals that are not monotonous. Their own needs and desires are subordinated.

using an Armenian expression that loosely translated means "they just don't know the taste of their own mouths."

Years later when I wrote my autobiographically based doctoral dissertation, food was a major character. In fact, a group of friends and colleagues who read each chapter as it came out of the printer complained that my detailed descriptions of food and meals made them ravenous. Later when the dissertation was published as a memoir, even reviewers commented on the role of food.* *Through the Kitchen Window* has grown out of the many conversations about food, eating, cooking, and feminism I have had with women and men, some of whom read my memoir and then told me their own food stories.

When I sent out the call for papers for this book, I was excited by the prospect of learning more about other feminists' relationship to food. When the first pieces came in I knew that I had embarked on an important project. The stories, poems, and essays I received evoked both tears and laughter. They spoke of oppression and resistance. They told of individual and cultural transformations. I knew I had the beginnings of a wonderful collection, but needing more material I sent out a second call for submissions. It was after this second call that I received the following letter from Ruth Hubbard, a feminist scientist who has been involved in women's and progressive movements for many years:

Dear Arlene,
I did not answer your . . . earlier letter because, to tell you the truth, I was irritated at the idea of collecting a set of feminist writings about women and food, in-

---

*Arlene Avakian, *Lion Woman's Legacy: An Armenian American Memoir* (New York: The Feminist Press: 1992).

cluding recipes. Haven't we had enough of women being viewed through the kitchen window. . . . I don't find a feminist linking of *Kinder, Kuche, Kirche* much more inviting than the more standard one . . .

My mother was of the generation of Central European women . . . who escaped the kitchen by becoming first a music teacher and then a physician. As far as I remember, she never cooked a meal until we emigrated to the United States as a result of the Nazi takeover of Austria in 1938, at which point I was fourteen. After that, she cooked our meals and saw to it that they were nutritionally balanced, even when we had very little money. . . . But she was never invested in her culinary prowess, never cooked from recipes, and never baked a cake or prepared a "fancy" dish.

Her own mother, though a "housewife" . . . was an avid reader and considered her domestic obligations as interruptions. A kosher Jewess, she prepared the traditional sabbath and passover meals, but with no fanfare. This by contrast to my father's mother who was very much the Viennese Hausfrau. But in my childhood home this contrasting domesticity was the source of family jokes, not of pride or joy. Call it anti-woman, but that's the way it was. My father's mother was esteemed for her caring, including her always being there with a favorite dish when any of her seven grown children were sick, but the culinary art itself—the fact that she insisted that noodles must be made at home and never bought—seemed comical rather than praiseworthy . . .

I tend to cook and eat simply, and have memories of mostly discomfort around the festive meals where a hostess felt hurt because I was never able to eat more than I felt like eating—no more than enough to still my hunger. "I am sorry; I cannot eat any more" was, and still is, my standard phrase. . . . I assign no virtue to this, though some people seem to do so. I just sense a very strict line of demarcation between having eaten enough and too much. And too much doesn't feel good. Or rather, it feels awful.

The current American preoccupation with eating, overeating, weight, body shape, body image irritates me. I don't think there is an "ideal" body shape and the evidence that "obesity" is a health risk is far from clear. What is clear is that alternate binging and starving oneself is. I just hope that your book is not going to feed into the preoccupation with "overeating" in a world where not having enough to eat is such a pressing problem. I am not saying "think of the poor . . ." (fill in the blank with your current choice of starving population), but, to be perfectly honest, I cannot help but feel that it is self-indulgent to put together a U.S. collection on "women and food," when women and feminists are confronting so many problems and engaged in such important struggles in this country and elsewhere.

Please take these comments in the spirit of positive, sisterly criticism in which they are intended.
Sincerely,

*Ruth Hubbard*

I had been expecting criticism for a book on women and food. Because cooking has been conceptualized as part of our oppression, "liberation" has often meant freedom from being connected to food. Yet I never intended this book to contribute to the obsession of the over-privileged. It is, instead, a critical interrogation of women's relationship to food, of gender and domesticity as it has been constructed in various cultures, and of the ways that race, class, ethnicity, and sexuality impact our relationship to food. Just as we now look at the quilts crafted by African American women in slavery as both the result of enforced labor imposed upon them by the slaveholders and as the creations of enormously skillful craftswomen or even artists, I think we need to look again at food and its preparation. Cooking is something that was and continues to be imposed on women, but it is also an activity that can be a creative part of our daily lives. As such, the work of cooking is more complex than mere victimization.

Food preparation, like housework and what Michaela di Leonardo has called "kin work," is part of the invisible labor of women.* Though absolutely central to our survival, it is what is taken for granted. If we delve into the relationship between women and food we will discover the ways in which women have forged spaces within that oppression. Cooking becomes a vehicle for artistic expression, a source of sensual pleasure, an opportunity for resistance and even power. By reclaiming cooking we insure that we are not throwing the spaghetti out with the boiling water.

I conveyed these thoughts to Ruth Hubbard in a letter and received the following response:

> Dear Arlene,
>
> I found your letter very helpful. I now have much more understanding for why any number of friends of mine love to prepare meals for their friends, or even just for themselves. I had never thought about the really quite obvious fact that preparing a meal can be a sign of caring and of loving communication, because food just has never been an avenue of communication for me.

*Michaela di Leonardo, *The Varieties of Ethnic Experience: Kinship, Class and Gender Among California Italian Americans* (Ithaca: Cornell University Press, 1984).

It would be more correct to say, a positive avenue of communication. The fact is that as I have thought about the subject since our correspondence began, I have realized that I have quite negative connotations with food.

They mostly turn around people expecting me to eat more than I want to eat, starting in childhood with my mother. There was a time when I suppose I was around three or four, when I often used to throw up after going to bed. In retrospect, I think it simply was the result of being urged to eat too much. No one "forced" me, but there was sufficient fuss about my "not eating," meaning not eating more than I wanted, that I guess I habitually overate and then threw up. I don't know whether my mother caught on or what happened. I did stop throwing up after a while.

Your letter also helped me to understand why my husband George and also some friends are sometimes almost hurt by my lackadaisical attitude about preparing food. I guess it makes them feel that I don't care about *them*, whereas I just don't care about the food. . . . Of course, as with all such loaded issues, the more people want me to be positively involved with food, the more I couldn't care less about it . . .
In Sisterhood

*Ruth Hubbard*

In this volume, the explorations of women's relationships to food—the cooking, the eating, the sharing—offer the opportunity to delve into concrete and daily activities which are deeply embedded within their cultural and political contexts. The pieces span a wide range of topics by women of many different ethnicities from a variety of regions in the world. Neither professing the commonalities among women, nor locating women exclusively in their own particularities, these works address the complexity and interconnectedness of social constructions.

While feminists may debate the effect of various family forms on women, none would deny the centrality of family to the production and reproduction of gender. Notions of motherhood are inextricably entwined with feeding the family. Caroline Urvater writes movingly of the guilt she felt for not providing her young children with the proper home-cooked meals that symbolize what it means to be a good mother. Yet, the work of feeding a family can provide the opportunity for creativity for women who are denied other outlets. With her own dreams thwarted first by the ultimatums of her father and then by the demands of her family, Clare Coss's mother's kitchen became her "domain" and her cooking highly sensual. Gloria Wade-Gayles describes Black women's own kitchens as temples where wounds of oppression, often inflicted by the white women in the kitchens where Black women labored, were healed by creating wonderful food and finding the space to bond with each other.

Even as we focus on food as nourishment and creator of community, we must also consider its antithesis—hunger and the economic, political, and personal issues that surround it. In Ireland certain foods denote a history of famine and oppression. Marie Smyth sees her mother's choice to pass on her knowledge of culling the wild foods that once kept her ancestors alive as a political decision, insisting on facing the history of both the famine and British culpability. The food stamp program may stave off starvation for contemporary women and children in economic need in the United States, but we learn from Trudy Condido's essay that providing nutritious and pleasing meals for herself and her daughter on their meager allotment is an enormous struggle.

For many of the contributors who are immigrants to the United States, connections to food are profoundly impacted by feeling alien in an alien culture. Some, like Ketu Katrak, write of their longing for the taste and smell of home, food carrying culture and childhood. Others write about food as mediating conflicts between cultures and classes. Ester Shapiro, blends her two cultures through fantastic Cuban/Jewish feasts, borrowing one ingredient or process from one culture to transform the other, flaunting cultural traditions about food as she rejects traditional admonitions about women's sexuality. Dorothy Allison's emigration was from the south to the north. There she dreams of her vegetarian lovers cooking, eating, and feeding her the now forbidden foods of her poor childhood: barbecue, greens flavored with fat back or bacon, biscuits, and cornbread smothered with butter.

These stories about women and food provide glimpses into the lives of women in their various contexts and tell us about the meanings embedded in women's relationships to food. They introduce us to cooking and eating as a way to maintain once colonized and now fragile histories; as creativity, sensuality, nurturance, love; as imposed, compulsory, and oppressive; as a way to combine diverse, even opposing, traditions; to claim or reclaim food rituals, transforming them or creating new ones and in doing so revising personal or collective histories. Thinking about women and food can help us understand how women reproduce or resist and rebel against prevailing ideas of what they should be and codes that determine what they can do—gender constructions as varied as the worlds we see when we look in through their kitchen windows. The voices in these pieces and the recipes themselves provide a rich array of dishes, a sumptuous feast—food for thought about our histories, our current shifting contexts, and our future agendas.

▯▮ ▯▮ ▯▮

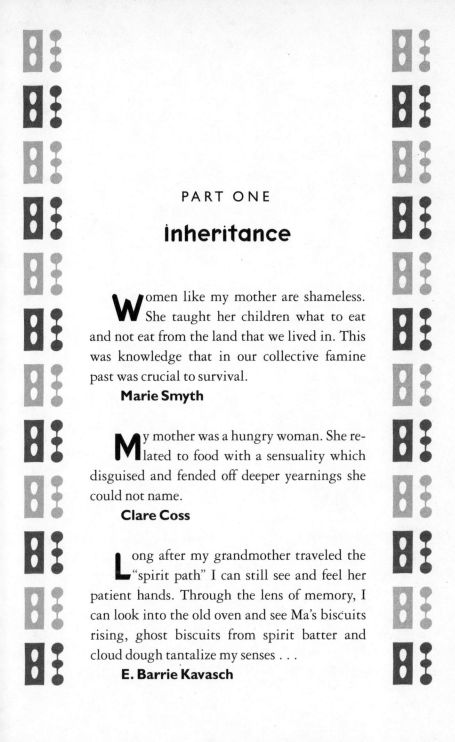

PART ONE

# Inheritance

**W**omen like my mother are shameless. She taught her children what to eat and not eat from the land that we lived in. This was knowledge that in our collective famine past was crucial to survival.

**Marie Smyth**

**M**y mother was a hungry woman. She related to food with a sensuality which disguised and fended off deeper yearnings she could not name.

**Clare Coss**

**L**ong after my grandmother traveled the "spirit path" I can still see and feel her patient hands. Through the lens of memory, I can look into the old oven and see Ma's biscuits rising, ghost biscuits from spirit batter and cloud dough tantalize my senses . . .

**E. Barrie Kavasch**

# My Mother/Her Kitchen

## Clare Coss

**M**y mother was a hungry woman. She related to food with a sensuality which disguised and fended off deeper yearnings she could not name. Her appetites never were satisfied.

She had wanted to be a nurse in New Orleans, her hometown. Her father did not permit it. "No daughter of mine will nurse strange men." She became a schoolteacher. Marriage to a Yankee delivered her from the hated classroom. They moved to New Jersey. She loved my father, my brother, and me. We became her focus. She dedicated her life to us. The kitchen in our home was her domain: "Cooking is my first love, my outlet."

I remember she had trouble getting through the hours of darkness, logged by the chimes of the mantelpiece clock. After her nights of phantasmagoric wanderings she sailed downstairs at dawn to drop anchor in the kitchen. Let out the dog, throw crumbs to the birds, take in the milk delivery, squeeze fresh orange juice. Feed-the-family rituals made nothing specific become something definite. Shopping, cooking, presenting, and consuming lashed down the corners of daylight, protection from the gusts of her oceanic energies.

A creative cook, she embellished her traditional New Orleans recipes: from gumbos to pralines to Spanish rice (each grain separate). Mother loved to eat, relished each bite: aroma, taste, texture. Her pleasingly zaftig body was a source of incredible heat and comfort. While my father and brother appreciated what she placed before us, I turned the dining table into territory for rebellion.

I challenged her over food. Became a picky eater. "You're too skinny. You have to eat more" was her litany as she forked my leftovers onto her plate. It was a necessary battlefield but a hard one because she was such a good cook. It was the one place I could separate from her overzealous solicitation for my welfare in a noticeably dramatic way. Too much. Too much. Gasping for air, my mutinous disinterest was sustenance that made me different from her and gave me space. From six to twelve years old, food was the weapon of war as she tried to fortify my active athletic being with the consistency and power of her balanced meals.

When I was sent off to boarding school for my high school years, I found I too had a ravenous appetite and really enjoyed new and international dishes. I was quite shocked to come across a raw onion in a salad. I thought people only ate cooked onions. At first the sharp flavor seemed barbaric. I began to appreciate and long for the classic Creole gifts from Mother's kitchen: crab gumbo and chicken jambalaya.

The last time Mother cooked for me she was visiting an old New Orleans friend out on Long Island who invited me to come out from the city for dinner and to stay overnight. They greeted me at the door, flushed and excited. The familiar fragrance of onions sautéed slowly in a heavy black iron skillet hung in the air. They had prepared chicken jambalaya for the three of us. Her friend kept saying, "Yawl won't believe Ali's been at it all afternoon. We've chopped and measured and peeled and seared and stirred each and every little ingredient." They were having a great time. I was glad to see Mother happy in the kitchen again. And she was pleased to see me enjoy seconds and thirds of her favorite dish.

❚❘ ❚❘ ❚❘

# Chicken Jambalaya

Jambalaya (a Creole word, means a diverse mixture)

This recipe was written out by my mother in 1959. She scrawled at the top, "I use the wedding present heavy iron Dutch Oven pot." My parents were married in 1921. I tried out this recipe in the same inherited pot, substituting only one ingredient: extra virgin olive oil for "oleo."

I four pound chicken
½ square inch of ham, if you have ham on hand
2 carrots
I stalk celery
2 large white onions
2 cloves garlic
I piece lemon peel (about a grated teaspoon full)
I bay leaf
2 whole cloves without seeds
I cup ripe tomatoes, skinned
3 sprigs thyme and parsley (each)
2 quarts water
2 tablespoons extra virgin olive oil
salt and pepper to taste
I cup rice

Clean, cut, and season chicken with salt and pepper. Brown well in olive oil in Dutch oven. Brown onions in olive oil in separate pan. Add to browned chicken. Add carrots and tomatoes chopped fine. Then add minced herbs, garlic, lemon peel, and bay leaf. Simmer gently for 10 minutes. Pour over 2 quarts of boiling water, stir, add ham, season with salt and pepper to taste. Set on low heat, cover, and simmer slowly 45 minutes or until near tender. Add I cup well-washed rice with diced celery stalk. Press down into the sauce and boil fast uncovered for 20 minutes, stirring occasionally to make sure rice does not stick to bottom of pan. Season again to taste. Serve chicken with rice in the sauce. Serves 4 to 6.

# Pecan Pralines

1 cup dark brown sugar
1 cup white sugar
2½ cups pecan meats
½ cup water
2 tablespoons butter

Dissolve sugar in water and boil to the thread stage, stirring constantly for about 4 minutes. Add butter and pecan halves and cook until syrup forms a soft ball when dropped in cool water. Cool without disturbing, then beat until somewhat thickened but not until it loses its gloss. Drop by teaspoon onto waxed paper on a cookie sheet. The candy will flatten out into cakes. Makes about 30 pralines.

  *Secret ingredient.* Mother scribbled at the bottom of her recipe, "The secret of delicious pralines is to have mostly pecans with just a little bit of sugar holding them together." Watching Mother make pralines was an incredibly sensual experience. After beating the mixture, she kneaded it bare-handed, then dropped a small portion onto the cookie sheet from her fingers. She licked her fingers constantly. I told her once to stop, but she forgot in a minute. I know the other secret ingredient in her recipe is the hand-to-mouth pleasuring of her palate.

❙❙ ❙❙ ❙❙

# Sand Plum Jelly

## Karen Coody Cooper

The women call an alarm.
"Car's coming!"
Shirttails fly to our faces
Arming us against the roostertail of dust.
The sand plums thrive on the shoulders of backwoods
   dirt roads.

The squat, frail sand plum trees,
Confronted by willowy aunts and uncles,
Yield tart golden orbs plunked into tin pails.

The jars of sand plum jelly,
    lined on storage shelves,
    look like a beekeeper's product
      tinged with pale rouge and glints of sun.

The jelly sparkles like jewels.
Amber, topaz, sunset and salmon colors.
Grandma knew each batch by its hue
"This was when Euless and his kids helped."
"The rosy ones are when you were here."
"The pale is from the drought."
The jelly was both bounty and art.

It recorded history, you see.
Events beyond the kitchen's reach,
Stacked in the root cellar,
In the memories of fledged offspring.
The jelly was riches and thrift.
The jelly was farm house repast.
The jelly was my family working together.

The jelly was summer and childhood.
The jelly was Grandma and everything I treasured.
The jelly was beautiful.

Light gently played through each jar
And cast a pink-gold aura throughout the tiny house
Where my strongest memories of women and love began.

There are no sand plums where I live.
But memory endures.

䷀䷀䷀

# Rice Culture

Julie Dash

I come from a family of rice eaters, a home where Uncle Ben was never invited to dinner. Uncle Ben's converted rice is not rice—it's "like rice." Kind of like what German *spritzal* is to elbow macaroni and cheese. Kind of like rice in a bag. If my great Aunt Gertie had lived long enough to see rice in a perforated plastic bag being tossed around a pot of boiling water—she would not have lived to the age ninety-nine. Aunt Gertie, the doyenne cook in our family, would have folded her apron in disgust and given up her title. My family is seriously radical about the cooking and serving of rice. We don't do bags floating in water. We don't do converted rice. In my house, Rice-a-Roni is totally unacceptable.

We come from South Carolina, a region where rice has always been an issue. We come from a long line of Geechees. We are the descendants of African captives that worked the low country and sea islands that stretch out along the coastlines of both South Carolina and Georgia. Geechees, or Gullahs as we are called by anthropologists, are rice eaters of the highest order. Some of our older family members, like Aunt Gertie, would have a serving of rice with *every* meal. For breakfast they would eat rice with milk, butter, and sugar; lunch was anything over rice. Dinner could include macaroni and cheese or any other starchy foods, but there would always be a serving of rice as well. Call it tradition, call it courage, call it what you may, the bottom line is Geechees gotta have it!

Before we were rice eaters we were rice planters and harvesters.

For centuries rice was cultivated along Africa's coastal regions; especially in the Senegal-Gambia region. During America's peculiar institution of slavery, that same Senegal-Gambia region of Africa supplied nearly 20 percent of all the slaves imported to South Carolina.

In 1685, Captain John Thurbar piloted one of many slave ships from Africa to South Carolina. Stashed among his human cargo was a bag of Golden Madagascar rice seeds. According to historians, Thurbar left a bushel of those seeds with his friend, a Dr. Woodward, when he reached Charleston, South Carolina. In the years that followed, the South Carolinian African captives played a major role in establishing a powerful rice culture in the antebellum South. Their labor and early technological knowledge of cultivating this difficult crop led to a rice aristocracy among southern planters long before cotton was King.

Carolina rice became renowned because of its superior quality compared with all other varieties of rice throughout the world.

Some 209 years after Captain Thurbar dropped off his cargo on Market Street, Gertrude Prunella Dash was born in Charleston, South Carolina. Born in 1894, Gertrude would become my Aunt Gertie.

Gertrude began her early education at Mrs. Saunder's School and the Avery Institute in Charleston. Gertrude believed in careful preparation. She had a love for music which led to studies as far away as New York's Columbia University and the Julliard School of Music. When she returned home, Gertrude Prunella Dash became the supervisor of music for the county of Charleston, for "Colored." She taught music, she married and raised three children, and she cooked. During those cooking, cleaning, toddler years, she became Aunt Gertie. Aunt Gertie was an exacting woman who brought the sensibilities of music and preparedness into her kitchen. She was a great cook. One of her specialties was Red Rice, a spicy dish made with onions, bell peppers, and bacon.

Like every other child in her community, Gertrude Prunella Dash learned the basics of rice preparation early. A ritual of scrubbing the grain, boiling, but *never* stirring (you shake the pot), and steaming till each kernel "stood on its own." Gertrude was taught to never, ever, use a colander to steam rice—she learned to do it by measurement. The ratio is—as it's always been—two parts water to one part rice.

To grow up a Geechee is to grow up tossed around the school of hard knocks. There was a lot of love in my family; on weekends we would all get together for big family meals. My family loved to eat good food, take photographs, smoke cigarettes with one eye closed, tell wild stories and argue. Everyone could cook, the men, women, and children. It was unheard of not to be able to "throw down" in the kitchen.

You never wanted to make any mistakes around my family because they would never let you forget it. I made a mistake when I was about ten. They never let me forget it. *I tried to stir a pot of Red Rice after it had started boiling!* To make matters worse, it happened on a Sunday. As far as Aunt Gertie was concerned, I was "too old for that kind of nonsense." A dozen Geechees, family members, rushed into the kitchen to take a look at me. I was still standing there with a big spoon in my hand. Looking like a fool. Laughing, some of my uncles wanted me to reenact the scene. Why hadn't my mother warned me? It was then I remembered that everyone always laughed at my mother's rice. Now they were laughing at me. I was forgiven because I had been born in New York and my mother had been born in the Piedmont section of South Carolina so that probably had something to do with my recklessness. Learning through humiliation and fear is certainly not the best way to acquire knowledge—but you damn sure never forget it! To this day I cannot put a spoon in a pot of rice that is cooking.

Like so many born of a South Carolina heritage, rice was more than just a staple food for Aunt Gertie. Rice was a way of life. Rice had been in her family for more than three hundred years—it was a science and art form. Aunt Gertie had a vested interest in a boiling pot of rice, and she taught us all that she knew, all that she recollected.

Before cooking, Aunt Gertie would wash her rice, really scrub it in a bowl of water until all the water was clear. Sometimes she would change the scrubbing water up to ten times! That's if you want each kernel to absorb her special red sauce! Every kernel of rice was scrubbed to a shiny translucence. When she was a child, they would use the cloudy rice water to starch their clothes.

Today as I stand over a bowl of cold water and rice, scrubbing, I feel Aunt Gertie watching me. Checking on me. Perhaps behind her the old souls are watching all of us, checking on the seeds that they have planted.

# Aunt Gertie's Red Rice

1 cup South Carolina white rice
   (do not use converted rice)
2 cups water
1 clove garlic
$\frac{1}{2}$ cup chopped onions
$\frac{1}{2}$ cup chopped bell peppers
1 6-ounce can tomato paste
5 strips bacon (or smoked turkey)
$\frac{1}{4}$ cup vegetable oil

1. Place rice in a large bowl of water and scrub it between your hands. Keep changing water until it is clear of starch. Pour off water.

2. Use a deep, heavy pot with a lid. Cook bacon or, if you prefer, smoked turkey with $\frac{1}{4}$ cup of vegetable oil in the bottom of the pot.

3. Add onions, peppers, garlic, and cook until they are done.

4. Add tomato paste mixed with 2 cups of water. When sauce begins to boil, add rice. Use a fork to make sure rice is evenly distributed in tomato sauce. Never stir rice once it begins to boil: "Never put a spoon in rice that's cooking." When rice begins to boil, lower the heat.

5. Wrap a wet brown paper bag around the lid of the pot and cover. Slow-cook. "Every grain must stand on its own. Every grain must be red." Slow-cook until rice absorbs all of the sauce. Red Rice tastes even better the next day.

# A Beet Recipe

Joan Ormondroyd

**D**espite the heat today I walked through the kitchen garden several times, admiring the fat tomatoes turning yellow, the large yellow blossoms on the squash, and the small yellow blossoms on the cucumber vines. Yellow seemed the dominant color, next to green of course, but there were also the lovely purple flowers of the eggplant and the white hibiscus jewels put forth in vast numbers on our okra. I filled my basket with fruit from all of these plants and was about to leave the garden for the coolness of our house when I noticed that the beets had taken a great leap forward in just the last few days. I pulled one to see how big it was. What a sight! A big fist-sized red fellow, just waiting to be eaten. By the time I'd sorted through the bed and pulled all the largest ones I had an armload of beets and beet greens. What a dope! Now, on this very hot day I was going to have to DO something with them.

Well, no matter. Beets are my absolutely favorite vegetable and it came as a big shock to me the year Ed and I got married to learn that he'd planted no beets in the veggie garden because he didn't like them. "Plant them yourself," he suggested. But I do flowers, *he* does vegetables, and it seemed wrong, somehow, to change that routine when we'd just gotten it going well. So I bought my beets that year at the Farmers' Market and proceeded to teach Edward to like them.

How'd I do it? Not hard. I made him my grandmother's borscht and served it on a hot day like this one. It was love at first gulp.

My grandmother's borscht and I go back over fifty years now. I was ten when my mother first took me and my brother back to New York City to visit her parents. My parents had moved us to California in the heart of the depression when I was only two and my brother not yet born, hoping, I gather, to find work. Those hard years are another story, but in 1941 my dad had a job in the shipyards and was finally able to afford to send us east.

What a revelation the Bronx was for me. Yiddish! I had never heard it spoken in our home for my father was not Jewish and didn't speak it. Here my mother and her parents spoke Yiddish all the time. Shopping with Grandma Masha was a new and exciting experience. Fat chickens, still alive and in cages, were chosen by poking fingers in through the bars to feel the finest, choicest ones. Vegetables were hawked from carts on street corners by men and women who were ruder than any I'd ever encountered, but who yet always sent me off with a piece of fruit in my hand.

I learned about borscht the day Grandma bought a basketful of beets with the greens left on and brought them home. We stood together at the kitchen sink to clean them. "I like to peel mine first," she told me, "or they taste like the earth." The greens were washed too, then chopped, stems and all, and added with the beets to the pot. Several large onions, peeled and roughly chopped, went in as well.

While the vegetables cooked my grandmother told me stories of Regkis, her village in Russia, where she had lived as a child. She told me of having to leave school in third grade to go to work in the match factory—a factory she walked five miles to and from each day—to help her mother support the eleven children in the family. Her father was not a rabbi, but he was a studious and pious Jew who spent nearly every waking hour in the synagogue. Grandma's mother supported the family by selling pins, needles, and small trinkets in a kiosk in front of their tiny cottage. To describe the crowded conditions of their lives Grandma taught me a poem in Yiddish, which I can recite to this day:

A gazind zalbe acht / Un betn nor tzvey
Un kumpt on di nakht / Vi sholfn dan zey?
Dray mitn tatn, Un dray mit der mamen
Hentlekh un fislekh, geflokhtn tsuzamen

As an adult I learned that this is the first verse of a poem by Avrom Reisen, the well-known Yiddish poet. It translates as "A household of eight, / Beds are but two, / When it gets late, / What do they do? / Three sleep with the father / And three with the mother, / Hands and feet / Entwined together." This seems to me a pretty graphic description of what my grandmother's home must have been like.

Ah, but the beets. Tender, aromatic, ready! A large colander was placed over a big bowl and the red juice was drained from the pot. Carefully my grandmother separated out the tender beets from the onions and greens, which, despite their heat, she squeezed to add their juice to that already in the bowl. The onions and greens were then discarded. An old grater was pulled from a drawer, and I was awarded the task of grating the beets. I had to wait until they cooled down a bit. My hands were not the calloused, work-worn ones of my grandmother. The grated beets became part of the bright red juice—one of the most beautiful colors I'd ever seen. Then into the icebox went the bowl with beets and juice to cool down before the next step.

While we waited Grandma told me more stories about her early life. She had, she told me, left the match factory in 1908 when she was sixteen, having made up her mind to go to America where, she hoped, a young woman might have a chance to do something more with her life than marry, bear dozens of children, and have to feed them while her pious husband prayed and praised her for being his footstool. Even at age ten I could hear the bitterness in my grandmother's voice. Yes, she *did* manage to get to America, but there was no gold in the streets and life on New York's lower east side was as hard as it had been in Russia and not nearly as healthy. She roomed with a cousin and his family the first few months, but there were eight of them in two rooms. She slept on two hard chairs pushed together in the kitchen and had to ward off her cousin's attentions in the middle of the night to boot. She learned to sew shirtwaists in the Triangle Shirtwaist factory and was lucky to be sick at home the day of the Triangle fire when all the friends she had made were killed.

My grandfather would often interrupt my grandmother's narrative with "Always kvetching! Never happy. She lives for bad memories!" In a way it was true; my grandfather, whose life had also been no picnic, was far more optimistic than my grandmother, but on the other hand, his expectations had never been as high as hers.

By now it had begun to grow late and dinner time was approaching. Grandma took the bowl of beets and juice from the icebox. In another bowl she squeezed the juice of several lemons, added a handful of sugar and a dash of something she called "sour salt." (I later, much later, learned that it was citric acid.) Cucumbers and scallions were chopped into all of this, and big spoons of sour cream were also added. Sour cream was not common in those days, especially not in my WASP neighborhood in California, so I was not at all sure I would like this combination. As Grandma stirred the beets and juice into the lemon-sugar mixture, the color turned from wine red to a soft cerise. It was beautiful to look at. "Could I taste it please?" I asked. Not yet— another hour in the icebox to let the juices mix, and then . . .

Well, it was indeed all that had been promised. Cold, sweet, yet sour. Fresh and filling. A wonderful soup. Edward couldn't help but love it! Does he grow beets now? You bet he does!

❚❘ ❚❘ ❚❘

## Borscht: The Recipe

6 medium or 5 large beets, peeled, trimmed,
　　and cut in half
greens and stems saved from beets,
　　thoroughly washed
2 yellow onions, peeled and coarsely chopped
enough water to cover ingredients (about 6 cups)
juice of 1 lemon (or 2 tablespoons prepared
　　lemon juice)
2 tablespoons sugar
½ teaspoon sour salt (citric acid)
sour cream or yoghurt
cucumber and/or scallions, chopped

1. Place all ingredients in a large pot (with beets at bottom). Bring to boil and then simmer until beets are tender (about 25 minutes).

2. When beets are tender, cool slightly. Place colander over large bowl and pour contents of pot into colander. Set aside juice collected in bowl, and fish out beets from greens, stems, and onions in colander.

3. Shred beets in food processor or with hand shredder. Squeeze juice from greens, stems, and onions into bowl of beet juice. Add beet juice to shredded beets. Place beets and beet juice in refrigerator until fully cooled. (Beets and juice may be frozen at this point to use at a later date; freeze in plastic containers.)

4. Squeeze juice of 1 lemon (or use 2 tablespoons prepared lemon juice) into large bowl. Add 2 heaping tablespoons sugar, ½ teaspoon sour salt (citric acid), 2 heaping tablespoons sour cream or yoghurt. Stir until smooth. Add beets and juice. Return to refrigerator for 1 hour or more

and then correct for seasoning. If you like it sweeter, add more sugar; if you like it less sweet, add more lemon juice.

5. Place scant handful of peeled, chopped cucumber and/or chopped scallions in bottom of each soup bowl. Fill bowl with beets and juice and top with generous dab of sour cream or yoghurt in middle of soup. Serves 4.

6. If you like more liquid and fewer beets in the borscht, save a couple of the cooked beets and eat them separately rather than shred them— they're delicious! Grate only the number of beets you want to use for your borscht.

*Note.* Sour salt (or citric acid) can usually be found in the Jewish foods department of any large grocery store.

# Zarouhe's Easter Gift

## Arlene Voski Avakian

Scrubbed until their purple black shells shone, the mussels were ready to be opened and stuffed. Zarouhe's feet ached and the small of her back was tired. She had been standing all morning—first chopping pounds of onions, sautéing them gently in olive oil, adding the carefully washed rice, pine nuts, and currants, then cleaning the dozens of mussels. Now she would have a little something to eat with her daughter Anahid, then she would finish the job.

Early that morning, just after Sarkis had left for work, she had had another argument with Anahid. It had been a week of disagreements beginning with the menu for the Easter dinner. Having just celebrated her eightieth birthday the previous month, Zarouhe was feeling expansive and wanted to make both *media*, stuffed mussels, and *enginar*, artichokes cooked in oil and lemon. Anahid insisted that preparing both dishes was too much work, that they never had two first courses, and besides both dishes were cooked in olive oil and lemon and would not complement each other well. Equally insistent, Zarouhe said that she didn't know how long she would be around, that no one else in the family made *media*, and while Anahid did sometimes make *enginar* everyone knew Zarouhe's were the best. Even Sarkis's Persian Armenian family praised Zarouhe's *enginar*. She wanted to make them for her grandchildren, she said, and she had risen early that morning to begin the preparations expecting Anahid to help her with the onerous task of cleaning the mussels. But when Zarouhe passed through the dining room on her way to the kitchen, she saw the silver serving pieces and cutlery on the dining room table, waiting to have their brilliance restored, and she knew Anahid would be polishing silver for the bulk of the morning. Well, Zarouhe thought, I don't really need any help. I have scrubbed mussels many times in my life. But now she was tired from the work and the tension she had felt all morning. She and Anahid had not spoken, each of them silently tending their work and their resentment. Zarouhe knew that Anahid was angry at her for not waiting to start cleaning the mussels until the afternoon when they could share the work.

Anahid came in from the dining room, washed her hands, silently went to the refrigerator, took out the left-over *messov fassoulia*, and heated it for their lunch. Zarouhe took her place at the kitchen table to wait. It felt so good to sit down and soon the food was ready. The steaming dish of lamb and string beans cooked in tomato sauce soothed and refreshed her. Anahid commented that the mussels looked very good. She had carefully picked out the largest ones, the best kind to stuff. Zarouhe nodded, pleased that her daughter had finally broken the silence.

Looking at the clock over the stove Zarouhe realized that she didn't have much time. Her stories would begin in a few minutes and she still had to set up her work space. When she began to spread newspaper on the living room floor, Anahid rose to get the aluminum TV tables out of the closet and put them on the newspapers. Zarouhe sat in her chair, the one nearest the television, and pulled the TV table as close as she could. Anahid carried the stuffing, the mussels, and Zarouhe's small sharp knife into the living room. Zarouhe's stories had begun, and while she watched that other world of the Americans on the television, she pulled the little hairy beard off of each mussel, opened it with her knife, and filled it with the stuffing. Later, she would begin the artichokes, pulling off the outer leaves until she got down to the tender ones, reaching into the center with a spoon to scrape out the choke, then rubbing lemon over the whole artichoke and dropping it into a bowl of acidified water to keep the light green flesh from darkening.

Zarouhe noticed that the silver was almost finished and hoped Anahid would be able to help her with the *enginar*. Like the other women in the family, Anahid and Zarouhe each had their specialties, one could help the other but there was never any confusion about who was in charge for each dish. *Media* and *enginar* were Zarouhe's domain, while Anahid presided over Persian pilaf, the marinating of shish kebab, and *abour*, a hearty yoghurt soup. Zabel, Zarouhe's other daughter, worked outside the home as well as doing all the housework and cooking for her husband and nearly grown sons, yet one of her specialties was *manti*, a kind of Armenian ravioli, one of the most time-consuming dishes.

Sometimes the three women would come together, usually in Zabel's home to help her prepare a feast of *manti* for their husbands and children and their brother Levon's family. Preparations had to begin the previous day or at least very early in the morning of the feast because the lamb bones had to be boiled for hours to make a rich broth. They bought whole legs or shoulders of lamb from the Armenian grocer when they lived in the city, but now that they lived in Jersey they had learned to negotiate with the butchers behind the glass windows in the meat departments at the supermarkets. All of the women in the family ground their own meat with hand-turned metal meat grinders clamped to the edge of the kitchen table. Grinding their own meat meant they could control both the amount of fat in the meat and the fineness of the grind and they would also have bones for broth or for various lamb stews they ate regularly. The ground lamb for *manti* had to be very lean and fine, and would therefore require careful removal of the fat, and be put through the grinder at least three times. *Manti* also required the making of an egg dough, kneaded and allowed to rest before it was rolled out paper thin and cut into small squares. A dab of the meat, mixed with finely minced onions, herbs, and spices was put in the center of each of the squares which were pinched on two sides with floured fingers to form a tiny boat. These little vessels were arranged in open baking pans, brushed with butter, and baked until crisp. They were eaten in broth with yoghurt, homemade of course. Even after Dannon began marketing yoghurt in the supermarket in the 1960s, no self-respecting Armenian woman of Zarouhe's or even Anahid's and Zabel's generation would serve her family anything but homemade yoghurt. They kept the culture alive from one batch to the next, sharing it with a relative in the rare case that someone's yoghurt failed to ferment.

The mussels were finally stuffed just as the last of Zarouhe's stories ended. Arranged carefully in layers, they filled the heavy aluminum pot she always used for this purpose and were ready to be cooked. She was pleased that almost all of the mussels had resisted her knife indicating that the mollusks were still alive and therefore fit to eat. There would be enough *media* for each person to have three or four with a few left over. Zarouhe always liked to have extra portions of her specialties so that she could give more to her favorite people. Anahid's son Johnny was her undisputed pet, but even Zarouhe had to admit that the boy was a strange eater. He didn't like anything that was too Armenian, doused even the wonderful Persian rice his mother made with ketchup, and had never even tasted *media*. Zarouhe held his older sister Diane responsible for his rejection of anything Armenian. The girl had yelled at the poor boy whenever he uttered an Armenian word: "Speak English. We are Americans." And he had listened to her, learning only a few Armenian words. Diane had spoken such beautiful Armenian when she was a young child. She had been a quiet, obedient girl, but then she went to school, learned English, and had been troublesome ever since. It seemed to Zarouhe that only Diane's palate remained Armenian. The girl loved Armenian food. Zarouhe would give an extra *media* and *enginar* to her son Levon, to Sarkis, the son-in-law who had provided her with such a good home, and to her headstrong granddaughter, Diane.

She mused for a minute on Diane's rejection of everything Armenian. Well, knowing about the food was important. They all knew that. When she and her children came to America, they had been glad for any morsel after the terrible privation in Turkey during and after the genocide. She had lost so much—husband, home, relatives. They had been so lucky to escape the dreaded death march into the desert where so many Armenians died from thirst and exposure and others were killed, women raped and abducted. Life had been hard, but she and her children were alive. And finally they had managed to come to America. Anahid had been eleven and the only one to finish high school. Zarouhe worked in a factory beading clothing. During the busy season she was required to bring work home, though her eyes were too tired to do the close work at night. Anahid had helped her without complaint when she came home from school. They had gotten by. And then Anahid had married Sarkis, and they all crowded into that five-room apartment with Zabel and her husband and their three children.

What feasts they had had then—all the women cooking together on that enamel stove standing on its long legs at the end of the narrow kitchen. She felt then that life was more like it had been on the other side. Armenians all around her on the streets, their church and market a few blocks away. Afternoons spent with friends drinking Turkish coffee, telling fortunes. They said she had a gift for that and it was true; when she was in the mood, she could "see" into the shapes formed by the coffee grounds.

Years later they had moved, like many of the other Armenians in the neighborhood. Different kinds of people were moving in, and Sarkis and Anahid insisted that they had to move for Diane and Johnny. They found a house in Jersey, and the funny thing was that Diane hated the move and went back to the city to visit her friends as much as she could. Zarouhe sometimes went too, to see the few friends who still lived there, drink coffee, and reminisce. In Jersey there was no Armenian church, no market, and nothing that she could walk to. But she did have a garden where she could grow basil, tarragon, parsley, and dill alongside the tomatoes and cucumbers Sarkis planted.

Her life was still good, but she missed going to church. The first few years after they had moved, Sarkis drove them back into the city for the Easter service. Sarkis and Anahid didn't usually attend church and she knew they had made the effort to get to church on Easter for her. She was touched, but would have preferred being able to get there on her own or to meet her son Levon on the corner between their apartment and his in the next block and walk the short distance to the church with him. For a short while, when she was about ten years old, Diane said that she wanted to go to church. Zarouhe had been delighted. She had taken the girl's hand and even spoke a little English to please her on their way to church. But Diane had stopped as quickly as she started, declaring one Sunday that she was not going to that church anymore. She said she didn't like all that Armenian stuff and the Sunday school class was boring. That girl would say anything and there seemed to be no way to stop her.

Now all that was left of her Easter rituals were the dinners, and she and Anahid were responsible for it all. No matter. Friday night, Good Friday, eggs and spinach, pilaf and chicken. In the old country they would not have had meat. Here they ate the spinach and eggs to mark that meatless time. Zarouhe didn't like to deprive herself of any food for any reason. She had had enough of hunger. Yes, it was good that they had chicken. Saturday they would all go to Vahan's home for dinner. He was Sarkis's older brother and a real gentleman who always treated Zarouhe like an important lady. He had always made her feel young, even flirtatious. Generations ago Sarkis's family had fled from Turkey to Persia and had started an importing business in America. Anahid had been lucky to marry into this family. Miriam, Vahan's wife, was a good enough cook for a Persian Armenian, but the food would not be special.

Not like the dinner they would have on Easter Sunday. She knew she had gone overboard this time, but the meal would be glorious. Somehow, this Easter she was glad to be alive and she wanted to celebrate with her children and grandchildren around her and thank God with a full table.

◧ ◌ ◧

# Media
### (Stuffed Mussel Appetizer)

3 cups finely chopped onions
$1/2$ cup olive oil
$1/2$ cup uncooked rice
$1/4$ cup currants
$1/2$ cup finely chopped Italian parsley
$1/4$ cup pine nuts
$1/4$ cup tomato sauce
$1/4$ teaspoon allspice
$1/4$ teaspoon cinnamon
juice of $1/2$ lemon
$1 1/2$ cups water
3 dozen mussels
salt and pepper to taste

1. Prepare mussels for stuffing by scrubbing with metal scrubber and remove beard. Force mussels open with knife, but *do not* separate shells. If they open easily, discard. Remove any waste matter attached to flesh. Rinse and then soak in cold water while you prepare the filling.

2. Make the filling by sautéing onions slowly in olive oil until translucent. Be careful not to brown. Add rice and stir until coated with oil. Stir in allspice, cinnamon, salt, and pepper. Add currants, parsley, pine nuts, and tomato sauce. Remove filling from heat and set aside to cool.

3. Rinse mussels and drain. Stuff each mussel with about a teaspoon of the filling, close shell, and carefully arrange them in a heavy bottomed pot. Add water and lemon juice. Bring to boil and lower heat to simmer. Cook for 1 hour or until rice is cooked. Uncover and cool to room temperature. The mussels may be made a day ahead and kept in a cool place. If you must refrigerate, remove before serving to bring them to room temperature.

4. Serve with lemon wedges. In my family we used one of the shells to scoop out the filling rather than a fork or spoon. Six mussels per person is a generous serving.

◻◻ ◻ ◻◻

## Enginar

(Artichoke Cooked in Oil and Lemon—A First Course)

6 large artichokes
12 small white onions
12 small white potatoes, peeled
½ cup fruity olive oil
2 to 3 lemons
a few sprigs of fresh dill
salt to taste

1. You will need a sharp knife, a pair of kitchen shears, a grapefruit spoon, and a large pot of water into which you have squeezed a lemon.

2. Remove tough outer leaves of artichoke and peel stem. Cut top half of each leaf with shears, or holding your thumb about halfway up a leaf snap off top part of leaf and pull it down to remove outer layer of leaf. When you have gotten to very tender inner leaves, cut tips off so that they are even with other leaves. You should be able to stand artichokes on this cut end. Open leaves and reach into the artichoke with your grapefruit spoon and scrape out choke. Be sure to get it all out as it is inedible. Rub artichoke with a cut lemon to prevent discoloring and drop into water.

3. When all artichokes are prepared, stand them in a heavy bottomed pot and surround with peeled onions and potatoes. Add water, juice of 1 lemon, salt, and dill. Bring to a boil. Lower heat to simmer. Lemons vary greatly in acidity so taste the water. It should be sour. If it is not, add more lemon. Simmer for about 30 minutes and then add olive oil. Cook another 20–30 minutes or until artichokes are tender. Pull off a leaf to test for doneness. When done, remove from heat and cool to room temperature. The artichokes may be made a day ahead and kept in a cool place. If you must refrigerate, remove at least an hour before serving to bring to room temperature. Serve with lemon wedges. Serves 6 very generously.

❒ ❒ ❒

# Persian Pilaf

3 cups rice, preferably basmati
6 cups water
¾ cup melted butter
peeled and thinly sliced potatoes or *lavash*
    (very thin, soft Armenian flatbread)
salt to taste

1. Soak rice overnight in salted water.

2. Preheat oven to 350 degrees. Drain and wash rice in bowl until water is clear. Drain again. Bring water to a boil and add rice. Boil for

about 10 minutes. The center of the rice should still be hard. Drain rice in colander.

3. Butter bottom of ovenproof pot that is large enough to cook rice, and cover bottom of pot with potatoes or lavash.

4. Add rice and pour melted butter over it. Cover and cook in oven for one hour. Serves 9 to 12 people.

# Gravy

## Sally Bellerose

**N**o religion, no politics, no sex at the supper table. Mother does the cooking. Mother makes the rules.

My father invites me and my lover to dinner. Last time we ate dinner at my parents' house my father implied that my lover was not a lesbian because of the way she devoured a drumstick. I'm a vegetarian. My father believes that all lesbians are vegetarians. My lover was invited tonight. She declined.

My mother cooks a stew, calls it vegetarian stew even though it has two-inch chunks of beef in it. I eat my mother's stew even though I call myself a vegetarian. My mother assures me that the meat she buys is so lean that there's not a chance in hell that one fat globule could melt into the gravy. I don't tell her it's blood, not fat, that alarms me. She picks out the meat with plastic pickle tongs that she got free at a tupperware party, before passing me a plateful. She discards my meat on my father's plate.

"Who ever heard of broccoli in stew?" my father says, picking out the little green trees and piling them on my plate. I eat the top off a tiny one, after smelling it. I want to ask my parents if they think the broccoli smells like meat but I'm afraid that might lead to breaking Mother's rules.

I get pumpernickel bread out of the freezer and nuke it in the microwave for thirty seconds so we can sop up the nonfat gravy. When I sit back down my mother is trading green beans for pearl onions with my father.

"Anybody want to trade gravy?" I ask.

My father says, "No thank you. I don't eat vegetarian gravy."

"This isn't vegetarian gravy. It's brown," I say.

"Alright, I don't eat a vegetarian's gravy," my father says.

Mother says, "Vegetarian gravy can be brown. You just add a little Worcestershire and a little Gravymaster."

Father takes a spoonful of gravy from my bowl, tastes it, shakes his head. Says, "No protein. You got unnatural gravy."

I take the spoon out of his hand and have a taste of his gravy. "Hormones," I say. "Antibiotics. Pesticides."

We must be talking about religion, politics, or sex because Mother is pissed. She gives us both a disgusted look and takes her plate into the den.

I follow her. "Ma, do you like the smell of broccoli?" I ask, contrite, by way of polite conversation.

"Ask me after I finish my meal," she says.

Father comes in with a second plate of meat-laden stew.

Mother gives us both a warning glance. "Put on *Wheel of Fortune*," she says.

My father and I sit on the couch, on opposite sides of my mother. We finish our stew and watch Vanna turn letters. We behave during *Wheel of Fortune. Jeopardy* is a different story, but the meal is over by then.

◻⋮ ◻⋮ ◻⋮

# Song of My Mother

Tahira Naqvi

Today, she is in my kitchen. Tall still, her lean and shrunken face mapped with lines too fine to count, her small black eyes sunk deep into their sockets, she cradles an emerald green *karela* in the palm of her hand, her fingers closing over the gourd gently, as if it were a child's face she is stroking.

"You haven't been patient," she says with a shake of her head, her eyes clouded as they are when she expresses disappointment at being alone. Your children leave to go to another country and you putter around in a big, silent house all day long wondering why you're alone. It is not to me she will say this. It will be to someone else, a guest, a relative, a friend's mother. As a matter of fact she will avoid looking at me so that I may not observe the reproof in her eyes.

She sighs.

"It isn't me," I protest, "it's the *karela*."

"You have to prepare the *karela* properly if you want the bitterness to go away." Tiny strands of grey hair, playing truant from her long, thin plait, have wandered on her furrowed brow, floating across the darkness of her skin like faint brush strokes.

I cannot tell her that often, beleaguered by memory's sharp resonance, I have tried to cook *karelas* her way. The words, reeking of failure, sit on my tongue like the bitter aftertaste of *karelas* that have been done in a hurry. Long and hard I had labored, until my hands ached and my fingers became numb, and then a full day the smooth-skinned gourds sat in a colander while I waited; much later I realized I had forgotten the salt, and so when the rinds were sharp and acrid still, I shrugged and thought, Ah, it's because I forgot to use the salt. How could I tell her I had neglected to use salt before I washed the skins? She would look at me in disbelief, and then, lifting her fine eyebrows, would ask, in a soft voice tinged with a hint of a reprimand, How could you forget something so important?

"Amma, *karelas* in Lahore are different," I say bravely. "These come from Mexico and God knows where else, and look," I point accusingly, "look how large the bumps are on these. How can you expect them to turn out like the ones from your garden?" They're small, delicate in shape and fine-skinned in her garden.

Her garden is in Lahore. But this afternoon she is in my town, a small New England town where summer recklessly crowds life into foliage with such abandon that the blue of the sky and the brown of the earth assume distant, foggy faces. And here, even though summer temperatures may rise to a hundred, *karelas* cannot grow. Summer is too short a season, too rapid in its abundance, too impatient.

"I'll show you," she says, a small, bony hand reaching for the vegetable knife. "You can get the same results from this *karela*, only you must know what to do."

Silently I watch as she pulls the plastic colander full of *karelas* toward her and begins scraping the thick nodular skin of the gourd in her hand with a slow, rhythmic movement. *Khrach, khrach, khrach.* Tiny sparks of icy cold juice fly in all directions, a wet, green speck lands on Amma's hollowed cheek and sits there like a bead. Her eyes are lowered, her brows furrowed, her mouth set tightly in concentration. *Khrach, khrach, khrach.*

The process of scraping the *karelas* is not new to me. I grew up watching my aunts do it too; every step of the ritual is deeply etched in my memory. I remember the cool, wet sensation of the juice as it flew into my face, the sharp acrid aroma of the skins combining with the smoke from my grandmother's hookah and filling my nose until I could smell nothing else, the brisk chatter of conversation interjected with laughter and head-slapping gestures that passed between my aunts, Amma, and my grandmother, the picture of the naked, cone-shaped vegetables after they had been fully cleaned, each smooth and clear as a baby's behind, and myself, a girl-child who had no taste for such a bitter vegetable.

Next, she slices them and disgorges the seeds, which if they are swelled and orange-toned, predict an overripe vegetable and thus are cause for dismay. Small and bottle green today, they spill out from Amma's hand and form a mound in the colander. She peers at them closely.

"At one time I used to fry them and toss them in with the rinds," Amma says, always reluctant to throw out what may have even the most insignificant use. "But let's not worry about that now." She has begun to cut up the slices into narrow bands.

Birds, blue-feathered and red-breasted, are creating a din. I think I also hear the plaintive *kuhoo, kuhoo, kuhoo* of a cuckoo in a tree outside my kitchen window. The sun, visible only as brightness filtering through thickly leaved trees, is now dipping toward a horizon we can only imagine exists somewhere behind the jungle of woods at the western boundary of our lawn. The air is cooler; a quiet breeze blows strands of hair in Amma's face as she stands before the sink at the kitchen window, ready now to wash and rub the rinds. Turning the tap on, she lets the water run through her fingers and onto the *karela* skins in the colander. Then she bends and, taking handfuls between the palms of her hands, rubs them, vigorously, energetically, until she is out of breath. Tiny beads of perspiration mark her forehead and there is a film of moisture on her upper lip.

"Let me do this," I say, placing my hand on her arm.

She shakes her head without pausing for a moment in her endeavors.

We dry the rinds with a paper towel and Amma sprinkles

salt on them. Now they must sit in the colander for an hour at least.

The kettle whistles. I get up and make tea in a pot. She sits down at the kitchen table and wipes her face with her *dupatta*, the long scarf that winds around her neck and covers the front of her body. A vein pulsates agitatedly in her neck, just where the long keloid scar from her bypass begins.

"Make sure the milk is boiling," she says as I remove the milk jug from the microwave. Quickly I slip it in for another ten seconds. It boils over.

An hour later she washes the skins again, rubbing them down vigorously once more. All the salt has to be removed. Another patting with paper towels follows. I pour oil from a small cup into the frying pan and wait for it to heat. Amma drops in the skins. They sizzle. A bittersweet smell fills the kitchen.

"The idea is not to deep-fry," she says. "Just have the normal amount of oil you would have to cook any other vegetable." She turns the pieces around with a wooden spatula, watching the pan intently, keeping a close eye on them as they gradually darken, first to a ginger-tinged orange, then brown.

I have already sliced one large onion, diced a tomato, and chopped two long, slender, dark green chilies into tiny bits. Ground coriander and sharply pointed cumin seeds have also been set aside on the counter to her right. She does not like peering into the spice rack or rummaging through the bottles there.

She signals and I drop the onions into the pan. Increasing the heat under the pan, she moves the mixture around. The smell of onions cooking in oil draws water in my mouth. She waits until the whiteness of the onions is dissipated, then throws in a spoonful of cumin seeds and coriander. The gold bangles on her slim wrists, thinned from years of wearing, tinkle as she moves the spatula around, her eyes grow restful, the look in them calm. Tendrils of smoke, thick with the vapor of spices and onions, rise above the pan and move lazily upward. She places the spatula on the counter, leans back, a hand set on her hip, and watches the *karelas* through half-shut, dreamy eyes. I don't know what she's thinking.

The tomato and the chilies go in next. Gently everything is turned over. A lid is placed on the frying pan. Amma lowers the heat to simmer.

I turn on the light in the kitchen and we return to tea. A second cup for us both. I heat the milk again. Outside the birds are silenced. The sound of an occasional car on the road snaps the evening hush, a cricket breaks into song, my teenage son ambles in for orange juice.

"What's for dinner?" he asks, reaching for a glass from the dish rack.

"*Karelas*," I say.

"Not that bitter stuff again Mom!" he wails.

Amma purses her lips and sighs.

"It's not bitter," I say. "Nanima made it her way. She knows this trick which makes all the bitterness go away." Ten minutes of simmering and the *karelas* will be ready. I lift the lid for a quick peek. My face is warmed by a sudden gush of steam.

The boy looks inquiringly at his grandmother.

"Yes," she smiles knowingly, stretching out her hand toward him to draw him into her embrace.

❏  ❏  ❏

# Vermont Kitchen

Janet Dike Rood

**S**ince I was brought up by, or in the home of, my grandparents, I observed my grandmother's kitchen productivity as a part of "simply what was done." Clearest in my mind's eye is all the cookery that took place at their summer camp (a Vermont colloquialism for what out-of-staters call a "cottage.")

Up in West Swanton the tap water did not run hot. It was heated on the large black wood- and coal-burning kitchen stove during inclement weather or on the two-burner oil stove on the back porch where we had our meals. Raspberries and currants were picked over on the back porch eating table, to be made into jelly. Good "buys" in meats (pork and beef) were "put up" in pint or quart jars for winter consumption as meat pies, topped with flaky baking powder biscuits. Mincemeat was worked by hand in a large crockery bowl and then canned. And pickles of each variety were produced here. The cukes were tended, washed, and carried in by my grandfather, and the endless preparations were carried out by my grandmother while I came and went, from school, summer camp, college . . . loving them and leaving them.

Reality of what was involved in my grandparents' summer camp did not come home to me until after World War II when I found myself pregnant, with a two-and-a-half-year-old, a husband in a New York City graduate school, and without a place to live. The war years' summers had found me returning to West Swanton, the first time pregnant, and the next with child in arms. That's where I gravitated once again and was taken in. God love them.

No longer a flitty schoolgirl, of course I shared in all the duties. And then my grandmother had a stroke. She was paralyzed, bedridden, and couldn't speak. Since they were living on their Social Security and my $10.00 a week for food, there was no money for nursing care. And there was no question about it either. I picked up the mantle and took care of them both. But this isn't about nursing care. It's about what was to happen to the vegetables in the garden. While my grandfather worried about Gram, his finances, and his summer crops, I did what needed to be done. I learned to can. On the wood-burning stove.

How? I racked my brain for memories of what I had half-witnessed and then I sat beside Gram's bed and asked her to help me through the process. I asked her to blink her eyes once or twice to my questions of this way or that and how long—while my grandfather harvested his rows and found the jars. I started with beets. Pickled beets. They were safe.

But I knew that this question and answer by blinking would never do for more complicated procedures. I had one more place to turn. Warner Home, a Haven for Little Wanderers, was the orphanage in St. Albans which had also been one of *my* havens during wartime homelessness. My husband had been reared there, his mother was the matron. Among the other employees were two Mrs. Murphys. The one way upstairs was the girl's caretaker and the one way downstairs was the cook whom my daughter had already given a name, "Mrs. Murphy-with-the-apron-on." With my mother-in-law matron's approval and my grandfather's assurance that he could handle the home front in my absence, I traveled the seventeen miles to get instructions from Mrs. Murphy-with-the-apron-on. Not only was she a teacher of merit, but also someone with a big heart who recognized my problem fully and set about to walk me through the process of canning string beans. (Unlike pickled beets, string beans were and still are *not* safe.) While my little daughter was upstairs being looked after by her grandmother, Mrs. Murphy-with-the-apron-on led me step by step—from the bushel of fresh, crisp yellow wax beans (just picked from the orphanage's garden) to the up-ended ball jars set on a clean white cloth in a cool dark place. Here they awaited the next day's ministrations. Never overhelpful and with comments such as "I know you want to know how to do it yourself, so I'll just *let* you—but help where you need me," she proved to be exactly what was called for. And all this happened during her afternoon "rest" between meals for thirty-five people.

Half a century passed before I thought of those two ladies in that exact context again. While gazing at my youngest daughter's garden and seeing a bounty of oversized cucumbers ready to be heaved to the compost, I suddenly saw Gram and Mrs. Murphy as well. In my mind's eye they were bustling industriously over their labors of love in their respective kitchens. I was moved to join them in my very own way, and after having done so I need to share that doing with the one who named the downstairs Mrs. Murphy long ago.

Sherrill,

I did a real memory trip last weekend with the baker's dozen (one-half bushel) large ripe cucumbers from Allison's garden. Saturday afternoon I sat and thought about Gram and Mrs. Murphy-with-the-apron-on (!) while I peeled and seeded and sectioned those great things in the shade of my courtyard. I had to peruse many books to find the meaning of "weak brine." Even the University of Vermont Extension Service's *Complete Guide to Preserving* didn't call it by name. Eventually I discovered it—2 tablespoons to 1 quart $H_2O$. Then I did it wrong. It also said 1 teaspoon alum. So I put these ingredients in my quart measure and poured it over the two huge mixing bowls filled with cukes (Gram's word, like glads for gladiolus). I needed much more so I repeated the process three times and stood back happily to observe my results. That's when I realized that I had 4 teaspoons of alum in there. So I drained and rinsed everything and started over. Now I know that for "one-half bushel cukes—large, ripe," take 1 gallon water, 8 tablespoons salt, and 1 teaspoon alum for the overnight soak with a plate on top to keep them from floating. As I looked at them floating away I suddenly had the vision of either Mrs. Murphy or Gram putting upended plates on top.

After Sunday church in Shelburne and breakfast at Leunig's I started the next step. I had bought one dozen new canning jars with lids at the Grand Union for $7.59 as I had given all mine away long before moving here twelve years ago.

Drain and rinse cukes (again) and cook in "weak vinegar." Those who should know at the Farmers' Market said "half 'n half" for "weak vinegar." Today my friend Doris said: "Oh, no! One-third vinegar to two-thirds water, or weaker. Didn't you taste it?" Of course not.

So . . . white vinegar and tap water to cover the cukes, now very reduced in size. Using my erroneous information, it took 1 quart of each to cover. But then I realized I had only *drained*, not *rinsed*, so I threw them all in the colander and did it again. And did it right.

Boil until tender. OK. Also put the 4 pounds brown sugar, 1 quart vinegar, and a little bag of pickling spices on to boil. Eureka! At the very bottom of my deep drawer for everything was a little folded piece of cheese-cloth . . . from another life.

All this while I am totally relaxed and enjoying myself. Then—wash the new jars and boil the lids (from ancient memories) and already the cukes are tender. Off the heat and drain. This time don't rinse. Oh, oh! I rescued the boiling sugar and vinegar as it rose just to the brim, poured it over my limp collection of cukes, and brought it back to a boil.

I should have bought pint jars, not quarts, I now realized, as I ladled my pickles into only four half-filled jars. "Much too dark," I told my friend Doris. "Didn't you use light brown sugar?" "Was it white vinegar?" Where was she when I was trying to think of someone whose youth included this stuff?

There they stand now, cleaned off and cooled, and too dark and probably too soft and I don't care. I had a lovely time. They cost me only about $20.00 including the jars which I may or may not ever use again. But Gram in her kitchen and in her garden back where I grew up, and Gram on that back porch at camp was always in my mind's eye . . . and Mrs. Murphy-with-the-apron-on, whose directions had made it possible for me to do the things I had *seen* Gram do but never knew the hows and whys.

The recipe looks like this.

### Sweet Pickles

½ Bu cukes
soak cut-up overnite in weak brine & 1 tsp alum
Rinse and cook until tender in weak vinegar

Boil 1 qt vinegar, 4 lbs brown sugar & mixed spices
in a bag
Pour over drained cukes.
Heat thoroughly.
Pack in jars.

*Gram and Mrs. Murphy*

Sounds simple enough.

*Love, Mom*

⚏ ⚏ ⚏

# The Sweet and Vinegary Taste

*For my grandmother, Rose LeBlanc Meunier*

## Cheryl Savageau

Summer overflowed the kitchen
where Memere made pepper relish
and piccalilli,
cooked up tons of beans,
and served us cucumbers and tomatoes
three times a day.

Every morning I followed her
down the cellar stairs
and out the back door
a load of laundry in her arms,
a bag of clothespins in mine.

A big girl now,
I grabbed the pole
and lowered the clothesline.
I hung the little things,
socks, underwear,
while Memere hung the sheets.

The line heavy with clothes,
Memere helped me push the pole
until the sheets swung
above my head,
closer to the wind, Memere said,
and safe from dogs.

But laundry was just an excuse.
The garden was what pulled us out,
and after clothes were hung
we walked our usual path
in and out among the beans and squash,

pulling a weed here, flicking a caterpillar
from the tender vines.
We buried fish
to make the plants grow.
We tied tin pie plates to strings
to keep the birds away, and
Memere wasn't bothered if
it didn't work. Birds flew
above and walked through the corn.
When I raised my arms and ran
to chase them Memere's voice would come,
Bury the fish, she said, and let the birds be.

Her knobby hands
working in the dark grown
New England soil
never seemed to doubt
there'd be enough.
This piece of earth
we called garden
was home, she knew,
to many, and not ours alone.

Bury the fish and let the birds be,
she said. There will be enough.

And there was enough.
Enough for everybody,
for birds, and rabbits,
and caterpillars, enough
and more than enough
to overflow the kitchen,
to fill the winter shelves
with the sweet and vinegary taste
of life, the mystery
flowing from the earth
through her hands
to our open mouths.

# "Family Liked 1956": My Mother's Recipes

Sharon L. Jansen

If I were to tell my mother she was an accomplished writer, she would deny it. Concerned about her grammar, her spelling, and her punctuation, my mother has apologized about her writing in every letter she has ever sent me. Even her handwriting bothers her. "IF I TYPE IN CAPS THEN I WON'T HAVE TO REMEMBER TO PRESS THAT KEY," she wrote just before Christmas, "CAN YOU GUESS IT HAS BEEN A YEAR SINCE I HAVE EVEN TOUCHED A TYPEWRITTER ? HA. . . . GUESS IT IS BETTER THAN MY HANDWRITTING THO."

As the first person in her family ever to graduate from high school, my mother worries that she doesn't have the necessary training or practice to know how to put her ideas into writing and on paper. Yet she is one of the most engaging writers I know. Once she's gotten past the self-conscious disclaimers that always preface her letters, she writes in a voice that is distinctive and personal. Her spelling and punctuation are unconventional, even flamboyant, yet this creativity is part of her unique style—my mother has never been interested in following rules.

Although the letters she writes to me are her most frequent compositions, her special genre is the recipe. For most, a recipe is a straightforward exercise in giving directions: a list of ingredients, step-by-step instructions, perhaps a few serving suggestions. But for my mother, a recipe presents an opportunity to experiment with composing as well as cooking. Her recipes are exercises in narration, description, analysis, even argument. For me, they raise questions about texts and context, about text and subtext, about textual authority and textual subversion. They are like nothing Betty Crocker ever imagined.

As I look through the collection of her recipes spread out in front of me now, I notice for the first time their studied casualness. Why is it, I wonder, that my mother never sends her recipes on recipe cards or at least on 3 by 5 inch cards? They come, instead, scrawled on a bewildering variety of scraps and sheets. She's never actually sent a recipe scratched on a paper sack or on the back of an envelope, but if she did, I wouldn't be surprised.

Sometimes, of course, she approaches conventionality. A recipe for "Dirt Cake" is copied neatly on a piece of yellow lined paper from a standard 8½ by 11 inch tablet, while "One Minute Dressing" and its multiple variations are found on six sheets of white stationery. The pages aren't numbered, though. Everything else has arrived on oddly sized scraps of paper or unidentifiable remnants of cardstock. Where, I wonder, did my mother come across this fragment of track-feed computer paper? And why did she use it, since it is so small (2¼ by 3¾ inches, not counting the perforated strip of holes) that the narrative surrounding the list of instructions for "Ranch Dressing Mix" is microscopic? "Old-Fashioned Coffee Cake" comes on a slip of paper almost as thin as tissue. The typed words could almost be read like Braille, except that this recipe and its accompanying commentary occupy both sides of the paper. If the typewriter ribbon had been new, the back-to-back typing would have been illegible, but since the ribbon is faded, I find instead two lines of gray impressions juxtaposed, the few periods piercing the tissue-thin paper. I can't imagine how it emerged safely from her old manual typewriter once, much less twice.

Their format suggests that my mother might regard these recipes as ephemeral documents, not meant for actual use. Perhaps they only provide an occasion for writing, since they are always accompanied by a commentary, often extended, that provides a context for the dish being described. Usually my mother's recipes come folded up inside her letters, which describe the dish, when she made it, who she made it for, how they liked it. And always what they said to one another—who is fighting with her husband over what, whose son or daughter is expecting a baby, who has the most annoying neighbors. I don't know any of the women she writes about, nor do I know their husbands and children. At least I've never met these women, except through my mother's recipes.

On occasion the recipe is embedded in the text of the letter itself, like the recipe for "Ginger Crinkles." I had written to my mother asking her for her molasses cookie recipe. I don't know why, now, I had come to think about that particular cookie since I couldn't remember when I had last eaten one and certainly had never wanted to make molasses cookies ever before—I usually confine myself to recipes in which chocolate is the principal ingredient. But any request to my mother, no matter how trivial, receives her immediate attention.

By return mail came a recipe for molasses cookies, but the cookies it produced were nothing like those I was expecting. I remembered a crisp yet chewy cookie, with crater-like cracks on the top, sugary too, and perfectly round. A letter noting my disappointment brought a second recipe from my mother, then a third, then a fourth, all of which I made, increasingly frustrated. The products were all wrong—too hard, too cakey, too much like gingersnaps or too much like gingerbread. Finally a letter arrived which began, "If you still want the old ginger cookie recipe I have looked for for so long here it is. In the cookbook it says 'Family liked 1956.' " The letter goes on to tell me that, at first, she couldn't remember ever having made molasses cookies. She certainly hadn't made them in years, didn't think I'd remember them either, and had simply sent the first recipe she could find. "You were only five then," she reminded me. I knew immediately this was the right recipe—my mother's directions concluded, "Drop by teaspoonful in sugar & form into balls coated with sugar. Cookies flatten & crinkle. Have fun!" The recipe was accompanied by a description of the house we lived in when she made those cookies and by speculation about why she might have made them originally and when she had made them last.

I read that letter whenever I make those cookies, which isn't often. I haven't recopied the recipe, or cut it out of the letter either, since, in effect, the recipe has become a part of my mother's reminiscence and reflection. Like nearly all of her recipes, the text has become a part of a larger whole, an occasion for a comment at least, more often for a story into which the recipe has been inserted. If the recipe is the text, it has been submerged in the story of which it is a part. Or it may be that the recipe is only an excuse for the larger narrative, which itself is the text that my mother wants to write.

Sometimes the comments that surround her recipes are only passing allusions: about "Artichoke Dip" she remarks cryptically, "My friend Joy tells me she loves it cold too." I am left with a textual puzzle. Who, I wonder, is Joy? Am I supposed to know her? I've never heard of her before—or since, for that matter—and what am I to make of the statement that Joy "loves it cold *too*." What untold story lies behind the recipe? I wonder about Joy and about when she enjoyed the artichoke dip *warm*.

My mother is more expansive in the coffee cake recipe typed on the slip of fragile paper. "Hope you enjoy it, we like it warm or cold," she writes. "A special favorite with the teachers at break and the little ones enjoy it too."

My mother cooked in an elementary school cafeteria for years, which provides the context for many of her recipes. Instructions for making a salad-dressing mix and several variations, for example, come with the comment, "I use the basic always but prefer to add the herb stuff & mixed green—very hearty! Use at home & school. Very well received by adults & kids at school." Each version of the basic recipe is accompanied by suggestions for use: the honey dressing is "good on fruit," she directs, the Indienne, with curry added to the vinegar-and-oil base, is "good on greens, fish, egg." The whole is followed by a brief discussion of the variety of vinegars available (cider, malt, red wine, garlic, tarragon, among others) and ends with a final helpful hint: "For a thicker dressing that is slow to separate add 1 uncooked egg to ½ c of dressing & beat thoroughly."

My mother's experiences in the school cafeteria may account for the more admonitory tone in some of her recipes. Appended to her salsa recipe is the note, "You can add the cilantro chopped if you want, but I don't like it." On a recipe calling for buttermilk she advises, "Buttermilk—1 tablespoon of vinegar in cup, fill rest with regular milk this makes sour milk which is same in baking as using buttermilk which you usually have to buy extra." Following a few more paragraphs of instructions about mixing and possible additions to the recipe (chocolate chips or nuts sprinkled on top, she says, can be "a nice touch"), she returns to her concern about the buttermilk: "If you use dry powdered milk mix as directed on the box and add 1 T vinegar to this and it works very well and is also cheaper."

Expense is frequently an issue in my mother's recipes. A recipe for another dressing mix, this one for the dry ingredients needed to spice a ranch dressing, is embedded in a narrative of my father and brother's eating habits and preferences. She is a little concerned about the amount of garlic in the mix ("Add more mayo and buttermilk if you think too strong"), but assures me, "We use so much here that I mix up about 5x's the batch & put in a jar then if I'm not home the guys can mix up a batch easily or add to sour cream for dip. In this case I use about 3 T mix to make dressing." Then the cost: "We like & it's about .07¢ for dry spices."

As I read through the collection of recipes I have assembled here on my desk, I am intrigued by the way my mother has treated her writing. The stories themselves might not be enough, these recipes seem to say, they must be accompanied by a reason for writing, perhaps by something useful. The recipe becomes the excuse for the narrative, then, as well as the occasion.

Or have I, her reader, mistaken the text here? Have I been tricked by the apparent form, have I been distracted by the recipe, fooled into believing the recipe itself *is* the text? Have I confused text and context? Have I misread the text and subtext? Are her warnings and bits of advice really comments on my own competence—or lack of competence? Is her concern with cost a covert comment on my handling of my money?

And what am I to make of my mother's frequent undercutting of the recipes she sends? Sometimes her attacks are parenthetical. To every list of ingredients that contains butter, my mother always adds, "(I use margarine)." I have been getting recipes in the mail from my mother for twenty years now. Does this constant—"1 c butter (I use margarine)"—constitute a helpful culinary hint to a daughter too dim to have caught on? Is it a comment on my extravagance since (I use butter)? Does it represent a health tip, an indirect way of reducing cholesterol in my diet? Or is it something more, a subversion of her own text?

I am more and more convinced that these asides represent a subtle attack on the authority of the recipes she includes. She writes "3 cups sifted flour" followed by "(I don't sift)"; "½ c almonds" is countered by "(I use walnuts)." To the salsa recipe I mentioned earlier, which calls for "8–10 chopped jalapeño peppers seeds & all" she comments, helpfully, "(Del Monte has one, 'Hot Chili Peppers,' 7¾ oz. jar)," then adds, in a second and more challenging parenthesis, "(To make better add more hot chilies)."

My mother's recipe for "Dirt Cake" is a long one, longer than most, since my mother tends to cut to the essentials where cooking is concerned, and she doesn't like any recipe that is too complicated. "Dirt Cake" is copied quite neatly on a regular-sized piece of paper. It comes with an elaborate diagram of a flower pot, along with quite specific dimensions, "7 inches high, 8 inch top diameter." The list of ingredients includes—in addition to the flower pot—a small shovel, a plastic flower, and a bag of Gummy Worms. Perhaps she knew I would never read further if she listed "1¼ pkg. Oreo cookies and 1 box Vanilla Wafers," cream cheese, powdered sugar, "½ cube butter (I use margarine)," "2 reg. size packages of French Vanilla *Instant* pudding," and "one 12 oz. container of La Creme Topping" right there at the top of the recipe. But I got through the recipe, stuck it away, even remembered it when trying to decide last summer what I should take to a friend's surprise forty-fifth birthday party. Then I was left to puzzle over her final comments, on the back of the page, which I had overlooked before: "Linda & I both think it would be better to *chill* but not freeze over-nite. This is cuter served in a play wheelbarrow or wagon. Have fun!"

As with the butter/margarine, sifted/unsifted flour, what do I make of my mother's deconstruction of her own recipes? Do I stick to the text itself, making the recipe as written and respecting its independent and anonymous authority, or do I follow my mother's emendations, participate with her in her guerrilla attack on the recipe's textual authority? As the author of her recipes, or at least as a participant in their transmission, she could simply incorporate her changes into the recipes as she sends them to me. Why doesn't she simply revise them—to include more garlic or less cinnamon, to include unsifted flour or margarine? Why doesn't she write the recipes as she has made them? I wonder if she is restrained by some sense of her text's autonomy or whether her subversion is another manifestation of her resistance to prescription of any sort. I have worried, too, that perhaps the choices I am offered are a test of some sort. Do I, as a daughter, choose the power of the word over the bond of motherhood?

There must be something going on. Toward recipes that aren't her own—recipes she's gotten from my sister, Vickie, for instance—she has a different attitude. "Vic's Cape Cod Oatmeal Cookies" is free of her hit-and-run tactics. She lists "1½ c flour" (no comments at all about sifting), "½ c melted butter" (no reminder about margarine), and "½ c chopped nuts" (no mention of which kind). The instructions are minimal. The flour, baking soda, cinnamon, salt are bracketed with a terse "mix together." The egg, sugar, melted shortening, melted butter, molasses, milk, and uncooked oatmeal are followed by "stir into above." About the raisins and nuts she indicates, "add to above." She writes nothing else except "350°, about 12 min., about 60 cookies." The recipe itself is flat, lifeless, devoid of her helpful hints and her encouragement to "Eat!" "Enjoy!" or "Have fun!" There is no indication of how many of these cookies she allows herself with her cup of tea in the afternoon, no comment about the book she is reading while she drinks her tea, no description of the flowers now in bloom on the patio where she sits.

My son, now fifteen, recently asked me to put together a collection of recipes for him so he would know how to make all the dishes he enjoys. He's watched me cook for years, and is already something of an accomplished cook himself, so his request was not surprising. But what intrigued me was that he asked me not to copy all the recipes out for him. He wanted them photocopied so he would have them in exactly the form he's accustomed to seeing. That's what made me realize that my mother's recipes are much more than lists of ingredients and instructions.

My own recipes fade by comparison. Aside from a few oddities—"Karen Cooley's Delicious Fudge" copied out in my tenth-grade hand or "Killer Brownies" scribbled down while I was in a studio audience watching Dinah Shore bake and subsequently named by a friend who had eaten too many—my recipes are nothing. Mostly they're ripped out of magazines; I don't even bother to recopy them. Some are in a friend's handwriting, certainly, and for me they do bring back the place, the occasion. But generally, if I've had to write the recipe down myself, it's strictly functional. "Isabel's Lemon Bars" is only a list of the ingredients in Isabel's lemon bars. I didn't even bother to write down her instructions for making them. I knew I would remember.

But as I sorted through my mother's recipes, really noticing them for the first time, I realized that they were more than ingredients and directions. They were the rich and varied compositions of a writer who had chosen her own form and then pushed beyond the usual limits defining that form.

My mother is a terrific writer.

And her recipe for molasses cookies really is good:

### Ginger Crinkles

| | |
|---|---|
| ⅔ cup oil | 350° |
| 1 cup sugar | 15 minutes |
| 1 egg | 3 inches apart |
| 4 tablespoons molasses | ungreased sheet |
| 2 cups sifted flour (I don't sift) | |
| 2 teaspoons soda | |
| ½ teaspoon salt | |

1 teaspoon cinnamon
1 teaspoon ginger
¼ cup granulated sugar for dipping

Mix oil, & sugar well. Add egg & beat well. Stir in molasses, add dry ingredients. Drop by teaspoonful in sugar & form into balls coated with sugar. Cookies flatten & crinkle.

Have fun!

# Follow the Food

Barbara Haber

People often ask me why the Schlesinger Library, devoted to women's history, has always collected cookbooks. Behind the question there is usually the assumption that a library that chronicles the progress of women's rights ought not also to be amassing books that are a testament to women's traditional role in the kitchen, thought by many feminists to be the epitome of patriarchal oppression.

Confronted with what seems a paradox, I respond with what is by now a rather well-rehearsed defense of the cookbook collection. The speech I give begins with a summary of the contents of many nineteenth-century books on domestic economy that, in addition to recipes, contain otherwise hard-to-find information about the running of homes of the period. We are told how women managed servants or, alas, managed without them. We find out how the sick were cared for not only with "invalid cookery" but also with herbal remedies prepared at home. We discover how women used homemade formulas for cleaning everything from mahogany furniture to kerosene spills. And, from this mass of information emerges a fully elaborated picture of the white middle-class nineteenth-century woman and her daily life. "This too is women's history," I tell my questioners, who usually back off from challenging me, better educated now, better persons than before. Or at least better understanding of the value twentieth-century cookbooks might have for twenty-first-century women's history scholars.

But during all of this high-minded speech-making I feel myself less than forthright. My set piece is sincere enough and accurate, but what I have not yet stated publicly is that I think that food—like gender—is a legitimate category of inquiry that can lead to important social and psychological insights.

The possibility of using food as an instrument of analysis dawned on me innocently some time ago when I started to notice amusing and revealing aspects of people's behavior regarding food and its preparation. Far from being a compulsive house-keeper, I nevertheless found myself irritated with friends who put their knives in the dishwasher, where blades can rust and wooden handles swell. Concerned cooks wash, dry, and carefully store away their knives, treating them like any other well-regarded tools, so that I was not surprised when these cutlery abusers turned out also to be indifferent cooks.

I turned this new awareness to popular culture. On viewing *Thelma and Louise* a second time, I noticed that our first sight of Thelma has her nibbling surreptitiously on a candy bar for breakfast, signaling her childish impulsiveness and irresponsi-bility that accounts for so many of the catastrophes that occur in the movie. In *Mermaids*, another film which focuses on two women, Winona Ryder plays the embarrassed teenage daughter of Cher, a counterculture single mother with even odder food habits. Averse to ritual or tradition, she serves meals that consist entirely of hors d'oeuvres—fun finger foods like cheeseballs and miniature franks on the ends of toothpicks, with marshmallow kabobs for dessert. "That's all the woman cooks," her daughter says. "Anything more is too big a commitment." For the mother, a 1960s type, standard meals with entrées represent conven-tional living and therefore are to be avoided.

Literature, of course, is filled with examples of food scenes that bring the reader straight to the heart of a situation or a char-acter. The famous dinner party scene in Virginia Woolf's *To the Lighthouse* has Mrs. Ramsay, the one character in the novel who successfully connects with others, serving her family and guests a beautifully prepared Beef en Daube. Woolf's description of the dish and how it is served and received makes clear that the food embodies all of the nurturance and good will that Mrs. Ramsay has displayed throughout the novel. Moreover, we know that Woolf herself respected good food: in *A Room of One's Own* she comments that "one cannot think well, love well, sleep well, if one has not dined well,"* conclusions she draws after contrasting the food served in the women's dining hall at Oxford with what was served to the men. They got succulent roast beef, fresh vegetables, and wine, while the women ate dry, stringy meat and overboiled Brussels sprouts, with only water to wash it all down. It is no wonder, she says, that men achieve higher status in the world.

Margaret Atwood is a more recent writer who understands the power of food in the lives of her characters. In *The Edible Woman*, the heroine finds that the closer she comes to her wedding day, the harder it is for her to eat. At first she gives up meat, seeing it as "part of a real cow that once moved and ate and was killed, knocked on the head as it stood in a queue like someone waiting for a streetcar."† Before long, she is unable to eat vegetables, her empathy extending to a carrot she imagines is pleading for mercy as she starts to peel it. These aversions are linked to her feelings about her relationship to her fiancé, a young attorney on the fast track, who treats her as an extension of himself. The novel is about her recognition of her own individuality and her newly found ability to detach herself from a man who is destroying her by devouring and assimilating her. In her case, an inability to eat is a sign that she must save herself from the sinister outside forces he represents, and indeed she does. At the end of the novel, the heroine is joyously eating a

---

*Virginia Woolf, *A Room of One's Own* (New York: Harcourt, Brace and Company, 1929); *To the Lighthouse* (New York: Harcourt, Brace and Company, 1927).
†Margaret Atwood, *The Edible Woman* (Toronto: McClelland and Stewart, 1969).

cake she baked in the shape of a woman, representing the end of her old life and the beginning of the new woman she is creating for herself.

While Virginia Woolf and Margaret Atwood write intentionally feminist work with food operating as powerful metaphors, most contemporary feminist writers have shied away from the subject of kitchens and cooking, seeing them as symbols of subservience rather than pleasure and fulfillment, and rarely as topics for feminist investigation. Typically, when feminist scholars have looked at food, their investigations have focused on eating disorders and the victimization of females, especially young girls, reflecting an intellectual framework that sees food and its preparation as fraught with conflict, coercion, and frustration. More generally, greater emphasis has been put on the value of women's public roles than on private lives as scholars have successfully brought new visibility to the accomplishments of women. The by-product of these attitudes is that women's domestic roles, which preoccupy most women most of the time, have been seen as impediments to women's success, ignoring the possibility that domestic life can be acknowledged and even celebrated without buying into an oppressive value system. Need this be? Can we not care about the sensual pleasures of good food and the personal relationships it nurtures without sacrificing our stands on equal employment opportunities, abortion rights, or anything else feminists have been fighting for?

No less a feminist than Emma Goldman thought we could. Imprisoned in 1919 for conspiracy to obstruct draft registration, she had the good fortune of having a lover who not only shared her political beliefs but also owned a delicatessen store and could cater to her food longings. From the Missouri State Prison Goldman coyly wrote:

Now dear boy you have yourself to blame if you make me cry out with David Copperfield for some of the good things you carry in your delicatessen store. So send us another box soon, don't think you can send too much, there are too many hungry souls here.

Among the things we liked most in your box was crabmeat, sardines, the sausage—quite a different kind from what we get here. Kate O'Hare altho married to an Irishman has a great liking for Jewish food. She likes smoked salmon awfully well, so you can send that also and a variety of canned fruits, we have preserves. Anyway, send along a mixture and it will be appreciated.*

A little shaky on her Dickens—it was Oliver Twist who wanted "more" to eat—Goldman was clear and precise about food. This fragment from a letter gives us a glimpse of Goldman appealing sweetly to a lover as she tries to make the best of a grim and isolated situation by providing delicacies for herself, her friend, and others in the prison.

These references come by way of providing a fuller answer to those who would question the legitimacy of food as an acceptable area of feminist study. Looking closely at the food habits of people—collectively and individually—can reveal them in new and unexpected ways; furthermore, the interpretation of attitudes and customs about food can be a shortcut to understanding the deepest or most hidden truths of people and groups. Just as "Deep Throat" advised Watergate reporters Woodward and Bernstein to follow the money when it came to learning the truth, I say, follow the food.

*Emma Goldman, Letter to Leon Malamed from prison, Jefferson City, Missouri, 17 July 1919. Goldman-Malamed Collections. Schlesinger Library, folder no. 23.

Following the food has in fact led African American writers to important parts of their history. In her foreword to Kathy Starr's *The Soul of Southern Cooking*, Vertamae Smart Grosvenor insists on the relevance of food and cooking:

> I was raised in a time and place where we African-Americans were expected to believe all sorts of foolishness about ourselves and our history. We were led to believe we had few, if any cultural links to Africa. Nobody even mentioned a culinary heritage. Even so, something always told me that soul food didn't no mo' jest grow from Massa's leftovers than a peach jest grows on a watermelon vine.*

Two other African American writers, Norma Jean and Carole Darden, express similar sentiments in *Spoonbread and Strawberry Wine*, a combination cookbook and family memoir:

> We are two sisters who love to cook. . . . our grandfather, Papa Darden, had been a slave and a great-grandmother whom we knew nothing about had been a Cherokee Amerind. . . . As children we had always been intrigued by the women in our family as they moved about in their kitchens, often preparing meals for large numbers of people. Each one worked in a distinct rhythm, and from the essence of who they were came unique culinary expressions. . . . We felt it was time to capture that elusive magic, strengthen family ties, and learn more about our ancestors' history and traditions.†

*Kathy Starr, *The Soul of Southern Cooking*, with a foreword by Vertamae Smart Grosvenor (Jackson: University Press of Mississippi, 1989).
†Norma Jean Darden and Carole Darden, *Spoonbread and Strawberry Wine: Recipes of a Family* (New York: Anchor Press/Doubleday, 1978).

By visiting family members, many of whom they had never before met, and by asking them for recipes and watching them cook, the Darden sisters came to know their relatives. Their book is filled with descriptions of touching reunions and delicious food.

Poignant in a different way are the gustatory remembrances of two contemporary writers—Mimi Sheraton and Madeleine Kamman. Sheraton, who grew up in a household of gifted cooks, captures the flavors of her childhood in *From My Mother's Kitchen*, both a memoir and a collection of cherished family recipes. Of particular appeal are her simplest recipes, which she ties to ordinary family rituals. She tells us, for instance, about fried egg and bacon sandwiches—"something my mother would prepare as a picnic breakfast to be eaten in the car when we drove to and from our country house in the Catskills. . . . Somewhere along the route we ate these sandwiches, which were still ever so gently warm and lusciously soggy and fragrant."\* The engaged reader desires not only the sandwich, but also the entire experience of being that well-cared-for child riding in that car.

Madeleine Kamman's *When French Women Cook* offers the reader the same kind of gift. Her childhood, however, was spent in war-torn France, and these recollections are organized in chapters that center on the different women who influenced her life. Kammen communicates her connections to those who lived in various regions of France, meticulously describing the women and providing precise instructions for recreating the regional cooking and baking, including "a solid, chewy, loaf of bread with cracked wheat, corn flour, and wheat flour" and *pain de fournier*, "a nice combination of light and dark doughs mixed beautifully into each other."† Her book reminds us that the best writ-

---

\*Mimi Sheraton, *From My Mother's Kitchen: Recipes and Reminiscences* (New York: Harper and Row, 1979).
†Madeleine Kamman, *When French Women Cook: A Gastronomic Memoir* (New York: Atheneum, 1976).

ing about food has to be not only good writing, but about good food.

Writing thoughtfully about food can bring comfort to readers. In 1942 M. F. K. Fisher, everybody's favorite food writer, wrote a book called *How to Cook a Wolf* when she was living in England at the height of wartime shortages. She offers her readers recipes geared to bring solace and comfort in the absence of butter and eggs—dishes like polenta and Southern spoon bread, and meatless sauces for spaghetti. Her credo, elegantly stated at the end of the book, is that "one of the most dignified ways we are capable of, to assert and then reassert our dignity in the face of poverty and war's fears and pains, is to nourish ourselves with all possible skill, delicacy, and ever-increasing enjoyment."* Like Goldman, Fisher had set out to make the best of a bad world by expecting and receiving the simple pleasure of good food.

Many of the books mentioned above have dedications to grandmothers and other female kin. Madeleine Kamman dedicates *When French Women Cook* "to the millions of women who have spent millennia in kitchens creating unrecognized masterpieces." And the theme recurs whenever women and cooking are spoken about in the same breath by people who elect to study the history of food and its preparation. That is why the Schlesinger Library's culinary collection should be seen as a part of a women's history collection. The cookbooks prove that the preparation of good food is a serious and often satisfying pursuit in which women have always engaged and excelled. It is a piece of our history in which we can take pride.

But enough of high-mindedness. Just to prove that food can be taken too seriously and that writing about food can be funny as well as informative, let me turn to the slightly irrever-

*M. F. K. Fisher, *How to Cook a Wolf* (New York: Duell, Sloan and Pearce, 1942).

ent Laurie Colwin who characterizes certain kinds of "fussy eaters" in *Home Cooking: A Writer in the Kitchen*. Future scholars who may someday attempt to sort out current conflicting notions of dietary correctness will appreciate her account of the way these contradictions play themselves out.

> Vegetarians, for example, are enough to drive anyone crazy. Like Protestants, they come in a number of denominations. Lactovegetarians will eat dairy, eggs and usually fish, but some lactovegetarians will not eat fish. Vegans will not eat dairy products or eggs or fish. And some people say they are vegetarians when they mean they do not eat red meat, leading you to realize that for some people chicken is a vegetable.*

It will be a great relief to me when feminists allow themselves the liberty to be as light-hearted as Colwin in dealing with such serious issues as food and eating, when they can see food as a way in which women have historically sustained and celebrated life. Some June, for instance, when the rigors of the academic year are over, I would like to invite the women's studies scholars I know to a banquet where we would cook and serve things like Emily Dickinson's bread and Elizabeth Cady Stanton's pudding (the kind she was always asking Susan B. Anthony to cook for her so that she had time to write a speech). We could then move on inventively to such dishes as the roast duckling that we think Dolly Madison might have served, or a chocolate rum mousse cake that we know Isadora Duncan would have loved. Teetotalers could enjoy an alternative dessert of an angel food cake with whipped cream as prepared by Women's Christian Temperance Union founder Frances Willard. The possi-

*Laurie Colwin, *Home Cooking: A Writer in the Kitchen* (New York: Alfred A. Knopf, 1988).

bilities are tantalizing so long as we accept that an interest in scholarship is not incompatible with an interest in cooking.

◻︎◻︎◻︎

## The Soup of Soups

I know it's winter every year when I begin to crave this soup. This is the soup that my mother learned to cook from her mother, and both of them used to tell me that it was the first solid food I was given as an infant. Their descriptions always included funny imitations of a happy baby smacking its lips, so that whenever I make the soup these days, I am always reminded of them, the two most important women in my life.

1½ pounds short ribs of beef
1 cup (8 ounces or half the package) green split peas
1 cup (8 ounces or half the package) large dried
    lima beans
8 cups cold water
1 medium onion
1 cup carrots, peeled and sliced
1 cup sliced celery
salt and pepper to taste

1. In a large pot with a cover, put in the beef and water and bring to a boil. Skim off scum that comes to the top.

2. When clear, add split peas, lima beans, and onion. Cook for 1 hour.

3. Add carrots and celery and cook for 1 more hour. Add salt and pepper. And serve. That's all there is to it!

One can make two courses of this dish. First, the soup with its vegetables, and then the beef which is delicious served with mustard. If you have any left over, just reheat the next day and add water if the soup appears to be too thick.

◻︎◻︎◻︎

# Grandmother's Pickles: Creating a Space

Beheroze F. Shroff

Grandmother Homai stirs the vinegar into the jar, next chili powder cascades into the jar from a packet—salted, dried mango cubes tumble in. Grandmother is making her *gor keri* pickle.

**W**hen I was ten years old, maternal grandmother Homai came to live with us. It was a year of great excitement. We had moved into a bigger flat, my younger brother Sorab was born, and my older sister Khursheed came to live with us along with Homai. That summer vacation, grandmother Homai began introducing us to her vast repertory of cooking of which I remember the pickles the most.

I smell the pungency of vinegar, the chili powder— my tongue dances against the roof of my mouth in anticipation of what will emerge from the confluence of ingredients in the jar.

Homai hardly looks up from her work. My paternal grandmother Dhunmai and the cook Madhu assist Homai—the three of them weave a magical web of words—the past year's pickles are evaluated—quality of ingredients and prices assessed—in the past there was plentitude, the present is full of deprivation. In the time of the British, everything was available, now only leftovers after exports.

Into the pungent vinegar the ingredients plunge—
garlic pods, cloves, peppercorns, cinnamon sticks, red
chili peppers.

The major meals of the household were prepared by our cook
Madhu. Madhu came to work for us when I was born and stayed
with us for the next forty years. Madhu, a Warli from Gujarat,
spoke the same language we did. At first, grandmother Dhunmai taught him to cook; later, grandmother Homai expanded
his culinary skills.

Madhu was totally in charge of the kitchen. Dhunmai was
the only person to whom he was accountable. Between him and
Dhunmai, the day's menu was prepared, vegetable shopping was
done, and three meals were cooked by Madhu. My mother, who
disliked household chores, was happily spared many responsibilities of the kitchen. Her main task was her new baby, her much-
awaited son after three daughters. She supervised her other children's homework and also assisted my father in his office.

Homai is a small, slightly pudgy woman with scant
hair tied back in a bun but her manner is authoritative.
Homai pours salt into the palm of her hand—years of
experience have taught her proportions by eye—she
stirs in the salt—swishing sounds emerge from the ce-
ramic jar.

There was this belief that only one hand must touch
the ingredients, and one hand pour them in; many hands
can alter the chemistry of the process, and the pickles
can turn out badly. No woman in her period could touch
the jar or the pickles were sure to turn out badly. So, if
my older sister Khursheed happened to have her period,
she was not allowed to enter the kitchen.

Paternal grandmother Dhunmai, who was already living with us when Homai came, was a frail, gentle, and soft-spoken person. She was the acknowledged elder of the family—a position she had earned after years of struggle. As a young widow she had shifted from place to place to create a space for herself and her only son, my father, and had given Indian vocal music lessons to make ends meet. Now, Dhunmai was finally in charge of her family, established as an elder, and no overbearing mother-in-law could soak up her power with just a look or a word—this was her domain.

Although Dhunmai welcomed Homai into the house as a sister would, Homai knew that she had stepped into the latitude and longitude of an enclosed geography in the household. She would have to sculpt out her space.

Lumps of jaggery (hardened molasses), the crowning glory of the pickle called *gor* (jaggery) *keri* (mango). I wriggle between the knees jutting out—I nab a piece of jaggery and waft off in search of my older siblings. In the May vacation heat, they loll in bed reading Mills and Boon pulp romances, or play records on our Murphy radio-gram.

"In our time we never lazed in bed like this. You girls should learn to cook a few things. Now's the time, or, what will you do in your husbands' homes?" Grandmother Homai proclaimed.

Dizzy with pulp romances and pop songs, in my ten-year-old head, husbands did not exist, at least not the kind my grandmother referred to as "good decent men" for my thirteen-year-old sister Khursheed. Khursheed had her eye on Prince Charles, prince of Wales, and the men who frequented my fantasies vaguely resembled

Ricky Nelson or Elvis Presley or the Indian-born British singer Cliff Richard, and pickles did not enter this dream world.

The jar is a bottomless pit—now dried fruit is tossed in, raisins, apricots, cashews, dried dates—the three conspirators ponder over quantity—Homai is the final authority: "More!" More raisins are tipped in.

During our school vacations, Homai made elaborate plans. "I'll make delicacies for the children"—she made *mesur-pak*, a sweet candy; *burfee*, *dal-pori*, *khajur-ni-ghari*, *bhakra*, all sweet snacks; *patrel*, a spicy snack; and pickles. "For the children" was merely an excuse. My father's eyes lit up when Homai made her specialties—Dhunmai too loved the *pori* and *patrel*. My father began to request his favorite foods from time to time—most often pickles. Homai had conquered new territory—she had found the proverbial way to her son-in-law's heart and created her sphere of purposeful activity in our home.

By the end of April, raw mangoes started appearing in Madhu's shopping bags. My sisters and I stole some as soon as the bags were emptied—"Leave these alone! They've been ordered for the pickles!" Madhu screamed.

Grandmother would skin the mangoes, cut them into cubes, salt the cubes, and put them to dry in the sun on a cane mat. Between the crows and us three sisters many cubes melted in our mouths.

When Grandfather died, Homai was forced to leave Poona where Grandfather had worked as a manager for the Tata Estate and Property. She could no longer stay in the manager's quarters. She had to pack her belongings and leave for Bombay with my mother who was ten.

Space was, and still is an incredible problem in Bombay, so

Homai had to stay with her sister's family in a cramped flat. Years later, when space also became a problem for my own parents with a growing family, they had to send my sister Khursheed to live with Homai. When Khursheed was thirteen, and my parents could afford a bigger flat, both Homai and Khursheed came to live with us.

For women of Homai's generation there was some awkwardness about living with a married daughter and son-in-law. Living with one's son was acceptable, but having no son and keeping poor health, at my mother's request, Homai came to stay with us.

Seems like everything was gone into the jar—Grandmother Homai places the lid on the jar. The lip of the lid ringing against the mouth of the jar has a finality. Dhunmai ties a white cloth around the lid to make it airtight. The mangoes will be transformed into *gor keri* pickle after a month. The circle is going to break up. Homai seems tired. She has a heart condition.

Very reluctantly, Madhu had given up his space and time in the kitchen for Homai and Dhunmai, so his cooperation in the pickle-making process was essential. From being initially aloof, as merely an assistant, Madhu moved to become the chief of operations.

There was always great excitement when pickles were to be made. Madhu served lunch early; the kitchen was swept and cleaned; the washed jar was laid out and the ingredients placed in orderly fashion. A sense of community and festivity was in the air around the kitchen. Children and adults dropped in to check the progress of the pickles, observe, and comment.

After my grandmother's death in 1972, her legacy was continued not by the other women of the family but by Madhu.

Having made the pickles with my grandmother for over ten years, he could recreate them from his memory and he continues to make them even today.

*Because Madhu is the only one who made pickles after my grandmother's death, no one bothered to learn pickle-making or even to acquire one recipe for pickles. When I asked Madhu for a recipe, he gave me an abbreviated version in Gujerati which I found difficult to translate for an American kitchen. So I offer two of my own concoctions instead.*

◻ ◻ ◻

## Kheema
### (Mincemeat)

2 pounds minced lamb, beef, or turkey
2 large onions
1 whole head garlic (medium) and same
    quantity of ginger
3 to 4 teaspoons garam masala
1/4 teaspoon turmeric
1/2 cup green peas
1 large potato (chopped into cubes)
2 or 3 large tomatoes
salt to taste
2 limes
fresh cilantro

1. Chop onions and add to minced meat in pan; sauté on low heat. When onions have softened slightly, add chopped garlic and ginger. Cover pan and simmer mixture for a few minutes or until meat loses redness.
2. Add green peas and chopped potato and cook for 5 minutes.

3. Add garam masala, stirring it into the mixture evenly. Allow the garam masala to fry for about 5 minutes. Stir frequently to make sure the garam masala does not stick to bottom of pan.

4. Add chopped tomatoes, cover, and cook until potatoes are done.

5. Add salt to taste.

6. Squeeze limes into the mincemeat, stir evenly, remove from heat, and add fresh cilantro leaves before serving. Serve with rice. Serves 6 generously.


░░ ░░ ░░


## Baingan Masala
### (Spicy Eggplant)

4 tablespoons vegetable oil
1 large eggplant, chopped
2 large onions, chopped
1 whole head garlic (medium) and same quantity
     ginger, both minced
1 teaspoon tumeric
$\frac{1}{4}$ teaspoon chili powder (Indian)
2–3 teaspoons of garam masala
$\frac{1}{2}$ cup green peas
$\frac{1}{2}$ cup cilantro
3 large tomatoes
1 lime

1. Fry onions in oil. When onions are pinkish in color, add minced ginger and fry for 2 minutes.

2. Add minced garlic and fry for 2 minutes.

3. Add chili powder, mixing it well. Stir in chopped eggplant, cover the pan, and cook for five minutes on low heat.

4. Add green peas and cook for five minutes.

5. Add tumeric and cook until it colors the eggplant.

6. Add garam masala, stirring it in evenly. Cover pan and cook for 5 to

10 minutes. Stir occasionally to make sure that mixture does not stick to bottom of pan.

7. Add chopped tomatoes, cover pan, and cook on low heat until the tomatoes melt into the eggplant.

8. Add salt to taste. If desired, before serving, add slightly chopped fresh cilantro leaves. Squeeze lime onto dish before serving and serve with rice. Serves 4 to 6.

# Mother I Hardly Knew You from *Deborah, Golda and Me*

## Letty Cottin Pogrebin

**M**y father always came home for dinner, usually at seven. But no matter how lovely my mother looked, or how interesting her conversation, or how delicious her meals, he didn't *stay* home. It wasn't another woman that propelled him out the door, it was a lifelong affair with meetings. Almost every night of the week, he went out to attend meetings—of the United Jewish Appeal or the Jewish War Veterans, or any of his other organizations devoted to the welfare of Jews or of Israel. At one time or other, he was the president, chairman, or county commander of every one of them.

My mother would beg him to stay home for my sake, to give me "a real father, a real family life." But a woman in a cotton housedress and a noisy little girl are no match for the lure of a room full of power and adulation.

Watching him leave the house, I lost faith in my mother's axioms for feminine success, yet she kept reciting them like a litany—not only "Freshen up for your husband," but "Don't show your brains; smart girls scare men," "Always laugh at his jokes," "Act interested in his work even if you're not," and "Have a hot meal waiting when he comes home." My mother lived by these bromides of the 1950s. She freshened up, listened, laughed, and cooked up a storm, but none of it stopped the man she loved from getting into his car and driving away.

Though she fought a losing battle against my father's meetings and organizations, she never gave up trying to lure her husband home by adorning herself, improving herself, and trying to win his heart the old-fashioned way—through his stomach. Her handwritten recipe cards attest to her efforts. In the 1940s and 1950s, when most housewives thought "gourmet" meant Jello molds, my mother was stuffing prunes with pecans and frosting the rims of ice tea glasses. To please me—a notoriously picky eater who was by Jewish standards "emaciated"—she created food art, making a pear into a bunny with clove eyes, almond ears, and a marshmallow tail, or getting me to eat fresh vegetables by presenting me with Salad Sally whose celery body packed cream cheese up its middle and wore a lettuce skirt and parsley belt.

Some of my mother's recipe entries are artifacts in themselves—reminders of the stuff of her everyday life in two separate worlds. Menus clipped from the Yiddish newspaper, the *Forward*, alternate with cuttings from the *Ladies Home Journal*. The recipe for huckleberry cake is scrawled on the back of a ticket for the Military Ball of the Jewish War Veterans' Ladies Auxiliary (November 25, 1942), while Beet Salad is written on the stationery of the City Patrol Corps. Both of my parents served as Air Raid Wardens during the war. I suspect my mother did civil defense work not as a public service but because it was one of the few activities she and Daddy did together.

Even more assiduously than recipes, my mother collected people. Her relatives were first in her heart, time, and devotion. After her family came her many friends in the Jewish community. She was a member of our temple Sisterhood, Haddassah, National Council of Jewish Women, Women's American ORT, and the JWV Ladies Auxiliary—and she had pals in each.

She also had a group of friends who played mah-jongg as if it were the Russian chess championships, but without the silence. I remember iced tea with mint in tall glasses and sandwiches without crusts—cream cheese, tomato, olives; tuna salad with Swiss—and above the clicking tiles and cacophonous cross talk, I remember hearing the women complain about demanding, helpless husbands who would be lost without them. The ladies of the mah-jongg group could forecast doomed marriages and fatal illness long before the principals knew they were in trouble. I learned to recognize the gravity of a person's condition from the voice levels of the narrator. Whispers meant polio and cancer. Heart attacks were discussed a little louder, the flu at full volume. When they forgot I was upstairs with my big ears, the women talked about sex—either they had too much or too little, or they suffered from physical problems that I couldn't understand and couldn't find listed in the copy of *Love Without Fear* that I kept hidden in a zippered bolster on my bed.

My mother died in 1955 when I was fifteen. At that age, the furthest thing from my mind was the possibility that I might someday want to cook the dishes she made, or that I might consider collecting her recipes on the chance that she might die. However, my sister Betty Cottin Miller (who is fourteen years my senior) was kind enough to give me a small book called *The Jewish Home Beautiful* which my mother had given to Betty on the occasion of her wedding in 1946. Betty passed it on to me when I got married in 1963, and I have been cooking from it ever since.

Written by Betty D. Greenberg and Althea O. Silverman, and published in 1941 by the Women's League of the United Synagogue of America, the book contains production notes for two pageants dramatizing Jewish holidays and traditions, plus recipes suitable for each observance, as well as advice on the proper and much-honored (but entirely home-based) role of the woman in Jewish life. The book is especially precious to me because it contains my mother's handwritten annotations of the recipes which she either improved upon or simplified over the years.

❑❑ ❑❑ ❑❑

*Recipes favored by my mother, Cyral Cottin (1901–1955)*

## Potato Latkes

Pancakes for Hanukkah, Passover, or anytime

4 large potatoes
2 eggs
1 teaspoon salt
dash pepper
3 tablespoons flour (In pencil, Mother added
　　"or ½ cup matzo meal" for Passover, a holiday
　　when cooking with flour is prohibited.)
1 teaspoon grated onion (I use more, usually
　　a whole small onion because I like onion.)
½ teaspoon baking powder (must be omitted
　　on Passover)
dash of cinnamon (Optional. I don't add it because
　　it gives the pancakes a vaguely dessert flavor.)
fat for frying (Mother used Crisco. I use olive oil.)

1. Peel potatoes. (I don't bother because the peel is the healthiest part and leaving it on doesn't affect the taste or texture.)

2. Grate potatoes on a fine grater (I grate in the Cuisinart using the disc with the smallest holes). For a lighter texture, one cupful of cooked and mashed potatoes may be substituted for one of the raw potatoes.

3. Pour off half the liquid. (The potatoes do sweat a lot of liquid, but Mother added "not necessary to pour off liquid" and I've found that to be true.)

4. Beat eggs and add them to potatoes with other ingredients.

5. Drop mixture by the spoonful (you can use teaspoon or soupspoon depending on what size pancake you want) onto a hot well-greased frying pan.

6. Turn with a spatula and brown on both sides. (I let them get quite crisp on the first side before I turn them.)

7. Serve hot with applesauce or sugar. (I always serve them with sour

cream on the side, which is the only way my family eats them—and they eat them by the dozens. Latkes is the centerpiece of our festival meal on the first night of Hanukkah. Also, I often make small latkes for hors d'oeuvres, and serve them with sour cream and black caviar. I can't say how many people this will serve because I've always made four or five times the recipe. I freeze leftovers, if any.

◧ ▯ ◧

## Matzoh Meal Latkes

(These pancakes are an easy side dish or dessert.)

3 eggs (yolks and whites to be separated and
    beaten separately)
¾ cup milk or water (Kosher Jews would never
    use milk if the pancakes were to be served
    with a meat meal.)
½ cup matzoh meal
½ teaspoon sugar
dash of cinnamon
½ teaspoon salt
oil for frying

1. Separate egg whites from yolks. (My mother taught me to do this by cracking the egg in half but not letting any of the liquid out until you turn the egg in your hand so that one side of the egg's shell becomes a cup. Then open the shell and keep the yolk in one half and tilt that side and let the white fall into a small bowl. Transfer the yolk to the other half of the egg shell very carefully so that it doesn't break, letting more of the white fall into the bowl each time you go back and forth. Repeat this until as much white as possible is in the bowl. Then, if you're sure you haven't let even a speck of yolk into that bowl, transfer the white to a second bowl and put the leftover yolk in a third bowl. Repeat this process for all 3 eggs. This way, if the yolk breaks and gets into the first bowl of whites, you can discard one egg without contaminating the whole batch of whites. Egg

whites will not whip unless they're pure. Beat yolks in their bowl. Beat whites in their bowl. Keep them separate.)

2. Add all other ingredients to beaten yolks, folding in stiffly beaten white last. (Folding means lifting the batter, not mixing or beating it. This distributes the light froth of egg whites without breaking them down, and keeps the batter light and airy.)

3. Drop by spoonful onto well-greased griddle and brown on both sides. (I use Wesson oil. I make 3-inch pancakes.)

4. Serve hot with sugar or syrup. (I serve with grape or raspberry preserves, or with real maple syrup.) I'm not sure how many this will serve in someone else's house. In ours, it barely feeds 4 as a side dish.

# Hedge Nutrition, Hunger, and Irish Identity

## Marie Smyth

f, as Lin Yutang has said, patriotism is the memory of foods eaten in childhood, then my particular patriotism is formed of the plain white bread of childhood, soft and warm as flesh, pungent with yeasts that live and swell to fill the belly, like no other bread from no other land.* It is also made of bacon, oatmeal fried in bacon juices, strong sweet tea, soda bread, maize bread baked on a peat fire, melting with butter and eaten with buttermilk, not for hunger but for the ritual of mothers baking and gathered children waiting for each scone as it comes off the griddle. As children, we were swallowing a sense of home, hearth, and who we were. We were learning that a woman's work is to feed others, whether they are hungry or not. This constant feeding was in order that we would never know hunger.

As a child walking in the Irish countryside, my mother taught me that hawthorn berries and leaves are edible, but rowan is not. Blackberries, fitches (vetch), dandelion are also edible; soup made from nettles is full of iron, the fruit of the blackthorn—the sloe—is edible but slow to ripen and bitter before it is ripe.

During the Irish famine, which began in 1846, roughly one million Irish peasants died, and a further one million fled the country, many to America. People resorted to eating wild leaves and berries. My childhood lessons of "free food" and hedge nutrition were echoes of this history. The dietary dependence of Irish peasants on the potato—a dependence structured by the land-

*Lin Yutang, quoted in Erica Jong, *Parachutes and Kisses* (New York: Signet, 1985), p. 42.

lord system of the time—the persistent failure of the potato crop, and the Malthusian policies of the British ruling class led to disaster. In the contemporary Malthusian view, the famine provided a "natural" culling process of a population who were multiplying too rapidly: it was functional, rather than tragic.

In my own consciousness, images, gleaned from reading and scraps of discussion, flicker across my mind: images of dying people crawling into graveyards so that they could die on holy ground while grain which would have fed them was exported to England.

I have heard family stories of the famine. I know, for example, that maize was made available to people, but that they didn't know how to cook it. My mother baked maize or "indian" bread on a griddle over a peat fire. The famine also lives on in the Irish landscape: look at the mountains and you can gauge by the height of the reclamation line the severity of the famine and the resultant desperation of the people to clear more land. But even though it lives in our stories and our land, the famine as a subject is often wrapped in silence and mythology.

When I dwell on the Irish famine, its scale and recency, the boundaries begin to dissolve between my nineteenth-century Irish peasant ancestry and starving Ethiopians in the late twentieth century. Yet it is these boundaries which allow Irish people to see themselves as "white," as cultured, civilized, identified with and indistinguishable, from the colonizer. When I dwell on the Irish famine, I am confronted with our own history of being dubbed "savages," "primitives," subhuman and therefore not valuable as human lives. We have avoided and been steered away from dwelling on this history, so it is still there, freshly enraging and fueling contemporary battles and grievances.

When we dwell on the Irish famine as a people, the racism inherent in Anglo-Irish relations of the time reemerges. That racism consigns us, Irish people, to the role of the swollen-bellied, large-eyed, emaciated living corpse that we have seen on television—a persona which is associated with primitivism, with backwardness and that secretly, quietly, is associated with ignorance and indolence. Ultimately, we are taught to believe that tragedy befalls only those who are ignorant and indolent. Otherwise human fate is too fearful and painful to hold in the conscious mind. Thus, we, who do not define ourselves as ignorant or indolent, can distance ourselves from the famine of our ancestors. Given such a history, one can understand the resistance of present-day Northern Unionists to owning an Irish identity: to identify as British is, on the surface at least, less vulnerable.

Nor is it any wonder why the famine does not feature much in Irish literature. It is an unwelcome reminder of how ignoble the Irish struggle for survival has been, how costly and random, and how many people who understood little or nothing of the complexity of its dynamic, paid, nonetheless, with their lives. Remembrance of the famine rekindles that smoldering doubt we carry internally, ignited by the poisonous racist discourse about ourselves that we witness daily. Perhaps we are "savages." Perhaps we are cursed—incapable of living happily and creating our own prosperous independent lives. Perhaps we really are addicted to drink and fighting; perhaps we are inherently inferior; perhaps it was all our own fault after all.

In the current climate of "rightness" the revisionist question about the Irish famine is this: in what way did the Irish people call upon themselves such an experience? It is no longer fashionable to ask the question which must sit alongside this one, the question about the role and responsibility of the British and the landlords: victim-blaming is the convention these days.

We ask ourselves why should we remember the Irish famine, if remembering means that we are blamed for our own holocaust? So it is not much spoken of. Women like my mother are shameless. She taught her children what to eat and not eat from the land that we lived in. This was knowledge that in our collective famine past was crucial to survival. In more plentiful times, it is oral history: we would gather brambles and make blackberry pie. Her passing this knowledge on to me prevents me from forgetting who I am, where my people came from, and how we are interdependent on the environment. To this day, in parts of rural Ireland, a "respectable" family would prefer pie made with apples that were bought in a shop. A "respectable" family would not wish to acknowledge that they too knew about foraging in the hedges and ditches for wild food to eat.

If patriotism is the memory of foods eaten in childhood, then my memories are particular to these hedges and ditches, to our vegetable garden with its root vegetables, to these mountains full of turf, these fields of dairy herds, to the van from Ardglass that sold herrings around the houses on Fridays, to the journeyman who slaughtered your pigs in your own yard for you—a procedure from which children were banished until the yard had been hosed and all traces of blood and slaughter were removed. The taste of that memory was in the bacon.

If patriotism is the memory of foods eaten in childhood, then we are rearing a generation of children with memories of cheeseburgers and pizza. Their patriotism, their identity, and their links to the land they live in—to the soil—are more ephemeral than for any previous generation.

Most of today's Irish children prefer french fries to boiled potatoes, find buttermilk disgusting, eat only white massproduced bread, instant pot noodles, baked beans, or spaghetti hoops from cans. None of this children's food carries in it the same sense of place, nor nourishes in physically or psychically in the same way as the food I ate when I was a child.

Many of the American multinational fast food corporations target very young children in their marketing strategies. Mc-

Donald's, for example, targets children between the ages of three and eight years old with cartoon characters like Ronald McDonald, the children's "friend." These strategies have worked. Irish children who would balk at eating anything "foreign" will happily consume pizza or tacos from a fast food outlet. When abroad, one can solve the problem of children (and other's) food xenophobia by recourse to the local multinational fast food restaurant.

Food marketing, particularly the selling of fast foods by multinational food corporations such as McDonald's, has penetrated the world market to such an extent that today's children need never yearn—as I did when I first moved to the United States—for the foods of childhood. The foods of their childhood are converging into an American fast-food monoculture which is increasingly internationally available.

If the malnutrition is more than physical, if we are what we eat, who will this generation of children, reared on fast food, think they are? Where will they belong? Will they feel like citizens of the world, able to roll into the nearest fast food joint in Dublin or Dubai and feel at home, at one with themselves and the rest of humankind? Or will they feel that there is nowhere on earth that is truly theirs? Will they feel that even their minds and stomachs have been colonized? No longer able to respond to their own hunger, will they be subject to the whim of the next advertisement, salivating on cue, and purchasing the most persuasive rather than the most nourishing or satisfying food.

And what stories will the mothers of this generation tell their children? Will the knowledge I was given by my mother be lost? How will today's mothers feed their children's sense of place, of belonging, of nurturing and being nurtured? If famine is not the shortage of food but the absence of entitlement to access to food, then surely famine is an abiding threat for many of our fellow citizens.

And if patriotism is the memory of foods eaten in childhood, then what land will today's children love? Will all memories converge on the American hamburgers of childhood, or will we rescue some of our diverse food histories and cultures from the submerging tide of a fast-food monoculture?

⚏ ⚏ ⚏

# "Laying On Hands" through Cooking: Black Women's Majesty and Mystery in Their Own Kitchens

## Gloria Wade-Gayles

The cast-iron skillet was large. It was heavy and resistant to scratches or breakage. Invincible. But it was plain and, like its name, rather ugly. A long uninteresting handle attached to a circle deep enough for the oil to cover chicken dusted with flour, fish coated with meal, and inexpensive cuts of steak hammered hard for tenderness. That's all it was: iron cast in a circle and a handle. I could scrub it with a hundred steel pads soaked in the strongest of cleaners, and still it would not shine and the blackness would not go away. I would have preferred a pretty skillet, a pretty silver skillet that emerged from the soapy water with a shiny smoothness in which I could see the reflection of my face, but only the cast-iron skillet understood that boarding in our kitchen was a privilege no cooking utensil should take lightly. Unlike the silver newcomer, it had a century-old memory of the hands, voices, and aromas of black women drawing family portraits in meals they prepared in their own kitchens. It had the weight of character to belong and, according to my mother, the needed know-how to fry everything to a just-right brown and not over-cooked succulence. For her, pretty was in the taste of the food, not in the appearance of the skillet and since she was the final arbiter of all things related to the kitchen, no box tied with ribbons and bearing her name ever contained a pretty silver lightweight skillet.

Its place unchallenged for decades, the cast-iron skillet sat in arrogant grandeur on top of the stove and my mother moved in majesty within our small kitchen, her woman's room. Her house shoes dancing on the linoleum, Mama moved from the stove to the refrigerator to the sink to the stove past the old treadle sewing machine to the white enameled metal cabinet standing flush against the back wall. Working to this rhythm, she produced full-course meals with swiftness and with love, always from "scratch" and always without the aid of a cookbook. She knew from a memory passed down through the generations how to mix the right amount of baking soda, yeast, salt, water, and flour to make homemade biscuits that were so light if you threw them into the air they would float down slowly and gracefully like feathers. She knew how much cold water (that is, water she had chilled with ice cubes from the trays in the refrigerator) was needed (and a drop could be a disaster) to make a pie crust that crumbled to your touch. She measured with the tip of her fingers—a "pinch" of this, a "smattering" of that. Other times, she measured with her eyes. She could see when she needed to add something—just a "bit," however—stir more vigorously, knead a little longer, or let the mixture be. She had a natural talent for cooking.

We know a great deal (or believe we do) about black women who, like William Faulkner's Dilsey or Toni Morrison's Pauline Breedlove, take special delight in shoring up their cooking talents for white families. They are real, of course, but black women like those in my old community are in the majority, and I bear witness to the incontrovertible fact that they took pride in their cooking and considered their own kitchens temples in which they prepared sacraments for family rituals. They could differ in complexion and circumstance, but they were one when they poured cooking oil into cast-iron skillets. I am certain that gender definitions of responsibilities placed them in the kitchen rather than men, but I believe most of them converted what might have been a demand into a desire, a responsibility into a joy, a task into a talent.

Cooking was the centerpiece of their bonding. They shared how-to recipes (oral, not written), information on what was on sale at the grocery, cups of flour and sugar, and a sample of an old dish prepared in a new way. When the subject was a kitchen achievement, they were more generous with their compliments than they were if cooking were not involved; and the wording of their compliments focused on the talent of the cook, not simply on the good taste of the dish. Instead of saying, "That was a good cake," the women said, "You *know* you can cook a cake." In other words, go ahead and be vain because you know you are good.

Men went to the kitchen to eat and as soon as they finished, they left, returning to the imprint their bodies had made in sofas in the living room or parlor. Women, on the other hand, went to the kitchen to work, to serve, to think, to meditate, and to bond with one another. When our neighbor on the left, Miss Annie Bea, came to visit, she and Mama did not sit in the parlor. Instead they sat in the kitchen at the table, and often, while talking, they shelled peas or picked greens. In their kitchens, the women experienced influence, authority, achievement, and healing. When a woman had a crisis and needed to talk, she entered secretly and quietly through the kitchen door which was the back door in blueprints of the apartments, but the front door in the meaning of the women's lives. It was no accident, then, that they often ignored a knock on the front door (which probably meant a salesman coming for a check or a child calling for a playmate), but never one on the back door.

It was from the back door, from their kitchens, that the women emerged on market days and met like an army at the wagons that stopped in the driveway. They became one pair of hands checking tomatoes for bruises, collard greens for wilted leaves, and corn for small worms hidden in the silk; and they were one voice demanding that the price come down or they "wouldn't buy a thing. Not today. No way." Victorious, they would return to their individual kitchens and begin the preparation of family meals.

Mama was not given to bragging about her cooking, or, for that matter, about anything she did or anyone else in the family did. What you did well, she believed, you did well because you wanted to do it well, not because you wanted someone to pat you on the back. Besides, if you did it well, she said, people will know and sometimes, though not always, they will pay you a compliment. People knew Mama was an excellent cook and more than a few of them paid her compliments as in "Nobody can cook better than Bertha" or "Bertha *knows* she can cook some collard greens."

If Mama's gift for cooking emerged from her love for us, watching us gather around the family table and affirm ourselves over meals was one of her greatest joys. I'd swear Mama put some good juju in her food. Why else did it have a way of picking me up when I was feeling low, giving me confidence when I was experiencing doubt, and making me believe that all of my friends envied me because I belonged to Mama, to the family? She seemed to know without our telling her when, emotionally, we needed a certain meal—pot roast, candied yams, collard greens, and hotwater cornbread after a quarrel with a friend; peach cobbler for dessert after a quarrel with a sweetheart. How can I explain why certain meals healed me in a way that others could not except to say that for Mama, cooking was a spiritual experience? When my friends give a similar testimony about their mothers, I realize that there was a mystery about black women working in their own kitchens we do not and cannot understand. It is like the "laying on of hands" we talk about and testify to and about in the black community; the healing hands touch us through the food they prepare.

At a different time, under different circumstances and perhaps in a different life, Mama would not have had time to spend hours in the kitchen preparing full-course meals, so engrossed she would have been with research on the lectures she would deliver and the books she would write. When I think about her passion for ideas, books, and polemics, I have a keen sense of a void in her life and I believe that cooking was her way of filling that void. This does not mean, however, that her love for cooking was not authentic and did not bring her immeasurable joy. Rather, it means that lacking fulfillment in other areas of her life, Mama put her whole self into cooking, making that which was a natural talent and a natural love an extraordinary gift to the family. But I am guilty here of looking at black women's kitchens and cooking through the lens of an academician, an angle of vision that is as limited as duality of the body and the soul is problematic in that it creates oppositionality between realities and, worse, hierarchies based on nothing other than our own biases and our own overweening sense of importance. In an era that has forgotten the joy of service and the patience of love, it is easy to forget our mothers and minimize the mastery of their art in their own kitchens. I pull back, then, from a might-have-been reading of my mother's life and witness for her majesty in the kitchen. Like other women in the community, she saw the kitchen as hers, a place she breathed into existence, a place in which she experienced balance, achievement, recognition, and influence. Her language, like that of her peers, said as much: "Don't step on *my* kitchen floor. It's not dry." Or "I need some new curtains for *my* kitchen windows." She kept *her* kitchen immaculately clean, the floors shiny and the large windows through which the light entered in order to dance with her own so clear they seemed to have no panes.

The two persons she was, gifted cook and lover of ideas, found expression in Mama's kitchen. We never simply ate her cooking; we feasted on her love for polemics. Family meals were, for us, intellectual gatherings. I remember watching a television special on President John F. Kennedy which attributed his success to a family ritual of discussing ideas around the dining table and saying to myself that no one would believe a black family living in a segregated housing project in the South observed the same ritual. What was missing in the television explanation of the Kennedy ritual and present in ours was the magic of food and the majesty of Mama in her own kitchen. It was a ritual that began during slavery when my ancestors gathered to testify, to bond, to gain strength from one another, to image themselves free and empowered. It traveled through time to the housing project of my youth and to Mama's kitchen. It continued when Mama was older and in failing health, with my aunt, her spiritual twin and the family's anchor, preparing the meals that brought us together, but Mama, no less passionate about ideas and polemics, continued to direct us to intellectual dialogue.

The world was so different then, in the forties and fifties, from what it is now. We are not as close. Today we race in a hundred different directions to whatever it is we are trying to catch in this you-must-catch-something world, making one dinner hour convenient for everyone an impossibility. Then we sat in the kitchen around the table, so close we knocked knees and shared hearts. Today we sit in the parlor, or the den, propped in front of TV trays, our eyes fixed on prime time shows that air during the proverbial dinner hour. Then we ate home-cooked and full-course meals prepared from "scratch" and with love, each dish calling our name. Today we eat meals scooped from large metal pans sitting dispassionately beneath distorted lights in a cafeteria serving line or bagged at fast-food restaurants that thicken the air with the smell of grease. We eat surrounded by strangers.

Of course this is progress for black people because now we can eat in those places. In the past the signs and laws and madness locked us out, and we wanted in, but only for the "principle of the thing," not the food or the service. We had everything we needed in our mothers' kitchens. This is progress also for many black women, giving them time off from the demanding work of love-meals: the picking and washing of greens, the shelling of peas, and the kneading of dough for homemade biscuits. Perhaps in this world of microwave and frozen meals, of cafeteria and fast foods, those kitchens are rarely open and might, in fact, be disappearing, along with cast-iron skillets that held memory and the weight of character. Without them, how do we as mothers lay hands on future generations? How do we feed them and what do we feed them in this world of spiritual malnutrition? Where do we gather with them, and when, to affirm them and affirm ourselves?

The woman I am functions in two places: the kitchen and the study. The former has a microwave oven, a gas oven with a see-through door, and Mama's favorite coffee pot in which I keep a pretty green plant The latter has shelves filled with books that look over my shoulder as I sit at my computer, which only recently replaced the one my mother bought me. I enter my kitchen from my study, and my study from my kitchen. Only a door, which is never closed, separates them. Since I inherited my mother's love for books, but not her talent for cooking, I am far more capable in the study than I am in the kitchen. I can cook and when the children were younger, I did cook, but some of the dishes were what Mama jokingly called white folks' food. They were not juicy with pot liquor and gravy like black cooking.

They were dry. And unlike black meals that include pinto beans and greens and cornbread and macaroni and cheese and candied yams—all in *one* meal, I mean—they were what my mother considered snacks: a casserole, a few sprigs of broccoli, a salad, and rolls. But not always. Sometimes, I would do the kind of cooking that would make people say, if they knew how to speak the language, "Gloria, you *know* you can cook." And when we sat down to eat, we passed poignant questions about life along with the tender baked chicken, well-seasoned dressing, tasty cornbread, juicy pinto beans, bubbly macaroni and cheese, and earth-red candied yams.

With each passing day, I look more and more like my mother. I talk like her, move my hands like her, am becoming her, and wishing for her presence in each room I call my own. In the study, she would take delight in the speed with which I work on the computer and the number of books that look over my shoulders, some of which she would have read and others she would want to read. "You are some kind of wonderful," she would say to me. In the kitchen, I would be just okay. She would tell me, as she often did, not to expect my chicken to be a just-right brown. My silver skillet is good for image, but not for food.

As I retrace my steps from childhood to womanhood, from my mother's kitchen to rooms of my own which, in truth, her majesty helped create, I search for the cast-iron skillet. Did I take one with me when I left the housing project and went East to white academia? Did I ever in any of my kitchens own or use one? If a cast-iron skillet were ever present in my kitchen, when did it disappear? Did I miss it or even remember it? Like the old treadle sewing machine that sat unused in my mother's kitchen, the skillet could have sat in grandeur on top of my stove, not to fry foods, but rather to anchor me in memory. I realize that class is operative here because black women who live in the housing project of my youth continue to use and appreciate the know-how of the cast-iron skillet. I wonder if its absence from my kitchen and the kitchens of other black professional women who knew cast-iron way back when is an indication that we lack the weight of character, the weight of memory that our mothers had? I wonder. I wonder.

# My Grandmother's Hands

E. Barrie Kavasch

**B**irdlike, deeply veined, and lightly floured . . . I can still see them firmly kneading—patting—rolling out biscuit dough on the old maple board. The fragrance of raw wheat dough rising in summer heat perfumes my recollections. One of my earliest childhood memories is of my grandmother's hands and of her soft voice drifting somewhere above them . . . in her deep southern drawl telling me of the farm "things" I would ask about—endlessly. Days ooooozed by like molasses then.

Cutting biscuits from the large white circle of dough was a daily activity on the Old Ferguson Farm. This task was so ordinary and essential that we just did it—like morning and evening meditations, filled with love and sweet energies, and the strength of my grandmother's hands. The various food transformations she performed were thrilling. Steaming hot biscuits and pan breads, okra cakes and hushpuppies, flapjacks and griddle cakes with homemade sausages and redeye gravy, hand-churned butter and Pa's own sorghum . . . float through my dreams, nurturing my love of foods and their joyous preparations.

Lucid dreams take me back again to our Appalachian foothills, and the rich red earth of Tennessee heartland, resonant with rasping crickets and the cicadas' liquid sounds of summer, rolling on the heat rising from the earth. A mockingbird's fluid trills and dazzling imitations explode nearby, ripe with territorial pleasures. The range of summer sounds siphon off all concerns.

And, birdlike—again—I see her hands milking the cows in

early morning, as I joined her in the cool barn and asked to help. Carefully she taught me how to firmly grasp the warm teats and pull down, repeating a natural rhythmic motion that bonded me with each huge, warm, munching cow. I felt such amazing closeness and pride, being able to milk "my own cow" in about the same time that my grandmother milked three others. Yet she said I helped "speed her work," and she was grateful. I cannot imagine what the cows thought, as we moved through the small herd who patiently fed in the spidery recesses between hay-speckled timbers. Primal fragrances permeated the old barn, made sharper on hot humid mornings.

My grandmother's hands taught me to weave grasshopper tipis, and placemats, to embroider words and pictures on feed-sack towels in bright cotton threads, to pluck chickens before dinner, and play rook, and pick potato beetles, and catch craw-dads and cook them, too. I tried to tie myself to her apron strings so I could go everywhere with her.

Living on the land is a delicate dance of reciprocity that I learned on that farm in southern Tennessee five decades ago. I cannot take too much without continually giving back. Like the big fireflies of late spring illuminating the misty night like dancing stars, we must return to Mother Earth gifts for new life.

Perhaps it's only in the leaving that we fully reckon with our origins, and the strongly magnetic force they exert on our core. How did my native ancestors deal with this separation? We are the earth, water, and sky of our birthplace and homeplace, which are often the heartplaces of our rational existence. The foods that we eat, and the fasts without food and water that we journey on, compel us back into these dimensions. I dampen my finger and pick up the tiny black seeds of wild lamb's-quarters from a cupped hand. Food has always been a vehicle for my memories to travel on . . . wading through conflicts of identities and cultures,

I sometimes journey back in thoughts to southern Tennessee, and the lush communities of Viola, Asbury, Hillsboro, Ninth Model, Pocahontas, and Wartrace . . .

Like kneading biscuit dough, bloodlines are compressed and blended together rising in new bodies and living in other forms. The polygenesis of my personal being is not without scars from conflicting identities, even while nurtured by earth foods. My Scotch-Irish kinfolks struggled to reach these shores in the late 1600s, escaping the Covenant Wars that had gripped their homelands for hundreds of years. My Powhatan Indian ancestors encountered the earliest English settlers in what became known as the Virginia Tidewater. Recorded as the "Starving Times" in America's history books, they were also the times when Europeans learned many new foods, the corn, squash, and beans the Indians brought to them and without which more of them would have starved. I am one of many who is a fourteenth-generation direct descendant of Chief Powhatan's daughter, Pocahontas, through my paternal lineage, which also charts early Chickamauga Cherokee and Creek Indian bloodlines.

Perhaps it is not surprising that I have become a writer of cookbooks, a food historian, and ethnobotanist. Foods of the Native Americas have exerted magnetic pull over my life. Wild foods and the diverse ethnic politics of foods have conspired to fill my life with nourishment on many levels. Healing pathways lead me through the varieties of wild fungi and other organic elements, metaphysics, and magic. Enthusiasm for life and reverence for food are cornerposts of my existence, continually pushing the envelope of investigation. Strength and diversity come from the land through the foods, and can help us find new balance in our modern lives. Long after my grandmother traveled the "spirit path," I can still see and feel her patient hands. Through the lens of memory, I can look into the old oven and see

Ma's biscuits rising, ghost biscuits from spirit batter and cloud dough that tantalize my senses and transform the food of my soul into modern recipes.

⠃⠇ ⠃⠇ ⠃⠇

## Ma's Buttermilk Griddle Biscuits

Classic buttermilk biscuits are speedy, light, and flaky, and a light hand in kneading makes these popular treasures most desirable. Assemble all ingredients at room temperature (about 70°) except for the chilled butter or lard, unless substituting a light oil. Sift fine wheat or cake flour in advance of measuring.

> 2 cups cake flour, or 1 ¾ cups all-purpose flour
> 2 ½ teaspoons double-acting baking powder
> 1 teaspoon salt
> 1 teaspoon garlic powder, or chili powder
> 3 to 6 tablespoons chilled butter or lard or shortening
>     (or combinations of these, or olive oil)
> ¾ cup buttermilk

1. Sift together in a medium bowl flour, baking powder, salt, and garlic powder or chili powder.

2. Make a shallow well in center, and add butter (lard, shortening, olive oil).

3. Briefly but thoroughly cut solid ingredients into dry ingredients with knife or pastry blender, until mixture resembles coarse cornmeal.

4. Again, make a shallow well in center, and add buttermilk. Stir well together and work briefly until dough pulls away from sides of bowl.

5. Turn dough out onto lightly floured board and gently knead for about 30 seconds with lightly floured hands.

6. Roll dough out into broad circle with lightly floured rolling pin and

cut biscuits with lightly floured biscuit cutter or shape generous biscuits
with lightly floured hands.

7. Place biscuits on hot, lightly greased griddle or in large iron skillet
about half an inch apart. Cook over medium-high heat for 5 to 8 minutes,
then turn over to cook about the same amount on the other side. If baking, place biscuits on ungreased baking sheet and bake 12 to 15 minutes in
preheated 450° oven. Yields about twenty 1½-inch biscuits.

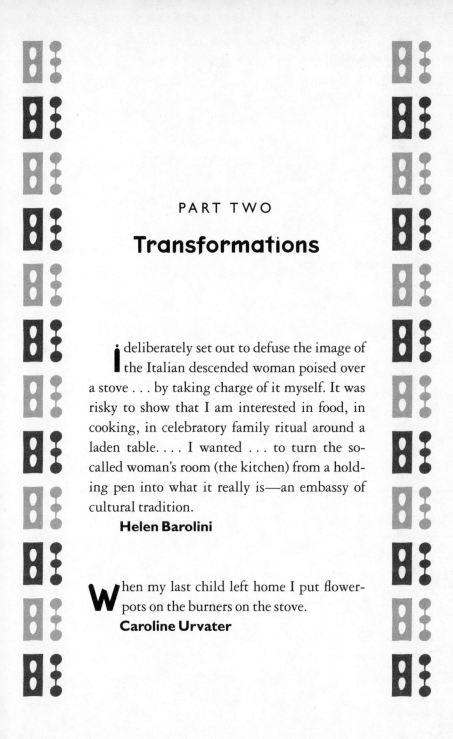

PART TWO

# Transformations

I deliberately set out to defuse the image of the Italian descended woman poised over a stove . . . by taking charge of it myself. It was risky to show that I am interested in food, in cooking, in celebratory family ritual around a laden table. . . . I wanted . . . to turn the so-called woman's room (the kitchen) from a holding pen into what it really is—an embassy of cultural tradition.

**Helen Barolini**

When my last child left home I put flower-pots on the burners on the stove.

**Caroline Urvater**

# What's that smell in the kitchen?

## Marge Piercy

All over America women are burning dinners.
It's lambchops in Peoria; it's haddock
in Providence; it's steak in Chicago;
tofu delight in Big Sur; red
rice and beans in Dallas.
All over America women are burning
food they're supposed to bring with calico
smile on platters glittering like wax.
Anger sputters in her brainpan, confined
but spewing out missiles of hot fat.
Carbonized despair presses like a clinker
from a barbecue against the back of her eyes.
If she wants to grill anything, it's
her husband spitted over a slow fire.
If she wants to serve him anything
it's a dead rat with a bomb in its belly
ticking like the heart of an insomniac.
Her life is cooked and digested,
nothing but leftovers in Tupperware.
Look, she says, once I was roast duck
on your platter with parsley but now I am Spam.
Burning dinner is not incompetence but war.

# The Cook, the Maid, and the Lady

Caroline Babayan

**B**efore I started school, I used to spend the days with my grandmother or Metzik as I called her, while my mother was at work. My father had died when I was still a baby. After his death, my mother and I moved in with my grandmother and my three aunts and uncle. My grandmother herself had become a single mother after her husband declared that he was unable to support so many people and had moved to another town. His departure meant that my grandmother was no longer subject to his state of utter gloom punctuated by violent fits of temper, aimed mainly at her.

Having been brought up by French nuns in a convent school, my grandmother was able to support her children by teaching, but she could not afford to give them the education she and they had dreamt of. This generated great resentment in her older children—my aunt, uncle, and mother—who had to work in order to contribute toward the upkeep of the two much younger sisters. By the time I was born, my grandmother was staying home looking after me and her youngest children who were only six and twelve years old.

Metzik and I were the first to get up in the mornings. She would send me to get washed while she got the samovar going and brewed a strong pot of tea. She would then make me something to drink, which depended on the season; in summers freshly squeezed sweet lemon juice, in winters a cup of cocoa or sometimes, if I fussed enough, some weak tea with milk and sugar. By the time the samovar was boiling, my uncle, who was the first to leave for work, was up. Metzik would pour them both some tea, while talking to him continuously in low tones. He would sip his drink without uttering a word. Naturally, I don't remember the subjects of these monologues, but I recall vividly her glass of tea. It was big as a drinking glass, through which I could see the spoonfuls of sugar accumulating in the amber liquid until it became half white. Metzik would then begin stirring, in rhythm with her soliloquy. She was a small thin woman who ate sparsely, but she had a gargantuan sweet tooth, which suited my taste perfectly.

After everyone had left for work or school, she and I would have breakfast. My favorites were omelette with honey and fresh "berberi" bread, a flat yeast bread sprinkled with poppy seeds or *gogli*, egg yolks beaten with sugar until creamy and pale, spread on white bread and butter.

While eating breakfast, she would discuss her biggest dilemma, choosing the day's dinner. She had six mouths to feed, each with his or her own caprice concerning food. I would offer suggestions which I now believe must not have been very helpful, since the dishes I liked best, besides shish kebab which I knew was a feast meal, were limited to three.

One was a Persian dish called *mossama*, which consisted of fried aubergines and cubes of lamb, cooked in a thick tomato and onion sauce, served with steamed saffron rice, and salad made with Romaine lettuce.

Number two was also a Persian specialty. Cubes of fried lamb or beef, cooked slowly together with black-eyed peas, chopped onions, and a huge amount of five sorts of herbs, finely chopped. Again served with steamed rice which had formed a thick bread crust underneath.

But my absolute favorite was vine leaf dolmas, which my grandmother was an expert at preparing. Even after so many years, and innumerable attempts at recapturing that taste, I have not eaten dolmas like hers. When fresh grape leaves were in season, she would have her greengrocer set them aside for her. Even then she always bought more than she needed because she would carefully choose the most delicate ones and discard the rest. After they were parboiled, I would help her separate the leaves while she carefully filled each leaf with a mixture of minced meat and onions, herbs, and rice. She made the filled leaves into little bundles and placed them gently into the casserole until it was full. Then she covered the dolmas with a plate and let them steam very slowly for several hours, until the natural juices had created a sauce. She would serve the dolmas with garlic yoghurt and lavash, a soft flat bread.

I would have gladly eaten these dishes twice a week, but the rest of the family didn't quite share my enthusiasm. They demanded more variety, and Metzik tried to comply.

Before the advent of freezers in Iran, most people went shopping every day. For me that was great fun because Metzik was incredibly popular with the shopkeepers and therefore I was always treated to some extra goodies. The reason for her popularity was a distinct ability that set her apart from all other grandmothers I knew.

There were a variety of nationalities in Iran, each specializing in certain food shops. The Persians sold meat, fruit, and vegetables. The Assyrians ran the delicatessens, the Turks the dairy shops, the Armenians and Russians the confectioneries, and so on. As we went into each new shop, Metzik would automatically begin to speak the shopkeeper's language. This incredible talent for languages endeared her to them, and I was the one to enjoy the fruits of their enthusiasm.

The shopping excursions I loved best were the days we went to the Russian confectionery to buy cakes for the afternoon tea. Monsieur Serge, the owner, who was probably in love with Metzik, would ignore all his other clients and bring us a big plate of petits fours in order to have a tête-à-tête with my grandmother.

I would happily stuff my face, while I listened to the soft melodious exchange, of which I understood nothing.

Home again, we would set on the Herculean task of washing, peeling, scraping, and chopping the mounds of vegetables and herbs needed for Persian and Armenian cooking. Sometimes I would keep her company, but mostly I would embark on one of my adventures. I would dress in the appropriate outfit, which Metzik somehow always found time to make for me. I would become Robin Hood, Peter Pan, D'Artagnan, Zorro, and so on. I only liked the male characters in the stories because they had the most fun. The women were either always waiting to be saved or were evil.

Sometimes Metzik would call me to give her a hand; to pour the milk in gradually when she was making mashed potatoes, or stir the yoghurt soup to prevent it from curdling. The smells from the kitchen always made me look forward to eating. However, the ambience at the dinner table was subject to the fluctuations within the family relationships, and was a great cause for anxiety, for both Metzik and me.

The memories of my early childhood dinner table in Iran are a mixture of idyllic scenes of family members swapping news, telling jokes, and eating heartily and the silence of repressed anger and jealousy manifesting themselves into the rituals of sniffing cautiously at the contents of the plate or carefully dissecting the food into an unappetizing mound. For my grandmother, however, those daily meals must have been an unmitigated nightmare. Metzik's children used food as a means to express their resentments and their anger at each other, or as was more often the case, at her. All of a sudden, one didn't like rice anymore, the other wouldn't eat meat. My eldest aunt would want more sophisticated continental cuisine, my uncle would demand simpler food. Even her choice of cakes could be a subject for endless squabble.

Metzik bore the anger for years. By the time I was nine, she had finally had enough. One day, I returned from school and found Metzik gone. She had left to live on her own, and we didn't see her for nearly a year. I felt desolate and betrayed, but I refused to listen to her children's slander of her.

When she reappeared, we hardly recognized her. Like most Armenian women her age, she had always dressed conservatively, dark blues and browns for winter, and white and beige for summer. Now she wore a silk dress, with a pattern of flowers in all the bright colors of autumn. Her hair, which was normally drawn back and held in place with hairpins, was now done in a nice round slightly bouffant style, accentuated by silver streaks. Her lovely hands, which had always been slightly stained from handling vegetables, were now immaculately manicured.

Metzik had found a job and rented a large comfortable room from an Armenian/Assyrian family who washed and cleaned for her. She bought take-away food now or ate out. She had stopped cooking and never made another dish again. Once, when my aunt had invited us all to dinner, she asked my grandmother to help her with the sweet and sour sauce she used to make for the cabbage dolmas. Metzik told her earnestly that she couldn't remember how to make it. She had never been a big eater, so her salary went to clothes, hairdressers, manicures, holidays, and rummy circles.

Whenever she came to visit any of us, she always brought a huge box of cream cakes, bought from her eternal admirer, Monsieur Serge. None of us liked cream cakes very much, but somehow we didn't dare to say anything until she had gone.

This metamorphosis of my grandmother from cook and maid to lady was considered, by her children and everyone else, as the pinnacle of egoism. But even though I missed Metzik terribly when she left, I could never bring myself to say anything else but "good for you!"

# What My Tongue Knows

## Margaret Randall

Mother rarely cooked in our family. She'd open a can of corned beef, which I remember Dad liked second only to his franks and sauerkraut. These remained his favorites as he struggled through the diminishing swamp of Alzheimer's exhaustion, right up to that bland wall of nursing home fare. In the last weeks of his life he clamped shut his lips, refused the force-feeding. It was the only gesture of control he had left.

When we were children Mom fashioned meat loaf or hamburgers, heated canned vegetables or cooked fresh ones till they paled. She was known for her spaghetti: boiled and then over-baked to a gummy mass of indistinguishable pasta, Campbell's tomato soup, and Velveeta American processed cheese. We loved it though. My sister, brother, and I thought our Mom's cooking was the best.

I cannot remember either of my grandmothers having culinary skills either. Nana Jo—my mother's mother—inhabits bathrooms rather than kitchens in my memory; her darkly circled eyes still frighten me thirty years beyond her grave. Nana Daisy, Dad's only parent by the time I came along, had a cook. Even so, no special dishes come to mind.

I am sure I am one of the American majority of my gender, class, and culture who nurtured an eating disorder long before I knew what that obsessive consumption might be called. Or that an array of industries would encourage it while others promised cures. Even when I became familiar with the psychological label, I was astounded by my condition. I looked upon it as if it had invaded someone else's body rather than my own. Three scoops of chocolate ice cream was a nightly staple, well into my mid-fifties. Gradually, year by year, the scales displayed more robust numbers, until I weighed in at two hundred pounds. I am five foot four.

I would frequently dream about food, often in connection with scenes of violent death. Some ten years back, this poem came to me complete. It is about a woman I knew only briefly before she became the accidental target of a bomb blast at a guerrilla press conference deep in the Costa Rican jungle:

## Fat

Standing beside me she is silent
as I part the flesh of bread,
wield soft cream cheese or unrepentant butter
generous across its open face.

She arrives as I ask myself
why I am eating yet another slice
of thick dough, and answer wordlessly:
this permanent gluttony of dreams.

In heavy dignified repose
she is dead. And with me.
Hands lightly clasped upon the counter,
briefly reticent within her body's spaciousness.

She has come before.
I know she will take her time,
will never speak my language,
and that I will understand.

In the violence of her loss
I search for bloody scars, missing limbs,
remembering how we met, spoke, forgot one another
until her last grenade.

Since then it has been visitation
at every kitchen counter,
her soft breath against my face, her silence
as purest fat swells pores of sourdough.

We are fat. Even in death she is fat
and I grow heavier as I cut and spread,
welcome her visits, accept her comfort.
Linda, hello again without question,

for I no longer wonder
what you are doing in my kitchen,
who also told you: if you can't say something nice,
please, don't say anything at all.

I knew that Linda was telling me that her burdensome poundage had prevented her from moving quickly enough to save her life, that when danger seared the air she had not been able to run. And I knew our bodies were joined, years before our casual meeting, in the repeating loop of a conditioning reserved for women.

When the contradictions became too painful (and the opportunity presented itself), I embarked upon the inevitable therapeutic journey. Memories began to surface. Incest, at the hands of my maternal grandfather, became an issue I had to confront head on. I even learned the origins of a lifelong phobia, though I couldn't erase its grip. Gradually I learned to deal with a number of ills: asthma, an off-balance security, vertigo. But a decade would pass before I was finally able to stop filling myself with too much food.

As I write this, and for the first time in my life, I savor what I eat; delight in it without that underside of cyclical anguish. And for the first time, I can admit without shame: I love to cook.

I love to bake, especially bread. I regularly set a day aside to knead and rise and shape the mounts of light whole wheat or oatmeal sunflower seed loaves. Raisin bread made with dried cranberries or tiny currants. Dark pumpernickel and its whiff of chocolate. The utensils are important: special earthenware pans I never wash are infused with the warm scents of many bread-baking mornings. A cobalt blue heavy duty mixer sits on my kitchen counter: the most powerful and elegant of sculptures.

I take sensual pleasure in working the dough with my hands, especially in winter when a cedar fire hums and sizzles in the pot-bellied corner stove. As heat permeates the room, the aromas of flowering yeast and loaves warm from the oven fill the house. I love those smells as I love the curve of my lover's neck or the full scent of chamisa in the air of an empowering New Mexico fall.

Now I cook as a woman, free at last of that feeling of enslavement with which a male culture has imbued the process of preparing food. I have always loved to cook, even when a complex web of stand-in and denial transformed the ritual into something it was not meant to be.

On my way to where I am now, I had to stop feeding people. That was important. I had to learn to prepare and place the food upon the table, allowing those I love to serve themselves—or not. My companion, Barbara, helped with that one. One day she simply refused to let me ladle all that food onto her plate. It prompted another phase of contemplation. And another poem:

## Yes, Something Did Happen in My Childhood

> I am a cook for others, a shameless feeder
> of lovers, children, friends.
> I plead guilty to this destiny or daily task
> this knowledge running from the succulent pores
> of a pork roast

lodged in the aftertaste of curry stew
rising in weekly dough of warm bread.
I give food as sustenance, stake well my territory,
unnerving tempers I spoon advice
to challenge hearts and minds.
On cold mornings I sit with recipe books,
*The Joy of Cooking* lived and died
five lifetimes in my hands.
There are full-color gourmet photographs
I preview heady scrapings from a bowl or pan
my energies rush to the fore
when no one waits or wishes to be served.
I am that woman over-filler of mouths
that plate-heaper learning late
to let my eaters serve themselves
come back for seconds on their own terms.
My food is not for thought
but for the belly, belt unbuckled,
every diet plan on hold.
I am the writer, teacher, political activist
who dreams of high praise for my apple pie
a note in the *Times Book Review*
for my oven-baked chicken enchiladas.
Yes, something *did* happen in my childhood.
No, I can't remember what it was.

The poem told me I couldn't remember. But by that time I
knew I could, and did in one way or another every day of my life.

Later I wondered if gaining control over my own runaway
food intake would keep me from the joy I'd always reaped from
creating meals for myself and others. Not at all. It's been quite
the opposite. Feeling better about my own relationship to what
I eat has freed me to delight more thoroughly in the cooking art.

How could it have been otherwise? When I think back
through my particular history, I remember that I never tasted
the food I prepared. I rarely sampled anything before I brought

it to the table (although I routinely snacked at any other time of day or night). It was always color rather than flavor that told me a dish had reached perfection. Over the years, trying to explain that I cook by color instead of taste has been a little like trying to explain how every word is possessed of a color in my eyes. People nod, but rarely understand.

The mysterious earth red of sun-dried tomatoes. Olive oil's serious but translucent amber-gold. Fresh shrimp, turning from mother-of-pearl green to a radiant pink, tight curves of coral just below a surface of gently boiling water. Broccoli or spinach at their moment of brightest green, steam exuding the scent of its freshness. Rich red-brown mole ladled over the pale ivory of a chicken breast, beside the reds and yellows and greens of enchiladas topped with shredded lettuce and cheese. The blue-black depth of home-cooked beans.

A powdery white—the sugared surface of a sweet—always caused me a slight shudder; it brought a clouded but nonetheless painful image of my grandfather's chalky face, too close to my own. Saffron yellow: there's a color dazzling as the sun. And there is deep comfort in the gray but not pink of a perfectly roasted pork shoulder. Dark chocolate is beautiful; light or milk chocolate too flippant for my taste.

In contemporary women's struggle to live our feminism, we have consistently been made to feel ashamed of loving to cook; just as prefeminist pressures shamed the women who did not enjoy this activity. And yet—each in our own milieu and according to our circumstance and need—we are most often the artists, organizers, and drudges of what passes the palates and fills the bellies of those we love.

And also of those we do not love.

Our creativity deserves a monument. The nightly meals set out by tens of thousands of single mothers defy the quick fix of Hamburger Helper or macaroni and cheese. Everyone knows that TV dinners are mainly the province of heterosexual males and the career woman who lives alone. Gay men often enjoy cooking and are generally as good at it as the most creative woman.

It's no accident that women feed a nation, while most of the prestigious highly paid chefs are men.

I lived in Cuba during the decade of the seventies. I raised my four children there, in an era of food-rationing in which no one had an overabundance, everyone had equal access, and intense innovation was the key to variety and satisfaction. I can remember long evenings doing neighborhood watch with other women on my block. We'd walk along the sea wall to the sound of the Caribbean's rhythmic slap of waves against old stone. And we'd exchange the most extraordinary recipes.

When tomatoes were in short supply we found ways to make "tomato sauce" without them; a little oil, some salt, and a lot of powdered redroot were the ingredients. Large Manilla mangoes were rare; we boiled the skins with sugar and a very little of the fruit, and came up with a delicious mango "preserve" to spread on our ration of bread.

There was food humor too. It helped get us through tough times. There must have been a hundred jokes about that staple, the split pea:

"Have you heard the latest recipe for making split pea soup?" one of the women would ask. We'd all lean forward, eager for her story. "After boiling them, you throw out the first water. Then the second. And the third . . ." The number of water changes depended upon the teller's skill in keeping her listeners' interest. Each change ended with the words "and then you throw that water out . . ." The punch line, of course, was "then you throw out water, peas and pot."

We'd all laugh, if for no other reason than to ease the tension of our own tired efforts.

Over the years I've joked about food, worried about it, worried about what it is doing to my body, and my mind. I've told myself I must not walk willingly into a madness coaxed by media images of women who are five foot ten and weigh little more than a hundred pounds. I have chided myself that I must resist the urge to pound my thighs or scream when my mother smiles and says something about how fat she's getting, she of nearly anorexic construct.

I have thought about my mother's childhood, reminded myself that we have no photographs of her before the age of nineteen or twenty. Not one. Even without her words, without her memories—which seem forever buried—I know there was abuse. For I no longer have doubts about my own abuse at the hands of her parents, my grandparents. Poems came in a rush as the images pulled themselves up into my conscious memory. I wrote this one the day the first of those images came into focus:

## The Green Clothes Hamper

Rain almost hides my mountains today.
Low clouds snag the rocky skirts.
Colors of rain and clouds clean everything.

I speak of the rain, the clouds, the living colors
of this land
because it seems impossible

to cut this silence with the words
my grandfather was a sick and evil man
posing as healer.

Now I retrieve his hands and eyes
his penis filling my tiny infant mouth
as he forced himself into a body, mine,

that still finds reason easier than feeling.
This is the green lucite top
of a clothes hamper where rape impaled diapers.

This is memory catching up with itself
overtaking asthma, compulsive food,
fear of that which is not itself.

This lost green hamper. My body, coming home.

My hesitant, stumbling, all too recently successful struggle
with my own eating disorder has had to force its way through the
needle's eye of my mother's persistent reminders that I am fat,
that she is thin, that an umbilical cord of control runs invisible
but ever-present between us.

Mixed messages. Like the TV commercial for three-cheese
pizza immediately following the one for Slim-Fast or Nordic
Track, my mother will exclaim her joy at my weight loss . . . then
offer me a second helping of dessert.

How did I begin to break this chain of punishment and reward? How did my relationship with food finally change? I
know it is about it finally being the right time. And I know exercise is an important component. I can talk about how it feels,
even point to some of the more obvious or tangible results. But I
am still exploring the richness of its language.

The physical moment happened like this. One brilliantly
delineated New Mexico morning, as I rode my bike along a favorite path, I knew it was time to make things different. It was
early September, 1993. I turned to Barbara and said: "I want to
begin working out, to eat differently, feel better."

My pattern had been to eat two or three meals in place of one,
feel confident I could break the pattern *just after* getting up from
each table, then inevitably repeat myself by the time the next

meal reared its seductive head. I recognized the absurdity of this cycle, but seemed unable to alter its dance.

My body felt like cargo, all the time. Although I possess my share of vanity, it wasn't only about appearance. It was about mobility, agility, how I felt. At the nursing home where I visited my father several times each week, I'd see dozens of old women and men, their inert bodies kept alive by a technology designed to profit from their continued presence on this earth. I didn't want to end up like these people. Increasingly, I became aware of a desire I had not recognized before: to keep healthy and delight in *using* my body—as long as it might serve me.

Of course that contributed to my understanding that I really didn't *possess* my body, not in the ways I might have believed. I could retrieve it, as I had my childhood stories. I could nurture it the way one nurtures one's children and then must let them go. But this new task would take a new and unfamiliar type of work.

Once I understood that, really understood it at a feeling level, the task ahead seemed disarmingly simple. Could it really be this easy? My partner and I joined a nearby gym. We got rudimentary advice about how to exercise. And we knew the basic food changes that were required: no rigorous diet or dietary aids—we were clear that these rarely work—but a set of simple rules: low fat, little or no red meat, cut out the three scoops of chocolate ice cream.

My fears centered on the changes I knew I would have to make in the way I consumed food. I would learn to eat more slowly, I told myself, tasting my favorite dishes, savoring them rather than gulping them down to fill those bottomless pits. I would learn to appreciate the succulence of the homemade breads I loved to knead and bake; not obscure them beneath butters or jams. I would delight in salads, fruits, vegetables. I liked these things; why not slow down and feed that liking?

But yes, I was worried. Worried about whether or not I

would be able to deal with such radical changes in my eating habits. At my age I might have worried about the exercising too: would I learn to use the machines, would I manage to be consistent, would I be willing to give time to this new activity—for as long as it took? And I knew it would take all the rest of the time.

Making weight loss and strength gain priorities requires a discipline. But I knew I had discipline. I had proven that to myself and others all my life.

I've been surprised that the radical change in my approach to food has not been more difficult. More painful. More back and forth, or up and down. When I made the decision, *this* decision, everything seemed to fall into place. It's not that I don't think about that chocolate ice cream (or amaretto cheesecake with fresh strawberry topping) once in a while. I still feel tempted to take that extra enchilada. But when this happens I am generally able to think about whether it's my food hunger I'm feeding, or that other, older, hunger: the holes left by the abuse.

Like so many things, cooking can be drudgery or it can be a source of resistance, even power. We cook for our children, nourishing them in a conscious continuation of the umbilical link— that connection that is never really severed, only changed. We cook for our lovers, delighting in offering the dishes they like best.

The first time I invited Barbara for dinner, I made a salmon soufflé: delicate yet pungent, and very light. She expressed the appropriate appreciation, and for at least a couple of years I continued to produce that soufflé every once in a while; it brought back memories of our first date.

It also brought Barbara a serious dilemma. In fact she hated salmon soufflé. She hated all soufflés, something about the consistency or texture of the dish. When she was finally able to tell me the truth about her food tastes and my cooking extravaganzas, we began to speak more honestly about other issues as well.

It initiated a complicated time for us, but one without which we might not have been able to struggle through to the deeply trusting relationship we have now.

Because we are women born and bred in patriarchy, Barbara and I both hold the pain of food abuse and damage in our lives. Now, for both of us, food moves from embodying and displaying the contradictions to speaking new words: a space and body of one's own. As the learned distances between mind and body close, as the heart finds its oneness in a particular configuration of cells, the dishes we prepare, eat, and offer to others are more and more an extension of those vivid colors—and tastes—our tongues have always known.

For, as Trin T. Minh-ha tells us, "Words empty out with age. Die and rise again, accordingly invested with new meanings, and always equipped with a second-hand memory." Women surviving patriarchy often need second- and third- or fourth-hand memories, each mirroring who we are with less subterfuge, with more of the power to bring us home.

❑❑ ❑❑ ❑❑

## Good Black Beans

> 1 pound good-quality black beans, cleaned but
>     not soaked
> 5 or 6 small cubes of bacon rind or ¼ cup olive oil
> 1 large or 2 small onions
> several cloves garlic
> 1 red bell pepper
> 2 large or 3 small tomatoes (8-ounce can of peeled
>     tomatoes may be substituted)
> water
> fresh cilantro

1. In large pot fry bacon rind until browned or heat olive oil.

2. When hot, add minced onions, garlic, and red bell pepper. Stir and continue to cook until vegetables are soft and run together. This is the all-important *sofrito*. If using fresh tomatoes, add them to the *sofrito*; if using canned tomatoes, wait and add them later.

3. Now add beans and cilantro (and tomatoes if canned), plus enough water to come within a couple of inches of the top of the pot.

4. Boil covered over medium heat for three or four hours, being careful to check the pot from time to time to make sure water has not evaporated. As beans cook, they will gradually thicken. Add more water whenever necessary. *Do not add salt* (beans don't really need it, especially if bacon rind is used—and even if it is not. Beans improve over several days, and if salt is added they tend to become much too salty).

5. These black beans are delicious with chicken and rice. For vegetarians, they are a meal in themselves when served with rice and perhaps some guacamole. A pot made from above ingredients easily serves eight—or four with several days' leftovers to look forward to.

❈ ❈ ❈

## Lemon Garlic Shrimp

1 pound extra large fresh shrimp, washed, deveined,
     and shelled
10 cloves fresh garlic, peeled
1 large onion
1 large sweet red pepper
3 tablespoons butter
2 cups lemon juice (fresh squeezed or bottled)
2 tablespoons fresh or dried mint

1. Melt butter in large skillet.

2. Press cloves of garlic to a gritty paste. Chop onion very fine. Cut red pepper into slender strips.

3. Cook garlic and onion over medium heat until most butter is ab-

sorbed and onion is translucent. During last five minutes or so, add red pepper strips and cleaned and deveined shrimp, stirring constantly until all shrimp cease to be greenish white and have just attained their pink color. Do not overcook at this stage.

4. Add lemon juice. Reduce heat to lowest possible level and cook 10 to 15 minutes more, until liquid becomes slightly opaque. At this point you may add a bit of water (if lemon juice reduces too quickly). Be sure not to allow the dish to absorb too much of the liquid. You want a succulent mixture to pour over rice.

5. Ladle over freshly cooked white basmati rice (2 cups dry rice, 4 cups water, a pinch of salt). Sprinkle with pulverized fresh or dried mint. Serve immediately. Serves four.

## Spanish Paella

This is a festive main dish which will amply serve ten to twelve people. Leftovers may be kept in refrigerator, heated, and served with more lemon juice the next day.

> 6 chicken thighs and 6 drumsticks
> ½ pound extra large raw shrimp
> 6 to 8 clams (be sure none of these are open
>     when purchased)
> 1 medium stick pepperoni (imported if possible)
> ½ pound lean pork (cubed)
> 2 red bell peppers
> 2 medium onions
> 4 large stalks celery
> 5 cloves garlic
> 1 large package frozen peas
> 1 large can good tomato sauce

2 cans peeled tomatoes

1 can medium or large black olives (without pits)

½ cup olive oil, plus several tablespoons for rice

3 or 4 packages saffron (this expensive item can
sometimes be purchased in large markets,
but most often must be obtained in specialty
food stores)

juice of 10 large lemons (or 1 cup bottled lemon
juice and 2 lemons for garnish)

1 bunch fresh parsley

1 jar pimento

salt and pepper to taste

4 cups white rice

1. Start by preparing meats. In a large skillet sauté in all but 2 tablespoons of oil, chicken, pork, and pepperoni cut into thick slices, along with onion, celery, garlic, and red bell pepper—all vegetables minced. Cook until meat is lightly browned and cooked almost through. Add tomato sauce, canned tomatoes, and canned black olives. Continue to simmer until meat products are thoroughly cooked, adding salt and pepper sparsely.

2. In separate pot, cook 4 cups of rice by lightly searing it in 2 tablespoons of olive oil to which saffron has been added. The rice should acquire a rich yellow color which intensifies once the water (8 cups) is added. Salt lightly, cover, and let simmer over low heat until all water is absorbed.

3. Back to the meat mixture. Add cleaned, deveined shrimp and cook until these are pink. Add clams in shells (shells will open with heat).

4. Combine rice mixture and meat and fish mixture, tossing lightly so that it is well blended. The paella is almost done.

5. Just before bringing paella to the table, add the frozen peas (so that they retain their bright green color and aren't cooked to death). Baste liberally with lemon juice. Garnish with parsley, strips of pimento, and lemon wedges.

# Buttermilk and Raisin Light Whole Wheat Bread

    2 packages dry yeast
    ¾ cup warm water
    1¼ cups buttermilk (room temperature or
        slightly warmed)
    1½ cups unbleached white flour
    3 cups whole wheat flour
    ¼ cup shortening (room temperature)
    2 tablespoons molasses
    2 teaspoons baking powder
    2 teaspoons salt
    1 cup golden raisins or currants, or mixture of both
    butter or margarine to grease pans

1. You will need a heavy duty electric mixer with dough hook, measuring cups, measuring spoons, clean cloth or large garbage bag, good
bread pans (preferably earthenware), large spoon, and a warm kitchen.

2. Arrange oven shelves so they are not too close to top or bottom
of oven, and preheat to 425° approximately 20 minutes before baking. If
yours is a convection oven, reduce heat by 40°.

3. Sprinkle dry yeast over warm water in electric mixer bowl. Stir to
dissolve and set aside until bubbly, 10 to 15 minutes. While yeast bubbles,
let buttermilk come to room temperature (or take chill off by warming
briefly for a few minutes over very low heat).

4. Pour buttermilk, white flour, 1 cup whole wheat flour, shortening,
molasses, baking powder, and salt into the yeast mixture. Blend at low
speed approximately two minutes or until ingredients are absorbed. Then
add remaining whole wheat flour, ½ cup at a time, continuing to beat on
low speed four to five minutes. During this part of the process you will
want to change regular mixer blade for a dough hook. If dough remains
sticky, add small amounts of white flour until it becomes soft but hang-
able. At this point also add raisins and/or currants. Ball of dough should
clear the sides of the mixer bowl.

5. Lightly flour work surface (clean top of kitchen counter will do),
and turn out the soft dough. Knead by hand for 8 to 10 minutes, until
dough is slightly elastic.

6. Divide dough and shape into as many pieces as you have greased pans. You may shape dough into ovals the length of the pans, fold each in half with seam down, and press them into pan. You may also push the dough into the corners of pan if you wish. Cover pans with a clean damp cloth or with a plastic garbage bag (just over the tops), and let rise approximately 1 hour in a place free from drafts, until unbaked loaves have risen 1 to 2 inches above the edges of pans.

7. Bake loaves until golden brown, 30 to 35 minutes. During last 10 minutes, cover with foil if crusts are browning too rapidly. Bread is perfect if thumping bottom produces a hard, hollow sound. Makes a light finely textured whole wheat bread. (I generally make twice as much as this recipe calls for—six medium sized loaves—for which I double all above measurements.)

# But Really, There Are No Recipes...

Elizabeth Kamarck Minnich

I think of myself as a woman who cooks even though it isn't really true anymore. I grew up with women who cook, apprenticing happily, and have neither renounced nor ever fully inhabited the art, the role, the identity.

My great-grandmother Nanny, in my memories of her, is either in the blue and white kitchen of her big country house in Luray, Virginia, or she is on the lower of the double porches of that house, built by her own grandfather, wearing her apron, welcoming us as we drove in from Washington, D.C., to visit. I can't remember her in the living room, certainly not in the bedroom, nor in the hall. She cooked fried chicken, mashed potatoes, biscuits. By my memories, that's all she cooked, and cooking is what she did. This makes her, my memory Nanny, a large, warm, important, and powerful figure.

Nanny died when I was—what? Twelve, I think. I do remember her in a bed in our house in D.C. I remember that the bed could be cranked up into a chairlike shape, and that transformation impressed me at the time in a way that old age and duty and illness could not, all those being abstractions to me then. Her final aging into death in D.C., away from the Luray Valley ringed by the enfolding, threatening softness of the Blue Ridge Mountains, was hard on my grandmother, her daughter, and on my mother, to whose house Nanny was brought when she was confined to bed. What disruptions and demands came with this infolding of the generations? Was it also a time of healing intimacy? My memories refuse almost all of that: the adult women in my child-life are not clear to me within their own stories, I'm afraid.

What I do remember is Nanny's smile, her white hair in a braid wrapped around the back of her head, a large mole on her cheek, her great height—but, even more, her fried chicken, mashed potatoes, and biscuits. And the Luray kitchen, blue and white (Vermeer paintings bespeak kitchens and Nanny to me), with various sizes of white tables with drawers in them lining the walls, interrupted only by the stove and the refrigerator, also white, large, humming, freighted with food. I sat often at the lowest of the odd lot of white tables, by the window facing the side yard, smelling bubbling fats (always, no matter what was cooking, it seemed), hearing roosters crowing (no matter what time), eating (something, no matter when), watching my large, white-haired Nanny move deftly around the kitchen, I ate when I was at Nanny's house, even as a teenage white girl who starved herself to be pretty, acceptable—thin. It never once occurred to me that Nanny was anything but beautiful and strong, and, with her, I ate.

Of course I want to think of myself as a woman who cooks. A cooking woman is strong, fragrant, capable unto magical, loving and very much in charge in a world my child's memories hold, still, as more real and more important than the world outside the house was then.

*This is not my recipe. This is a memory, retrievable only as memories are, by evocation and gesture and occasional concreteness that is not factual. And I resist making it a recipe. This is about art and love, not about technique. Some things to need to be learned standing beside someone.* Fried chicken pieces are dredged in flour with plenty of salt and pepper mixed in. They are cooked in huge black iron frying pans, in lots of butter. You star them on high heat so the flour makes a nice, crisp crust; then, before the pieces turn from very light gold to rich gold-tan, you lower the heat and cover the frying pan. I haven't the faintest idea of how long you cook the chicken; until it smells done, and feels done when you stick a fork into it. The liquid that bubbles out of the holes should be clear. Maybe half an hour? Meanwhile, you peel lots of potatoes, cut them, and throw them into a large pot of boiling water, which spits at you as the pieces go in. When they are done (Nanny could just tell; I stick a fork in. I am trying to catch them at the moment when the fork goes in smoothly, but before they are so soft they fall apart), you pour off the water and add just the right amount of warmed milk with butter melted in it, salt, and pepper. Then you mash the potatoes. By hand. With a strong, long-handled spoon. Actually, I use a beater. It's not as good; beaters make *whipped* potatoes. Some chunkiness makes them taste better. Between spoons and beaters, there are those metal things you can buy to mash things with; that's okay. Mashed potatoes are served in a big bowl with a chunk of butter in the middle, melting.

Nanny's daughter, Grammy, my mother's mother, was small to her mother/my Nanny's large. Small, quick, sharp-tongued, also very capable. Grammy could make the best chocolate chip cookies in the world. She used the Toll House recipe off the chocolate chip package, she said, but her cookies turned out different from anybody else's. She used lots of butter; she always added vanilla to almost everything and taught me also that a dash of almond extract in sweet things is almost always good; she knew how to use her wrist and not overstir; she knew just when to take the cookies out of the oven. By the smell, she said. They had crisp bottoms and soft tops.

Grammy, in her life as something other, and before Grammydom, married a man with a Ph.D. in the then very new field of economics who was determined to save the world from poverty. He was a refugee first from Russia and then from Germany, a Jew, an atheist, an admirer of Bertrand Russell, a short, intense, brilliant man with a shock of white hair, and a Chesterfield always dangling from his fingers. He talked seriously to me in the living room and allowed me to be with him silently in his study. He banned everybody else from that study. I therefore adored him. I think he adored my grandmother, whose sharpness matched his own and whose sphere was utterly different from his. From Luray, Virginia, and Kiev, Russia, they came together, working in different spheres, proud of each other. (But once my grandmother said, "I told Manuel I wished I could understand his work so he could talk to me about it. But he said he did that all day and wanted to get away from it.")

My grandmother was small and dark in a family of tall blonds (so she told me; I don't remember anything but white hair on her mother or my great-uncle Nick, and never met any of the others in her family). She had an "olive" complexion, as she called it, once had dark hair, and brown eyes. I believe this was hard on her, growing up in the white community of segregated Virginia, though she only alluded to it and never discussed it. Perhaps it had something to do with why she fell in love with a Jew from Russia, himself short and dark. In any case, my mother grew up with these two caring about justice.

*This is not my recipe either because I learned it also by apprenticing to a woman whose cultural art had nothing to do with recipes.* Russian cutlets were normal in our house; Grammy made them up to feed her husband's homesickness. Ground meat, mixed with thoroughly soggy bread that has been soaked in a lightly whipped whole egg, and with chopped onions . . . and what else? I've done all sorts of things through the years. A little Worcestershire sauce. Some garlic put through a press is very good. Freshly ground pepper. Some beef bouillon or stock, but just a little; a tablespoon for about a pound of meat, I think. A little beer; same, just a bit. Spices? Sometimes, if I feel like it. Oregano is okay, but not really proper; too Italian. Roll the meal/egg-soaked bread mixture into a large egg shaped form (four by three inches, maybe—it's up to you; the larger they are, the longer they have to cook, of course). Roll these in another whipped egg and then in bread crumbs (stale bread crumbled into butter in a frying pan and browned). Fry the cutlets in light butter, turning as each side becomes lightly golden (and a bit flattened). I usually prop them against the sides of the pan and each other to let the narrower sides cook, too. How long? Well, each side needs to get crisp and turn golden. On medium-high heat, maybe five minutes a side (four sides)? When all the sides are golden, I turn the heat down to low, cover the pan, and cook another fifteen minutes or so. I like them done clear through; pink in the middle doesn't seem right.

Nothing special; just a kind of miniature meat loaf, really, but surprisingly good. And anyhow, these are "Russian cutlets," designed for my grandfather, reminiscent of my grandmother, made for us often by my mother. When I asked my mother about what was special to her in her own cooking, with this essay in mind, my father looked up from reading his newspaper across the room (all men in my family read a lot, as do the women, but the men read also in the middle of social gatherings); "Russian cutlets," he said.

My father has a doctorate, too; my mother did not finish college. I am aware of having wanted a Ph.D. because of my grandfather's study, its silence and peacefulness, though, not because of my father (grandparents, I think, are safer to identify with). I wanted to have such a place as my own, and my grandfather, by allowing me and only me in while he was working, gave me permission. And I also think I learned to cook because of Nanny and my grandmother's equally loving, buttery cooking in kitchens they also made peaceful and productive.

Cooking, like writing as my grandfather did it, became to

me a kind of yoga (not that I knew about that). Absorption in a task for its own sake, for the pleasure and gift of it, both. I can think of it that way while I allow myself to think of Nanny, my grandmother and my grandfather, food, kitchens, and his study. Needless to say, there is a lot I move to the margins to remember those calm and feeding places. How much did my grandmother resent her husband not talking to her about his work? Did she at all? I don't know. She revered him, and held him and his life at the center as well as the firm encircling framing of her life. Her life was on the inside of the line, his on the outside; she in the home, he in the world. His was a wide world, international: my grandfather worked on many projects through which he hoped, as I have said, to make use of the new science of economics to get rid of poverty, or at least of the then considered to be inevitable swings between inflation and depression. My grandmother, I am told, refused to go to all the international gatherings and embassy receptions to which he was invited. But they had good friends from his world that they shared. I grew up with some of them; they remained friends of my parents. Remarkable people, of the group that came to Washington genuinely to be public servants. During the McCarthy era, many of them—and my father, who is also an economist involved with international issues—were either called before the House Un-American Activities Committee or ordered not to leave the country until they were "cleared." Some were professionally broken. They used to come to our house because it was one of the only places where people could speak freely about what was going on.

What I remember from that time mostly is a kind of heaviness in the house, and a funny record made by Stan Friedberg (however you spell his name), in which a parrot repeats, "Point of Order, Point of Order." I remember hearing that Friedberg and Walt Kelly, in his comic strip "Pogo," were among the few who were brave enough to publicly criticize McCarthy. Wiley the Cat was McCarthy in "Pogo," I think. "Pogo" was one of the primary works in our house, providing shared allusions and always reminding us that political courage was possible, and to be emulated.

My mother and father inherited my grandparents' New Year's Eve party, to which brave political people used to come. I stayed home to go to this cross-generational party, preferring it to parties of my own friends. They were warm, funny, welcoming, interesting people whom I loved talking to. Like my grandfather, they all treated me as if I were a real person, not an amusing child.

I learned how to make shrimp De Jonghe from my mother, because that was what she always served, at midnight. I used to sit on a stool in the kitchen for hours deveining shrimp and sometimes peeling mushrooms the day before the New Year's Eve party, listening to an old radio we had in the kitchen and looking out the window at a small patch of woods just behind our house. Cooking was rather like being part of the mystery of being grown up; fried chicken and shrimp De Jonghe were the things the women who made safe houses knew how to do.

I don't think of my father when I think of cooking (or of the New Year's Eve party, I realize: putting it on right was my mother's task). He ate, he was professionally involved with some of the party guests, and he was very active in our usually very long dinner table conversations. Actually, though, there were times we had meals for Daddy: baked beans and brown bread. The beans were heated in a thick ovenproof pot with a chunk of bacon fat and a touch of brown sugar, and the brown bread—which came in a can, and was dark, dense, very moist and slightly sweet—was warmed beside the bean pot in a moistened brown bag. We also had fish on Fridays. My father's parents were Polish Catholic immigrants who barely spoke English, and he grew up in a northern town near the paper mill in which his father worked (and fought for a union). We threaded some things from his past into our family life: the fish, although he was vehemently no longer Catholic ("it's brain food," and brains are to be developed: immigrants and refugees have nothing else when they arrive); the baked beans and brown bread; his presents on Christmas or his birthday, which we tried to remember to wrap in plain brown paper, because that's what he liked (it's all his parents had, when he was young). Memories have a way of shaping what makes something feel special, and particularly so for our more ritualized celebrations. My father once said he spent his life crossing class lines. He allowed himself baked beans and brown paper as remnants of a past to which he remained loyal.

My grandmother and my mother: both on occasion, but not often, self-conscious about being "uneducated," both assertive about their abilities and opinions despite their own (only barely glimpsed by their children and grandchildren) doubts. I was assuredly not brought up to defer to anyone. I think that was because they were what they were then supposed to be, good wives and mothers, and because they shared the values, the dangers, and hardships (the depression, world wars, McCarthyism) that the world brought and that were inherent in the backgrounds and chosen work of their husbands. The women in my family have not until my generation been educated, but certainly all their children were to be. Within the framing of these women's homes and rituals of hospitality, people treated each other with dignity and respect. All had known hatred, and what brought them together was a commitment to keep it from taking power again.

My grandfather was Jewish as well as Russian although he pronounced himself "American" and was not at all religious. His name was Goldenweiser; he would have been known to be Jewish, no matter what he himself thought. How did my grandmother handle that, being herself from Luray, Virginia, and probably having known no other Jewish people before her husband? She pronounced "Goldenweiser" with a German W—as a V. I always thought that was her way of participating in his foreignness, his international world, another kind of dignified formality. But perhaps it was ambivalence.

Sometimes my grandmother stumbled and was confused in the international world she encountered with her husband. She wasn't quite sure, either, how she was supposed to deal with Black people, with whom, I think, she also felt implicated. Something in her tone when she mentioned her "olive" complexion suggests to me that she was subject to racist "jokes," at the least, as she was growing up. As an adult she supported my mother's work on fair housing in our neighborhood; she supported our participation in the bus boycott in D.C.; she thought the Civil Rights Movement was right, needed, and good; she was pleased to meet the Africans my father often brought home. But she was sometimes unnerved by what she had learned in her youth. She said to me once, when I was seventeen and invited my friends and co-workers, white and Black, from the restaurant where I had a summer job to a party in my home: "The problem for me is that I just don't think Negroes are attractive. It's not anything wrong with them; it's just what I'm used to." Five minutes later she said, "The problem is, you know, that they are *too* attractive." Well, if I ever doubted the sexualization of racialization, there it is. Grammy lived her life off balance, a Luray, Virginia, olive-skinned white girl who grew up to live in Washington, D.C., married to a Jew who moved in international circles.

We weren't Jewish, after all. We weren't Christian either. We were "American." *Novus Ordo Seclorum.* We all lived our lives off balance. It's the American way, a dream, and a nightmare mixed together.

My mother, too, has always been a cook learning to take care of hungers of many kinds: to fried chicken, Russian cutlets, and baked beans she added meals that accustomed her children to still more tastes. When I was in my teens I wanted to bake, and though my mother never baked much she taught me well. My cooking was "special," the making of fancy desserts—marble cakes, vanilla and chocolate batter swirled together; coffee cakes made of dough dotted with butter, folded, rolled out again, buttered again, rolled up and the ends brought together, variously decorated; pecan sandies, rich with ground nuts and butter, rolled in confectioner's sugar; French Noel log cakes, which take a full day to make and come out really looking like a log, lying in the "snow" of confectioner's sugar.

Sometime in my teens I also took over my mother's occasional dinner parties. I made them my job, interviewing her about what she wanted to serve and then shopping, cooking, and serving. She was kind enough to pay me so I made a little money that way. My cooking however, stayed separate from hers: I did the Special Events and the desserts.

Cooking began to change for me when I lived with my first husband, a man who always thought he was too thin and had trouble eating. He craved what he refused himself, refused what he craved. I might have gone on wanting to give gifts of cooking, but to someone for whom eating was difficult? Perhaps I chose this, too: my attention went to my studies, teaching, my work, and friends. Later, when that was over and I married again, I lived (and now live) with a man who had been a single parent: three sons, all quite young when I arrived. We all cooked some, the boys too as soon as they were old enough. But producing meals was not the same as cooking, and my attention did not attach itself. Still not safe: cooking for a household of various ages of males, each of whom had a history that shaped his ability to accept the gift of artful food, risked a kind of engagement, as well as a role, I avoided almost by reflex. The role of feeding women is about as fraught as any I can think of: we tip-toed around it, all of us. We kept my family's tradition of the kitchen discussion of politics though.

This is curious to me: I grew up with cooking women who worked with skill and love and commitment. My mother still explores new recipes, creates wonderful meals that are more healthy than those she grew up learning how to prepare. She genuinely enjoys the art of cooking and is glad to feed people. But I have never tried to inhabit that role: I made Nanny's and Grammy's and Mother's art into something both more private and more social, skirting the familial. I cooked because I loved to cook, and I gave my cooking to friends. Meals? I took my turn at preparing them, not investing in them. Perhaps this was a step-mother's way of refusing the dangerous you are/you aren't that craved/feared eternal vanishing mystery: The Mother. Perhaps it was a way of avoiding the ambivalences that underlay the achieved harmony I grew up in. Perhaps it was also a way of holding onto another thread of sustaining identity, the one that anchored in the quiet of my grandfather's study. Who knows?

In this family, we are all now cooks and enjoy each other's creations when, as adults now, we visit. When our oldest son, who spent some time in China, comes home, we make Chinese meals together. He is a gourmet cook, actually, and often calls me when he is giving a dinner party to check a recipe. The next oldest son has become a vegetarian and a generous kind of cook, one who piles lots of things into every dish. He calls on occasion about basic things like pie crusts: the elaborations he does from his own imagination (last night he called to talk about how I might make "sweet potato chapatis"). The youngest, still only sixteen, thus far avoids cooking although he often feeds himself. He likes all kinds of exotic foods in restaurants . . . and persists in fixing himself disgusting things like canned ravioli at home. I sense that he prefers to be fed by strangers. A teenage male, defining himself away from family? For all of us, it is really as if cooking is something we do socially, as a special gift for a special occasion, as a kind of enactment of mutuality. Perhaps we are all still avoiding the sinkhole of need for a Feeding Mother, while we practice artfully creating our own cultured homes.

Now that the boys are grown, I am slowly returning to cooking, but I have to relearn how to do it. I still know how to cook with butter and vanilla, with sugar and chocolate, with sour cream and meat. Now I want to cook with vegetables and rice and yoghurt, but I don't have the kind of feel for it that, for me, real cooking requires: I have never used recipes, and it is hard to do it now. I mess around: I know how to use yoghurt for sauces, on fruits with lemon and cinnamon and a bit of honey; on chicken with paprika and garlic and cumin and coriander; and baked potatoes with cheddar cheese melting underneath, and sprouts on top . . . things like that. I cook a lot of fish in the summer, when we get to Cape Cod.

*This summer I did this with cod.* I heated something like a quarter cup of peanut oil in a large, heavy iron skillet. When the oil was hot, I put in some chopped-up garlic (maybe two cloves?), and about a half cup of chopped onion. When the onion was soft, I removed it and the garlic from the oil and put in about a cup of chopped red and yellow and green bell peppers, and a half cup of pitted, chopped dark olives. I just tossed them quickly, maybe three minutes, and removed them, too. Then I put a piece of cod in—of a size such that the whole piece could fit, so it could brown in the hot oil (See? It depends on the size of your frying pan. How should I know how much? Well . . .). About three minutes on each side, medium heat, hot oil. Then I put the onions, garlic, peppers and olives back in, and turned the fish over so that the flavors spread around. Added some capers (a tablespoon?) and a dash of Lillet (an aperitif—a white wine such as a chardonnay would do, or perhaps some dry vermouth). Covered the skillet and cooked about five minutes . . . served it with brown rice, crusty French bread heated in the oven, and some very crisp, quickly steamed broccoli. The extra sauce from the fish pan went nicely over the rice and the broccoli.

Occasionally, I still make pies and brownies (add a quarter cup of peanut butter to your brownie recipe just before you put it in the pan to bake—doesn't taste like peanut butter, just becomes richer still and chewier). But what I really like, these days, is seeing what is in the refrigerator and making something up with it, letting the ingredients tell me how they should be cooked, how they go together. It's a reflective sort of thing, such cooking. I like turning my attention inward to imagine how that would taste with that, how it might do to add this spice—how will it smell, taste? Smell it cooking: what does it need? A wonderful kind of concentration develops that is both very inward and as open as possible to what you are working with, a kind of communion of the sense that is also a social communion: how will it taste to the others for whom you are cooking, too? That's fascinating to me, and very intimate. Cooking has to do with intimate connections, self to others.

Still, there is something here about walking around the rim of a volcano, propitiating powerful spirits, dancing instead of fleeing or falling in: dancing *about* the balancing art of human being, in relation, mind to body, self to other, culture to cultures. From survival to art, with all of everyday life clamoring in between . . . that's cooking, but it is now also what for me studying and writing are. I rarely have time to really cook, nor to retreat as I dream of, to write. To be my grandmother and mother, grandfather and father, is of course to be none of them at all: my life is a smorgasbord with ingredients from them all and many others and differing times.

Still, I can locate my life, centering in thinking and politics, friends and family, between studies and kitchens and all they signify . . . I want them all, and I don't want to be solely in any.

Not kitchens or living rooms or meeting rooms or classrooms. Being from a family of Southern Baptists and Russian Jews and Polish Catholics, all of whom were suspicious of religious as well as political intolerance, all of whom overcame their ambivalences by acting and living by loving values, I was taught to cook, to study, and to be political. I begin to realize that cooking, study, and being political have in common taking the risks that always go with caring and trying to do something about it. Really, there are no recipes for the arts of connecting.

# Layers of Pleasure: Capirotada

## Pat Mora

**S**elf-defense. That's why you started baking," my mother, a woman with little interest in kitchens tells me, her daughter who craves sweets. Every night Mother prepared a good meal for us—meat loaf, roast and mashed potatoes, tuna casseroles, and on Fridays, our favorite, cheese enchiladas; but the kitchen wasn't a pleasure place for her. An occasional pineapple upside-down cake, Mom's only homemade dessert I remember, is the best I've ever eaten because she made it.

The kitchen became one way I created my place in our family, one that included a live-in maternal grandmother and an aunt, not that the eldest of four has to struggle for definition. But soon after I learned to read, I practiced the new skill on boxes of butterscotch pudding, standing at the kitchen counter reading the directions aloud while my grandmother watched, proud of her granddaughter who could read English. *"Necesito dos tasas de leche, Mamande."*

Neither she nor Mother were tamale-making or tortilla-rolling women. My grandmother would sauté rice, make a *sopa de tortilla*, or *arroz con leche*, the creamy rice dessert much like Indian *kheer*, but these women in the kitchen with me didn't turn the pages of recipe books savoring each description, rolling the very words around on their tongues, *blackberry jam, lemon cloud, flan de naranja con almendras*.

The kitchen became Pat's place, the special room in which I succeeded in bringing myself and others pleasure. I'd clip recipes from magazines, watch cooking shows on summer afternoons and copy down ingredients for peanut butter meltaways and chocolate dream cake, anticipating not only the mouth-pleasure, but even sweeter, the sound of my father's, "*Umm, umm, honey, is that cake good! How did you make that?*" and the others around the table asking for seconds. My aunt, Lobo, arriving home late from work, would sit at the kitchen table, tasting the cake, and say, "*¡Ay, Patricia, qué rico!* You are a very good cooker."

Years later she was still lavishing such praise, only now at a table with my husband and three children, again a group of enthusiastic eaters who grew to expect a homemade dessert most evenings. Once my three were in school all day, some friends and I began cooking for one another once a month. We prepared fresh pea soup or chicken *sopa*, lingering over them as we sat around a table, sharing ourselves and our family traditions. We gave one another advice on everything from dividing irises to foster blooming to our fears about our ability to nurture our family life.

As I began to spend more time writing in the early eighties, the time I once spent on my garden and in my kitchen began to be spent at the cafeteria table I use as a desk.

I cook now, but more the way Mother did, quick and easy, surprised when my daughter says she's learned to make corn tortillas. I'm glad she took a break from studying for law exams, and I resolve (again) that soon I'll do the same, resist the computer—maybe next week.

The recipe books and the interest in food remain, though, particularly as I finish a family memoir. While my children were growing, I'd bring daisies, phlox, and cushion mums from relatives' yards and transplant them in the late afternoon to protect them from our intense Texas sun, planting a bit of the family in my garden. I'd also copy down any recipe I could cajole from relatives, sometimes memorizing it as they spoke if they were the kind to hoard their secrets. And I had spies too. Lobo would say, "I watched how your aunt made that jello salad. I think I can tell you."

Books, like children, bring wrinkles and gifts, and a gift of my memoir is that I am able to braid together the threads of my life—gardening, cooking, writing. As I journeyed into the family's past, I discovered again that all we are and all we've lived, we bring to a book, whether as reader or writer. I pestered my family not only with questions about relatives, but also about their gardens and kitchens, about our places of communion, the joy of our heritage, *nuestra herencia*.

On visits to my home town of El Paso, I sat with Uncle Lalo and Aunt Carmen, my aunt by marriage who liked to be out watering her plants at six before the sun got hot, who every Christmas made sweets we coveted, perfect apricot and coconut candies, spritz cookies. Last year, at seventy-five, she had a Christmas party for fifteen couples. She wore a long skirt to the party, one she sewed herself and color-coordinated with the tablecloths. By phone she described the meal to me with great enthusiasm. I heard about each dish she'd made—jalapeño cream cheese dip, potatoes au-gratin, ham and turkey, platters of cookies, cakes, "and a new cake, honey, a recipe from my grandmother, lots of dates. Delicious." I made a mental note to pursue this. I want that recipe.

When I hung up the phone, I marveled at Aunt Carmen, who'd said to me, "I don't want to hear people complaining. I'm fine, honey. I'm fine." Before that December ended, my aunt had a stroke. She lost the power of speech, and I use the phrase with care, the power of speech. The first days her husband, my favorite uncle, just longed for her to live, her familiar body to continue, our loyalty to flesh. As her condition stabilized, he began to confront the silence. The aunt who moved through rooms like a small unstoppable sun ceased glowing. Humans adapt, and though Uncle Lalo's previous kitchen experience was limited to dishwashing, he began to perfect the art of making hot cereal. "I think I've got the idea now, honey. I can serve your aunt a good, hot breakfast with no lumps."

I come from a long line of determined women, and my aunt is relearning words, every correct syllable a small victory. For months, the only words she said were in English, and I missed the smooth transitions between the two languages in which she lived. Did she?

"How are you, Aunt Carmen?" I ask when I call. "I'm . . . fa-ine hon . . . ey," she says, her mind and mouth pushing each thought into careful syllables, pushing them from the throat, over the tongue, out the lips. "I'm . . . fa-ine." And today she said, "*Mu . . . uy bie . . . en.*"

"Aunt Carmen! You did it! You spoke Spanish again." My excitement surprised me; a part of her had returned to me in those few sounds.

Grateful that I'd visited her this past spring, I re-read the notes I wrote when she served me *capirotada*, a popular Mexican dessert. Compared with the verbal punch of the Spanish name for this dish, the English translation is anemic: bread pudding. Bread pudding with peanuts and cheese? Let's stick to its name in Spanish, pronounced cah-pee-ro-TAH-dah.

I pull out my Spanish dictionaries and assorted cookbooks to pursue the permutations of the word and of this unusual Lenten dish which added protein to the diet of Catholics who abstained from meat during the purple season, thereby gaining spiritual healing through mortification of the body. Cultures shrewdly navigate ideological and physical terrains. Cultures are into nutrition.

In Spain, the word seems to refer to a kind of dressing served with meat, perhaps as a kind of topping. I call friends who are Spanish professors, the word a good excuse to visit. Dictionaries in hand, we pursue braided roots, culinary and linguistic, discuss the versions of the dish we've eaten in the Southwest and the possible etymology of the name, savoring both its ingredients and the word, *capirotada*, on our tongues. We keep reading, deciphering. A *capirote* is a kind of hat, the root word probably *cappa*, Latin for hat or covering, the suffix *ada* suggesting a shape or likeness.

An elegant version of the layered dessert served in Mexico City is made with *biznaga*, candied cactus and the dish is covered with meringue. My friend, Diana, a native New Mexican, has always prepared the dish with an egg batter, "almost like a souffle, that puffed to make a kind of cap or top." If indeed that notion of a crust or covering is the origin of the word, any of the toppings could qualify, the syrup, cheese, coconut. The version that most made me smile given our quivering reaction to animal fat is in *The Good Life: New Mexico Traditions and Food* which was first published in 1949 by New Mexican writer Fabiola Cabeza de Baca Gilbert (not a name it would be easy to use in these days of answering machines and telephone tag).

One of Fabiola's versions includes wine, which is unusual, and instructs us to top the dish with "a heaping teaspoon of lard" before placing the bread pudding in the oven to thicken. I can anticipate my slender daughters' groans at such a thought. The various recipes I've read include quite an array of possibilities for the creative cook, layers of nourishment, walnuts, pecans, pine nuts, or almonds; longhorn, Velveeta (!), or *queso añejo*; dried pineapple, raisins, white raisins, or currants; water or milk; white bread, *bolillos*, or sweet yeast bread; cinnamon or cloves; brown sugar or *piloncillo*. One version even lines the baking dish with fried tortillas. Choices, options, like shaping a garden or an essay.

I see Aunt Carmen moving through her small kitchen like a surfer on a perfect wave. I hear her directions. "Come and look,

Pat. I think you're going to like this. I make it the way my mama did. It's got a layer of sliced French bread. Not fried. No, sir. I don't make mine all greasy like some people do. Just toast your bread in the oven, then layer it in a buttered nine by thirteen inch Pyrex dish. Layer your raisins, peanuts, pecans, coconut, and longhorn cheese, maybe about two layers of each and end with the cheese. Some people use pine nuts and pineapple. Add whatever you like, honey."

I scribble exact quantities for myself as she speaks.

◻ ◻ ◻

## Aunt Carmen's Capirotada

1 loaf of French bread, sliced and toasted
¾ cup raisins
¾ cup peanuts (unsalted)
¾ cup pecans
½ cup coconut, angel flake
¾ cup longhorn cheese

Syrup:
3 cups brown sugar
1 sliced orange
3 cinnamon sticks
3 cups water

"Boil your syrup for five minutes. My mama used *piloncillo*, do you know what that is? That cone of hard, raw sugar. I just use brown sugar and cinnamon sticks and water. AND one sliced orange. That's my secret. Boil your syrup for five minutes and then pour it over the layers. Decorate the top like this, with the cinnamon sticks and oranges, see honey? Don't waste things. Dot it with butter and bake it for about fifteen minutes. *Rica, pero rica.*"

Aunt Carmen can't say those words today. I ask Mother if my grandmother made *capirotada*. "Yes, but I can't tell you how," Mom says. "At almost eighty I just have too many memories in my head. They don't all fit up there."

Writing, gardening, and cooking are often solitary acts for personal and communal sustenance. We mull and mutter, retreat not from life but to our private life, for alchemy and transubstantiation, transforming what our hands touch and also ourselves. Eventually, we savor the layers of pleasure.

We need to get the recipes while we can, absorb *el pasado*, the past, nourishment and delight for the body, for the soul.

❙❘ ❘❙ ❙❘

# The Parable of the Lamb

## Martha A. Ayres

Arlene, my partner of eight years, decided to bring a leg of lamb (shish-ka-bob) as her contribution to my family reunion. I wanted her to be a part of the reunion and introduce her to the rest of my family. Of course, she knew my mom and dad and sister, Sally, as well as my nephews, Jay and Charlie. Until this reunion there was no easy way for Arlene to meet the relatives. Anyway, they are mostly very conservative, conventional people, and I didn't expect them to be very open to Arlene's and my relationship. However, a reunion was different. Everyone would have to be open and accepting and just wonder who this Arlene was and frankly, I just didn't care if they liked her or not as long as they were polite. I guess you might call this a coming-out reunion. Since my style has always been to bring my life wherever I wanted, we decided to go and if that wasn't acceptable to my parents or the rest of my family they would have to let me know. I had agreed to the lamb although I felt hesitant. I didn't know why but I did know it had something to do with my mother. I knew Mom didn't like lamb but that didn't seem reason enough to keep Arlene from bringing it and I knew Mom had never prepared lamb in this way, so maybe she would like it. I did have a fleeting thought that some of my hesitancy had to do with bringing Arlene into the extended family, but my long-developed skill at shoving worries into a dark corner and covering them with dust let me go full steam ahead with my plans.

Now you must know that Arlene's recipe for the shish-ka-bob is delicious. She takes a leg of lamb, cuts it into small pieces and marinates them for several days. Then she places the pieces of lamb on skewers alongside small onions and summer fresh tomatoes and cooks them on a grill until the vegetables are browned and tender and the meat is still a little pink inside. Since Arlene's Armenian, she grew up on shish-ka-bob and this lamb was a gift from her culture to mine.

My father had organized the reunion by sending a note to all family members with a postcard to send back saying yea or nay. Everyone was so happy to be invited that he got back all yeas. He arranged the cabin rentals at the state park near my grandmother's birthplace. She had been the matriarch and when she died in 1951 the family stopped getting together until this reunion in 1983. My father arranged cabins for each family which were close enough but not too close, so that we could hang out, talk and play together, and still have the privacy which my father valued.

People came from Texas, North Carolina, Virginia, Georgia, Florida, Massachusetts, New York City, and, of course, West Virginia.

I flew from my home in western Massachusetts to Fayetteville, West Virginia, to pick up my parents. Mom, and Dad, and I arrived at Blue Stone State Park a couple days ahead of Arlene. I think Dad was beginning not to trust his driving and in a very surreptitious way he ask me to drive his car. So I went to Fayetteville, my hometown, and picked up my parents with all the accompanying foods. They'd packed bread, fruit, cereal for breakfast, condiments such as mayo and mustard, and West Virginia ham or country ham as it is called so my father could make redeye gravy to cover our biscuits with one morning for breakfast. The major meats would be purchased from a grocer in a little town next to the park. There would be plenty of chicken, fried of course, grilled hot dogs and hamburgers, and that old standard, a big jar of peanut butter. We all loved peanut butter.

We arrived at the park, found our cabins, and began to unpack. I was already having a good time and was looking forward to Arlene's arrival. Aunts, uncles, and cousins started arriving and checking into their cabins. My father and I went around from cabin to cabin greeting everyone. My mother stayed in our cabin in order to get the kitchen organized and just be there if anyone dropped by. There were relatives coming whom I hadn't seen since I was a little girl. I just knew it was going to be a good week.

As the afternoon was passing I started looking for Arlene to arrive. She was driving down from Massachusetts and stopping in New York City to pick up my nephew Jay, who was in graduate school at Union Theological Seminary. He was important to Arlene and me because he was so accepting of our relationship and I knew that he would make being at the reunion a lot of fun. As it got later, I started worrying about them. I get so anxious when people are late. I think the worst because my grandmother whom I loved and who accepted me for who I was died when I was eleven.

Finally they arrived. I ran to the car wanting to hug them but Jay was the only one who got a hug. That old childhood fear of loss wouldn't let me hug Arlene. We both looked at each other as if to say, is everything ok? Finally, we were able to give each other a hug and the excitement of their arrival returned. After all the greetings I started to help unload the trunk. As soon as I opened the trunk door I smelled the leg of lamb marinating. Suddenly, I was confronted with all my conflicts. I thought, if I tell my mom that Arlene brought a leg of lamb to be turned into shish-ka-bob and cooked over the family fire for dinner, I just know she'll be angry. And, if I say to Arlene I don't think it's a good idea to cook the lamb she'll be confused since we had both decided that it's her gift to the family reunion's opening picnic. What in the hell was I going to do? Why would my mother be angry? I knew my mother's anger made me feel guilty, and I knew that I had to ignore the guilt or I wouldn't do anything that she didn't want me to. I was not about to give into her manipulations now. I said to myself, it's a wonderful gift so let it be.

The next morning I told Mom that Arlene had brought shish-ka-bob for her part of the evening picnic. As expected, Mom looked at me with such rage that it took my breath away. After a moment I finally opened my mouth and allowed air to pass across my vocal cords and ask, "What's wrong with shish-ka-bob?" In Mom's cloaked, angry style she whispered, "We have enough food." I, of course, increased my volume and said, "Mom, isn't a picnic about having too much food? What's wrong with Arlene adding to our family table? The lamb's a gift, so what's your problem?" Mom stared at me and lowering her voice even more said, "You do what you want, you always have." Then she fell silent. I knew her silence was the end of any rational discussion. I knew she did not want the lamb and that to serve it would appear a betrayal.

I decided to go against my mother and serve the lamb at the family picnic. This act put my relationship with Arlene above my relationship with my mother, and I knew it meant the end of my mother's control, albeit silent control but control nevertheless. I knew my father would like the lamb, and I also knew my father liked Arlene so this made it easier to add the shish-ka-bob to the picnic table laden with the "traditional" picnic fare of fried chicken, potato salad, green beans, sliced tomatoes, hot dogs for the kids, and pies and cakes. Of course there was strawberry and lime jello, a salad that Arlene had so little relationship to. Shish-ka-bob and jello are at opposite ends of the food spectrum. Some relatives loved the shish-ka-bob and others passed it over for fried chicken, but all in all it went over well. My mother wouldn't have one little bit of that lamb, and she stayed as far away as possible from Arlene and me.

That night, as Arlene and I were talking, I began to shine some light on those thoughts that I had pushed to the corner of the dark room and covered with dust. I realized once more that my mother had trouble with my relationship even though she seemed to like Arlene. She had always wanted everything to be perfect, especially in front of the relatives which meant in front of Dad's relatives. Mom's mother had died when she was thirteen, and she had been sent to live with Aunt Verge, her mother's sister, who had treated her badly. She was treated a lot like Cinderella and the glass slipper was my father and his family. Mom was afraid of being judged by Dad's family. She was so afraid to be different because she might lose what she had worked so hard to get and keep. Dad's family had became hers. Mom felt there was no way to compete with my grandmother or Dad's sisters in the cooking realm. My grandmother was known for her bread, her jams and jellys, as well as all her handwork, knitting, sewing, and crocheting. To me, Mom was a great cook but she never believed she had any ability to do anything. She never wanted to upset any member of the family in any way. So with Arlene's and my relationship in plain view she felt exposed enough and then we brought the lamb which further accentuated our difference and therefore her difference from the rest of the family. We got through that evening, but Arlene and I never, ever forgot the parable of the lamb and I never, ever forgot to listen to that little niggling in the back of my mind.

*Arlene was good enough to give me the recipe for shish-ka-bob, and she informed me that my spelling was unique.*

◘◘ ◘◘ ◘◘

## Shish Kebab

one 7-pound leg of lamb (bone in) boned and
    butterflied* or cut into 1½ inch squares
3 to 4 large yellow onions, very thinly sliced
5 to 6 cloves garlic
6 tablespoons ground cumin
2 tablespoons Middle Eastern red pepper (optional)
1 tablespoon each dried basil and oregano
juice of 2 lemons
3 to 4 tablespoons olive oil
½ cup red wine
pepper to taste

1. The amounts of herbs and spices vary both according to individual taste and strength of spices. You should be able to smell the cumin. If you can't, add more. If you like spicy food and cannot get Middle Eastern red pepper, use a little cayenne pepper. You should really experiment with the herbs and spices until you get the combination that pleases your palate.

2. Cover bottom of container large enough to hold meat with half of onions. Put half of garlic cloves through a press and spread over meat. Sprinkle half of herbs and spices on meat and rub them in. Sprinkle with olive oil and lemon juice. Turn meat over and repeat process. Cover meat with remaining onions and add wine. Cover container. The meat should be marinated for at least a day. The longer it is marinated the more flavorful it will be.

3. Thread cubes of meat onto skewers (*shishes* in Armenian) with sweet peppers, small onions, and other vegetables if you like. The meat

---

*A butcher will do this for you if you are not feeling adventurous.

should be cooked over hot coals about 10 minutes on each side (or about 15 minutes on each side if you do not cube the lamb). Do not overcook. The meat should be seared on the outside, but pink in the middle. The cubes can be served on the skewers or removed. (If you leave the lamb whole, slice before serving.) In my family the cook removed the meat from the skewers by grasping the meat with bread and sliding it off. The bread catches the juices and is delicious. Serves 8 to 10.

❚❙ ❚❙ ❚❙

# Fast, Free Delivery

## Paula Martinac

About eight years ago, I was living in Brooklyn and commuting to Manhattan every day to my job. A difficult relationship had ended, leaving me pretty drained, and I didn't have much desire to go out in the evenings. Most nights I ate dinner alone at home, leftovers of dishes I had cooked on the weekend. Nothing fancy—pots of soup in the winter, bowls of pasta salad in the summer. And there were always ingredients in the refrigerator that I could throw together in a pinch if I didn't want to have black bean soup three days in a row. I could have been living anywhere—the Jersey suburbs; my hometown of Pittsburgh; even Iowa.

At that time, I used to tease a friend of mine who lived in Manhattan about the state of her refrigerator. Whenever I visited her, I could open it up and find nothing more than a liter bottle of Diet Coke, a small tub of Parkay margarine, and a half-pint carton of milk past its freshness date. There was a fine layer of New York City dust across her stove that I once wrote her name in as a joke. She ordered out three meals a day. An egg on a roll from the coffee shop downstairs. Turkey on rye from a favorite deli near her office. Dinner from an array of menus that occupied their own special drawer in her living room wall unit, next to the phone—Chinese and Italian mostly, because those were her favorites. I loved to have dinner in her apartment. In my lower-middle-class, heterosexual-family-oriented Brooklyn neighborhood, there was almost no "fast, free delivery," except for greasy thin-crust pizza from Sal's or Tony's. In Manhattan, however, every taste imaginable was at a woman's fingertips: "Hi, I'd like to place an order to be delivered . . ."

My friend's food scenario was a result of the way she organized her life. She had a job, a girlfriend, and an active participation in the lesbian and gay community. Evenings meant meetings, and meetings meant no time to cook, let alone to grocery shop. Weekends meant rest, and rest meant movies and dinners out. Living in Manhattan gave her the freedom to set up her schedule without missing a meal.

Interestingly, "fast, free delivery" for my friend never meant a diminished enjoyment of food. It never meant "Let's get it over with." It didn't signify that food was an afterthought; in fact, it allowed her to integrate food into the myriad activities that packed her day. A favorite activity at meetings was either to order in (if the meeting was at someone's apartment) or to eat out after. The meeting, in fact, would continue at dinner; the best stuff might even happen during the entrée. Food and politics have always been a good mix. People loosen up with a good meal; they share ideas and reflections brought out by the camaraderie of eating together, particularly foods that lend themselves to being passed around and shared. ("Well, I didn't want to say this in the meeting, but . . . could you pass the dumplings? . . . I'm not really sold on What's-her-name's idea . . .")

The size of my friend's kitchen was also significant in her relationship to meals. Manhattan kitchens are more like aisles than rooms, with about a square foot of preparation space, hardly conducive to pleasurable cooking. In Brooklyn, where everything is bigger, my kitchen was the grandest room in my apartment, designed for "family use," with a full-sized table and chairs. Consequently, it was the room where I spent the most waking time—not just cooking and eating, but talking on the phone, paying bills, reading my mail, and writing.

About six years ago, I started publishing short stories, then novels. All my alone time in Brooklyn led to a productive outburst of creative writing. When a friend read my first novel, she remarked, "There's so much food in it!" It is, in fact, all take-out food. The characters order in during most of the significant scenes in the book. They relish food; what they eat helps define their personalities. A fortune cookie can lead to their deeper understanding of some situation. But then, they live in Manhattan.

What drew me, finally, to live in Manhattan after skirting around it for years—two years in Jersey, seven in Brooklyn? Sometimes I think it was the lure of take-out food—take-out as the realm of the possible, what my girlfriend calls "the constant flow" that happens on this little island. It is a great irony that in one of the most complicated cities in the world, food (as long as you have a home and a job) is extraordinarily easy.

My move was also, I believe, the final departure from my family and my class background. I am the only person in my family who has ever earned more than thirty thousand a year and has not had children to support. Somewhere along the way from college and graduate school, I switched economic classes, like many members of my generation, passing easily from the lower class into the middle. Unless I mention it, no one would suspect that neither of my parents finished high school, that my father worked two jobs most of my life, and that I went to a private college because my mother saved every penny. This meant painstaking consideration of food and its cost. If there was such a thing as "take-out" when I was a kid, we certainly couldn't have afforded it. Dinner out (we called it "supper") occurred only on occasions and almost always at Young's Restaurant, a neighborhood joint, where having fried shrimp with french fries was a very big deal.

I realize now that all the years that I lived on the outskirts of Manhattan, I mimicked my mother's pattern of food preparation, familiar to me from my Pittsburgh childhood: thinking ahead about what to cook during the week, making a grocery list, shopping for the whole week, making dinner every night, and washing the dishes immediately after. Though I had none of the demands my mother had as a cook—a husband who had to eat at five and didn't like surprises; finicky children who wouldn't touch most vegetables unless they were disguised—I inherited her basic routine. When I lived in New Jersey and Brooklyn, my parents used to buy me cookware and serving dishes for Christmas and birthdays, so much of it that a friend of mine, on helping me pack it all up to move, asked, "You're sure you weren't ever married?"

Marriage, of course, is what my parents wanted for me. They were building my "hope chest," or more accurately, theirs—they were *hoping* it couldn't be true that I was really a lesbian. It was confusing enough to them that what I was cooking in those pots and pans they gave me were foods they would have never imagined could taste good, things I never tried until I was an adult— chick peas, zucchini, eggplant, any kind of bean other than kidney, any kind of cheese other than American. The list would fill too many bytes of memory. Mine was a childhood of chicken, white potatoes, and corn, with an occasional "exotic" Polish dish from my mother's family thrown in, which, I have to admit, I detested. On the rare nights when my mother served *kluskis* (potato dumplings), stuffed cabbage, or kielbasa, I begged for peanut butter and jelly instead. It wasn't just a question of having a kid's picky eating habits, but one of survival.

In grade school, having a last name that teachers stumbled over ("Croatian? What's that?") and a father who worked as a tool-and-die maker ("Your father makes dye?") instead of as a "professional" already set me apart from my friends and classmates; kids are cruel, and I was the subject of scorn. Growing up in my white, middle-class, predominantly Catholic neighborhood in the sixties was about fitting in—looking, talking, dressing, worshipping, and eating alike—and though we *were* white and Catholic, we were definitely more "lower" than "middle" class, and therefore "different." I had a friend who actually wasn't allowed to accept a ride from my father because he was an undereducated blue-collar worker (and therefore, I presume, might molest her—"professional," educated men would never hurt children!). Early on, I learned the shame and stigma of class, and I didn't want to connect with my heritage through food or in any other way because I didn't understand that there was anything to be proud of.

I spent too many years with the same kind of people, in Catholic schools that thought they were teaching tolerance but were really instilling fear and hate. It was college that saved me, college in the early seventies when "working-class" became a catchword, and the upper-middle-class students I met at the fancy women's college in Pittsburgh that I attended envied my class background. Many wanted to disassociate from their parents, particularly fathers, who were bastions of the Establishment. Everyone wore blue jeans, which is what my father had always worn to work. Students escaped the blandness of cafeteria food to visit the kosher dairy restaurants of Squirrel Hill, the surrounding Jewish neighborhood, or hung out at a leftie bar called Wobblie Joe's, drinking pitchers of Iron City—a beer so working class, even my father wouldn't drink it!

I haven't lived in Pittsburgh in almost twenty years, but I visit my parents there once a year, and the smallness of the suburbs where I grew up always gives me pause. On a recent trip, my girlfriend and I had trouble finding a place to eat that wasn't a Burger King, Roy Rogers, or McDonald's. We settled on Eat'n' Park, which in the sixties was a drive-in restaurant where carhops came to take your order. In those days, they served mostly hamburgers, fries, and shakes, but now they have internationalized. The menu was a curious amalgam, with its "South of the Border" entrées, its stir-fry offerings, its Italian selections, and its awe-inspiring two-page spread of pies and ice cream. We both settled on the salad bar, where I ran into a friend of mine from high school, who was with his wife. If I had never left Pittsburgh, I wondered, would I have been eating there with my husband?

Given the narrowness of my childhood, the intolerance of difference that I grew up with, it doesn't really surprise me that I had to leave it all behind. As an adult and a lesbian, I needed to live in a city where anything is possible. In Manhattan, I might see women holding hands with men or with each other. I might hear four different languages just on my way to work. I might eat as many different kinds of food in a week.

Sometimes I worry that I have become cavalier, particularly about food, living in a city where so much is available so readily. ("Oh, no, not Brazilian food again! I had it on Tuesday!") My refrigerator at this moment contains only ground coffee, milk, juice, seltzer, and bread. But at least once a weekend, my girlfriend and I prepare a simple and frugal meal together from scratch—shopping, washing, chopping, measuring, sautéing—then eat by candlelight on the couch. Like so many Manhattan apartments, mine is the size of a Swanson's frozen dinner box; not only was its kitchen designed to be used by one person at a time, the apartment also won't accommodate a proper dinner table.

But it *is* rent-stabilized and centrally located, and there's a good restaurant nearby to get falafel and the eggplant dip *babaganoush* and one for northern Italian and another for kosher vegetarian Indian. And don't let me forget the great bagel shop around the corner . . .

# A Simple Chicken Marinade for Saturday Night

I pound thinly-sliced chicken breast or tenders
1½ tablespoons olive oil
I tablespoon red wine vinegar
1½ teaspoons chili powder
I tablespoon crushed coriander
2 tablespoons cold water
Black pepper to taste
4 individual pita pockets
Shredded lettuce
Chopped plum tomatoes
Salsa and/or sour cream

1. Wash chicken and place in a shallow backing dish.

2. In a separate bowl, combine oil, vinegar, chili powder, coriander, water, and black pepper.

3. Pour mixture over chicken and turn pieces to coat thoroughly. Cover dish and marinate in refrigerator at least one hour (but the longer you leave it, the better).

4. Broil chicken pieces for 2 to 4 minutes per side. Serve as sandwiches in pita bread with lettuce and tomatoes, topped with salsa and/or sour cream. A rice side dish is nice. Serves 2.

# On Becoming a Cuban Jewish Cook: A Memoir with Recipes

Ester Rebeca Shapiro

I was born into the Jewish Diaspora in Havana, Cuba, in 1952 and into a family which refused to look back at the shadow of the shtetl, embracing instead the Caribbean sunlight. I became part of the Cuban diaspora in 1960 when we fled from Castro's socialist revolution to Miami. Suddenly, there in Florida, new rules for survival and a rigid new family mythology fell into place. The bright landscape of my Cuban childhood became shrouded in darkness as we struggled to invent new, assimilated American selves. Ever since, I have tried to make my peace as a member of two dispersed communities, each infused with conflicts and contradictions in politics, religion, and values. As an adult I have become a fanatical cook and in the creative process of cooking have found a way to reconcile these contradictions. As a cook, I can achieve a rich and harmonious unity in my struggle to make sense of my conflicting identities.

Not that my relationship with food and cooking is at all simple: I am deeply driven by creative forces and subterranean needs that have found the preparation of just the right meal the most compelling form of expression. From my childhood in Cuba, I carry vivid, voluptuous memories of shopping for food in the old Havana street market. At the chicken vendor mother would select the chicken with the silkiest feathers and the brightest eyes, and its neck would be wrung as we watched. We would bring home the partially plucked bird and scrape its yellow skin clean of its last feathers. Once in the pot, this carcass was alchemically transformed into arroz con pollo, chicken and rice, and a sublime, gelatinous *Yeddishe* chicken soup was produced from its gizzards and feet.

My lifelong mission to understand human development in family and cultural contexts began as a strategy for personal survival. In the hothouse Havana atmosphere of our Cuban Jewish extended family, I realized with a painfully piercing clarity that I had an inner life and a will to understand the world and act in it on my own terms. My family experienced this as profoundly threatening to their safety and stability. After three generations of uprooting and loss, a private cult of family loyalty and financial security had replaced our family's severed connections to stable, enduring cultural and spiritual communities. After leaving Cuba, my parents and grandparents tried to forget their relatively brief sojourn there compared with our many centuries in Byelorussia believing they could best survive in the United States as American Jews. Betrayed by the Cuban revolution, whose ideals shaped the first six years of my own remembered life, my family reverted to the most ingrown *shtetl* life, albeit a *shtetl* community in which everyone spoke Spanish and ate *picadillo*.

My own personal search, both as a Cuban and a Jew, brought me into conflict with my family's values and became a source of ceaseless battles in my growing up. They did their best to reinvent our lives as American Jews as if Cuba had been a small, insignificant accident of fate in our diaspora wanderings. Cuba loomed much larger for me, compelling yet forbidden because of both political and religious prohibitions. I honored my family's ban on yearning for Cuba, and for many years went back only in my dreams. There were many other forbidden zones in my own freedom to explore and experience my Cuban heritage and identity, the hottest buttons being Communist politics and connections with non-Jews. But no walls were erected around food, and in cooking it has seemed possible to bridge our multiple cultural legacies and come up with a creative union in which the whole, indeed, is more than the sum of its parts.

The women who shaped my own intense relationship to cooking and food are the two cooks in my family who were both the most integrated in the Cuban/Eastern European traditions, and the most generous in their genuine desire to express their love and their own natural exuberance through their cooking— my mother's mother, Abuela Adela, and my father's sister, my tía Consuelo. Abuela Adela left Poland as a teenager in 1923 and lived for forty years in the small town of Cabaiguan, in the central Cuban province of Las Villas. Tía Consuelo, who left Poland for Cuba when she was eleven, lived her turbulent adolescence as an exotically beautiful, dangerously intelligent, sexually curious girl in Bolondron, a village just outside of Matanzas, hotly pursued by many ardent Cuban suitors. Consuelo was married off twice by the time she was seventeen, both times in arranged marriages. Abuela Adela and Consuelo were much more fully Cuban as well as Eastern European Jewish than the rest of my family. I used them as my models, even though to do so was to act deliberately against the family prohibitions that devalued my mother's side of the family in favor of my father's and devalued my aunt in favor of her brothers. When my father and his brother, my tío Noel, tried to curb my prohibited intellectual and sexual appetites, they often told me how dangerously I had become like Consuelo.

Abuela Adela was an exuberant, almost manic cook, driven in her generosity by a complicated need to fill her own private hungers. She never seemed to know when to stop. For her daughter, my ascetic mother, whose appetites for culinary luxury ran more to café con leche with barely buttered toast, her mother's insistent generosity seemed at best self-centered and at worst downright persecutory. Because Abuela Adela was relentless and unstoppable in her drive to make her daughter a more suitable reflection of her own glory, her outpourings of clothes and food were sources of endless torture for my mother. Abuela Adela would ride an hour on the bus from her house in Miami Beach to our house in Hollywood, Florida, laden with bundles and packages of food which would inevitably appear in a messy flurry of spilled juices and grease stains. I would eagerly pore over the bulging bags for the garlicky veal roast, fried ripe bananas, and homemade gefilte fish with fiery red horseradish sauce called *rein*, earning her glow of pleasure and a complimentary comparison for my fine appetite to her son, my equally voracious tio Nuñi. She could be relied on to make *lochschen kugel*, the traditional noodle kugel, with *guayaba* (guava) instead of the traditional apples. Her Eastern European recipe for gefilte fish began to blend and fuse with her fabulous seviche of marinated fish, so that her gefilte fish acquired a more and more aromatic use of garlic and bay leaf, while her seviche relied on the more European style of precooked fish marinated with rounds of carrots.

When I was younger, I found Abuela Adela's relentless insistence occasionally irritating, as I tried to put a limit on my eating somewhere prior to stupefaction. Her exaggerated generosity was touching, at times, a bit of a burden: having once praised the incomparable *pastelitos do guayabe* which she had procured from a baker around the corner from her, she made sure that anytime my sisters or I visited she sent us away with an entire baker's tray of fresh guava pastries. Convinced that more is inevitably better, she proudly declared the pastries had been made especially to her specifications, with lots of extra guava in the center. Have you ever tried to negotiate an airport with not only your own luggage but also a bag of forty or so extra dense guava pastries? But when I left home and discovered my own great love of cooking, I found myself more and more appreciative of her inventive culinary crossing of cultures, her talent for never leaving well enough alone. And I have become notorious, among friends and family, for my habit of appearing in their homes laden with food which I have transported in the back seat of my car, often sticky with inadvertently spilled *mojo criollo*, the Cuban-style citrus marinade.

Although I was a far more prodigious eater than cook while living in my parents' home, as soon as I went to college I discovered that cooking could join my other intense yet dangerous appetites to be refashioned into an image of myself as smart, sexy, affectionate, and good to my friends, in short a terrific cook who loved to prepare and share meals with others. As I entered the kitchens of my college and graduate school apartments, with roommates or alone, every evening meal became an opportunity to celebrate my emancipation and my own life. I cherished my freedom to live honoring the juicy, messy, and generous passions I felt and not have those feelings shrivel in a climate of threats and hurts, as desiccated as an overcooked flanken. I cooked to share lovingly with others, but cooked even if only for myself, a commitment which probably saved my sanity after my divorce.

My culinary excesses are probably most evident at my parties for 100 to 150 people, at which I do all the cooking myself. I now consider *lechon asado*, *picadillo*, and seafood *zarzuela* a menu I can pull together with about a week's anticipatory shopping and marinating, and with preparation time squeezed in between classes and appointments. It's the Jewish weddings and other Jewish events that give me more trouble, because after all, you can't serve only *treif* (Yiddish for non-Kosher; literally means unclean), in fact, sometimes you can't serve any *treif*. The first time I encountered the problem of having to expand my tried-and-true quantity Cuban menu was for the occasion of my sister Rachel's wedding. Rachel responded to our controlling family ways by concealing much and revealing little: my parents thought she had a lifelong indifference to dating, and had no idea she had a long-term involvement with a non-Jewish man.

When Rachel could no longer postpone introducing our parents to Bob, at the time they decided to get married, our father predictably blew a gasket. Born in Poland and immigrating to Cuba at age five, my father has been forever haunted by fears and insecurities which he has hidden behind authoritarian rages. As outraged as he was in talking to Rachel, he reserved his greatest vitriol for me. As his oldest daughter I had been duty-bound to dissuade Rachel from this marriage or at the very least to tell him so he could exercise his parental authority. My refusal to do so was clear evidence of my lifelong, systematic interference with his authority as a father, an interference that had resulted in both Rachel and our sister Miriam following in my disloyal footsteps. Father eventually announced that he would make an enormous concession and accept Rachel's relationship with Bob, but only if Bob converted. Bob, who had himself been fought over by his Roman Catholic father's and Greek Orthodox mother's clans, loved Judaism but did not cherish another battle over his everlasting soul. Ironically, when Rachel was finally able to say to Bob, I love you and will marry you whether or not you convert, he felt free to convert from personal desire rather than coerced ultimatum.

My then husband Jeff and I had agreed to throw the wedding. Now, suddenly, the party changed. It got bigger and more formal. For one thing, they would now be married by a rabbi and I could hardly prepare my usual Cuban *treif*. I also felt moved to recognize Bob's sacrifice of his own people's legacy by affirming the Greek heritage which would remain an important part of his family life even if the Greek Orthodox and Roman Catholic faiths were not. So I came up with a lovely menu: Greek *mezzas* or appetizers and roast leg of lamb with a fish dish for vegetarians, all of which could still be served informally, buffet style, right out of my kitchen pans and onto paper plates. As Rachel and Bob brought their relationship out from secrecy, and Rachel began to experience her right to her own life and to prepare to publicly acknowledge the rightness of this relationship, she began to feel that she deserved to be a beautiful bride at a lovely wedding. She and Bob decided to spend some of their savings on making the event a memorable one. The party plans entered another realm, complete with klezmer band, a tent in the backyard, rented tables with tablecloths, china, silver, and glassware—the *gantze tzimmes* (literally the whole thing, the Yiddish word for the deluxe version of a traditional carrot and sweet potato dish, to which you add meat in times of luxury). Through more luck than I should have expected, we survived the many culinary catastrophes that came with my inexperience.

The typical Cuban Jewish Miami wedding, long on formality and short on intimacy, could not have been more different from our homemade party. The visiting family was initially in shock. Yet the magical space created by our abundance of love transformed my backyard and the people in it. My tio Nuñi, as exuberant and generous as his mother Abuela Adela, had asked me if there was anything he could bring from Florida. I told him we were at the end of our New England strawberry and blueberry season so I would be enormously grateful if he could bring me some tropical fruit, mangoes would do it, as they were inaccessible to me. When he agreed, I should have remembered Abuela Adela's overstuffed guava pastries. Sunday afternoon, a black stretch limousine showed up at my door. An utterly infatuated driver, who had probably never seen the likes of this Miami mafioso look-alike adorned with gold chains featuring a huge diamond-studded Jewish star and an Afro-Cuban *azabache* (a good luck charm with an onyx fist holding a coral and gold circle), began to unload carton after fragrant carton of perfectly ripe mangoes, luscious *guanabanas*, and magnificent *mameyes* (both Caribbean fruits for which no American names exist), all somewhat bruised and warmed by their long trip and filling the house with their exotic aromatics. I set up the dessert table with its glorious fancy wedding cake, a generous bowl of the last New England berries, and these exotic tropical fruits. To everyone's surprise, the family enjoyed themselves enormously. Having grown accustomed to frequent, large, and relatively impersonal family gatherings, I felt the intimacy of the wedding was intensified by the fact that the food was cooked and served with my hands and heart, with all my love for my sister and her present friends and her future family. It moved everyone present to respond with far greater closeness to each other.

When I first read Anne Tyler's *Dinner at the Homesick Restaurant*, I identified with the brother Ethan's craving to cook the perfect meal with so much love it would transform his family from their irritable, feuding distance into the close and loving family of his dreams. With Rachel's wedding, I came very close to that ideal. Only my father wandered the party a lost soul. He confessed that when he saw the unexpected success of this extravagant event he saw his own image. Yet my accomplishments were a source of pride and satisfaction for him only if I remained completely within his orbit, only if I credited him with my achievements. We would need twelve more years, including my divorce and remarriage, to find the new balance of love and disappointment which allowed us to be close without rancor.

In 1990, after the post-divorce collapse and rebuilding of my life along lines much more of my making, I went back to Cuba and to Israel for the first time. I approached both of these places seeking a more inclusive exploration of who I might yet become. I needed to rediscover what had once been my family's most cherished value and the one they were forced to jettison by their urgency to insure personal survival—a sense of social mission larger than the needs of the individual and the family.

In going back to Cuba, I unleashed a storm of personal as well as family upheaval. The implacable prohibitions against returning to Cuba, at first, appeared to be based on the rabid anti-Communism characteristic of all Cuban exiles in my parents' generation. Yet closer scrutiny showed a much longer history of loyalty pacts between parents and children, necessary to any family's survival in diaspora, which I was violating by asking the questions: what might my life have been like if I had grown up building Eretz Yisrael or the Cuban Revolution, if I had been devoted to a historically meaningful social cause instead of my own personal fortune? In both Cuba and Israel I sought out the fragments of the family who could answer my questions, and discovered kin who shared the intellectual curiosity and sense of social obligation which my Miami family had long ago replaced with more material concerns. My willful disobedience, all the more unbecoming in a daughter, evoked fury, which turned to grief, which was then masked again by fury. Like Pandora I was opening a trunk of painful memory and potential meaning which could radically disrupt our carefully crafted peace, and could never again be shut at will.

I felt profoundly moved by our Cuban people's revolution and began to learn about a rich, culturally diverse national legacy from which I had been abruptly cut off. I found that my own experience and interpretation of *Yiddishkeit* and *Cubanidad* were surprisingly compatible, unified by their highest striving to create a just society which embraced enormous cultural difference, even as they were unified by their lapses in strictly insisting on ideological or religious tests for full participation.

The visit to Israel reassured me that our Jewish people had found a way to remain Jews while enlivening our traditions with the riches of our host cultures in diaspora. The *mestizaje* (or race mixing) which so informs our creative Cuban cultural traditions also characterizes the intermarriage of our Jewish people in exile, who joined the host culture and embraced its people and traditions, at least whenever permitted to do so. I was relieved to read

James Baldwin's 1980 essay in *Esquire*, "On Being White and Other Lies," which exposed the corrupt bargain the United States arranged with its brown European immigrants, that they could pass for white as long as they colluded in anti-Black racism. I am not white. I am a Jew, and I belong to a scattered Semitic tribe whose members have made the best of their many homes, whose cultures and complexions reflect shades from Ethiopia to Yemen, from Spain to Poland, all intermixing in Eretz Yisrael where the beauty of the Sabra, like that of the mulatta, is legendary. I brought that realization back with me to my life in Boston, to my new marriage with a Cuban whose soul is so Jewish I can assume there were Marranos in his Galician genealogy. I have promised myself that in life as in the kitchen I can create traditions which are satisfyingly coherent, continuous yet innovative, out of exile's inevitable losses.

❑: ❑: ❑:

## Mojo Criollo

(Cuban marinade for chicken, roast pork, or barbecued sweet potatoes)

    I cup orange juice
    juice of 2 lemons
    2 to 6 cloves garlic, mashed
    3 bay leaves
    2 tablespoons cumin
    I teaspoon dried basil or sweet marjoram
    salt and pepper (to taste)
    chili powder or hot sauce (optional, to taste)

Note that the proportion of orange juice to lemon juice, of sweet to tart, can vary with the food you plan to marinate; you want to balance the sweet and sour effect, although some foods like fish or chicken may be better tart, and other foods like sweet potatoes may be better sweeter. Rock Cornish game hens are most delectable with a higher proportion of sweet to tart. The amount of total juice may have to be increased, depending on the quantity you are marinating. The mix of herbs is also approximate; it depends partly on what you are making and what it takes to lightly coat with herbs. Cumin should be dusted lightly all over the food; basil and marjoram are used more sparsely as a little goes a long way; only you know your own garlic tolerance, and beware that mine is very high.

1. Place 1 chicken (cut up or whole) or pork (roast or chops) in a bowl and cover with all the above ingredients. If you have time, let meat marinate overnight in the refrigerator. Meat should be well coated with herbs and you should turn it over in the citrus juice mixture once. If you don't have time to marinate overnight, it will still be tasty; you should make sure the coating is thicker, with less juice and more herbs, so it comes out a little more like a paste which lightly coats the meat.

2. Chicken parts can be broiled or baked; whole chicken can be roasted. Roast pork and roasted chicken should be started in a 425° oven for 15 minutes, then finished in a 350° oven until they are fully cooked according to a meat thermometer. Pork chops are better broiled if they are thin, although those over half an inch thick can be baked.

3. Sweet potatoes should be cut up. Double the proportion of orange juice and halve the lemon juice. Spread potatoes in one layer in a baking dish with the marinade. Bake for about an hour and a half at 350°. These are good with some hot sauce like a mango or chile hot sauce, which gives them a more barbecued quality. Just be careful about your tolerance for hot sauce. The marinade is enough for 4 sweet potatoes.

❚❖ ❚❖ ❚❖

# Basic Cuban Tomato Sauce

(for *Picadillo*, *Zarzuela de Mariscos*/Seafood or Chicken,
*Arroz con Pollo*, Stove Top Paella)

olive oil (enough to cover bottom of your pot)
1 large onion, chopped
1 large green pepper, chopped
2 to 4 cloves garlic, crushed
one 16 ounce can of tomato puree
3 tablespoons cumin
2 teaspoons dried basil and/or marjoram
salt and pepper to taste
chili powder or hot sauce (optional, to taste)
half a can of beer, or ¼ cup sweet sherry (optional)

1. Cover bottom of a pot with olive oil.
2. Sauté chopped onions at medium heat until golden.
3. Add green peppers and cook until softened.
4. Add crushed garlic and cook until softened, but not browned.
5. Add tomato puree and herbs; lower the heat to medium low (or you'll get splashed by jumping tomato sauce). Adjust seasoning and add more herbs as desired. *You can also add the optional hot sauce, half a beer, or sweet sherry to the sauce at this time.*
6. Simmer 10 or 15 minutes, and then add ingredients from one of the following recipes:

**For *Picadillo*:**

1 ¼ pounds lean ground beef
¾ cup raisins
¾ cup green olives with pimentos

1. Crumble the beef into the simmering tomato sauce, and then thoroughly stir it into the sauce so there are no remaining lumps of meat.

2. Add the raisins and green olives with pimentos. Raise to medium heat and cook until mixture is boiling, then lower to medium low and cook the beef through, approximately another half hour.

3. Serve with white rice. Serves 4.

## For *Zarzuela de Mariscos* (seafood):

      1½ to 2 pounds mixed shellfish and fish (shrimp,
             scallops, squid, mussels, clams, cut up lobster in
             the shell, or any firm fish like monkfish, grouper,
             or red snapper fillet cut into 3-inch squares;
             if using flaky white fish, cut slightly larger
             and watch to keep from overcooking)
      ¾ cup frozen green peas

1. Add seafood to simmering tomato sauce as follows: first squid, then shrimp, then mussels and clams in the shell, then cut up lobster, then fish.

2. When fish is almost cooked through, add peas. Stir in peas and cook through.

3. Serve with white rice. Serves 4.

## For *Zarzuela de Mariscos* (chicken):

      olive oil to coat bottom of pot
      one 3½ to 5 pound chicken, quartered;
         skin may be removed
      ¾ cup frozen green peas

1. Heat the olive oil on medium-high heat and sauté chicken until golden, then remove from heat and place in a bowl.

2. Bring basic tomato sauce to a simmer.

3. Add chicken and cook through for another 40 minutes.

4. Stir in the peas and cook through. Serves 4 to 6.

## For *Arroz con Pollo*:

      chicken and tomato sauce ingredients as above
      2 cups white rice
      2 cups water and/or beer (approximate)

1. Cook chicken in tomato sauce as in the *zarzuela de mariscos* recipe, but do not add the peas.

2. Remove chicken from sauce and place in a covered bowl to keep warm.

3. Check the amount of sauce to make sure it adds up to 4 cups. If not, add up to 2 more cups of water or beer. Also make sure to adjust salt, pepper, and seasonings at this time.

4. Stir in white rice and bring liquid and rice to a boil. Then lower heat to low and cook rice about 20 minutes.

5. Add peas and cook another 5 minutes.

6. Add chicken and any sauce that remains in the bowl. Serves 6 to 8.

## For Stove Top Paella:

      seafood and tomato sauce ingredients above
      2 cups white rice
      I cup water and/or beer (approximate)

1. Cook seafood in tomato sauce until just barely cooked through, without adding the peas.

2. Remove seafood from tomato sauce with a slotted spoon and place in a covered bowl.

3. Follow above steps for adding and cooking rice, adjusting seasonings and liquid depending on how much liquid is released by the seafood.

4. When rice and peas are cooked through, add reserved seafood.

5. This same dish can combine chicken and seafood, following chicken and rice recipe above. Shellfish would be cooked in the tomato sauce after chicken has been cooked through and removed. Then same steps can be followed for stove top paella, with all ingredients stirred into rice after the peas have cooked through at the end. Serves 6 to 8.

▯: ▯: ▯:

# The Staff of Life

## Margaret Randall

Into the bottomless space his invasion left
back when your resistance took a turn
toward sublimation,
dissolve 2 packages dry yeast
in 3 cups lukewarm water.
This sea throws up a tangle
of passwords on its beach.
Stir in ¼ cup honey, molasses,

or brown sugar (1 cup dry milk
if milk is what you drink).
Then 4 cups whole wheat flour.
Beat well with a wooden spoon:
100 strokes.

No beating was necessary to seal your lips
back then, only the steel promise
of his gentleman's eyes.
Let rise until doubled in volume
and in meaning.
One day the rising of your rage
will dissolve the fear,
I promise you this.

But when you fold in 4 teaspoons salt
and ⅓ cup oil,
your heart may harden into rifts of terror.
Two cups unbleached white flour
and another of wheat
slowly build the mass you need
to "get on with life."

Your responsibility: to clean his image
with strong forearms, kneading
finger tips.
Slapping and gathering in the dough
is an exercise in pain control.
You have it now, have earned it

with a life remembered and cherished
as bread from the fire
calms this cusp of years.
We are always as strong
as our waiting need demands.

First rising: 50 to 60 minutes,
second 40 to 50.
Between them make a fist
and punch the risen dough,
but gently.
Remember: this is your food, not his face
flattened by dust and the sifting of time.

Shape loaves in greased pans,
let rise one last breath of air:
20 minutes to $\frac{1}{2}$ hour will do.
Finally, brush with a wash
of cold water or milk and egg.
Then bake. 350 degrees fahrenheit
for 25 minutes or until golden brown.

Remove from pans and cool
or eat right away.
Eat right away.

# Home Cookin'

## EL. Cortés

**S**he use to have her favorites, like Spanish omelette. I learned to make it real good for her. Just the way she liked it—not too runny and not dry, neither—just right. "Johnny," she'd say—she had everyone in the family callin' me that, Johnny, even though my name is Juan—"Johnny, oh Johnito, can I have a potato, please, Johnny, please?" and then before I could answer yes or no she'd sneak a golden brown one outta the pan, just fried in the olive oil, all oniony, right before I was gettin' ready to pour in the eggs, all beaten up, and I'd pretend to be angry, but she'd just laugh runnin' away with her stolen potato, tiny pieces of crispy, crunchy onion all over it, stuck on top of her fork, like it was a trophy she'd won by cheatin'. Runnin' and laughin', like she was gettin' away with murder. She has this sweet laugh—I use to make her laugh a lot, before. I loved that laugh, so honest, so clear. "A woman falls in love with a man that can make her laugh, ain't that important what he looks like," she said.

"How do I look, oh sweet babius mine?" That's what I'd ask her whenever we was gettin' ready to go out to some special place and she'd grin and say, "Ain't that important what a man looks like, funny-lookin' big teddy bear man." Then she'd hug me and hold me and keep me and hold me, my funny valentine, she laughed till she cried. Never meant to make her cry. All over the house she had these pictures of us, just the two of us together, to-gether forever, like they say in the old doo-wop songs, we clung to each other, each picture the same—like we was holdin' onto each other for dear life—she said once, then laughed. So many pictures of us two all over the house, of us on the shelves, of us on our altar, of us hung on the walls. Each safe in its own little frame, like a home. She had this thing 'bout framin' them right away, like she was afraid we'd forget 'bout them and they'd get old or messed up. Or lost.

"Look, Johnnyolo, isn't this a great frame," she said. "I had to touch it to know it was really fake. But it's a good fake. Looks like marble, but it's only cardboard. I got it at our favorite place—you know, the discount store." Then she put in our picture, held it up high and said, real proud, "Damn, don't we look pretty. We're something else."

Wonder if she's ate any omelette lately. Can't believe she'd throw away nine years just like that. She was always tellin' her friends how she loved havin' a man 'round who could cook—a real man—but one who really enjoyed cookin' and even cleanin' for his ole lady. She was always tellin' 'em what good care I took of her and her house. Made me feel so good—the way she use to brag 'bout me alla the time. And I just loved cookin' for my sweetcakes and I know I will again. It's just a matter of time. Time and luck. Didn't get a chance to do much cookin' before I moved in with her on account of I was livin' with my sister in the Bronx back then—just temporarily, of course—'cause of a little run of bad luck I happen to be havin' at that time. And, now, here I am back again at Dolores's. Kind of funny the way life is—filled with ups and downs. There's always too many people in this place, like Grand Central at rush hour and the kitchen's too cramp. But I don't worry, 'cause soon I'll be back, back home sweet home again cookin' for my darlin'.

She liked the way I always remembered to bring her flowers, even after nine years. Had said she never thought she'd last no more than five with no man. Had never done it before. Guess I fooled her. If I forgot the flowers for more than two weeks in a row she'd act real dramatic—cracked me up—how she made out like she was Barbra Streisand singing "You Don't Bring Me Flowers Anymore," except she use to sing it *"Ju Doan Breen Me Flores Nunca Más"*—half in Spanish—just to make me laugh and that was my cue to get her some more, which I always did. Use to make her so happy when she'd see me comin' up those stairs with a great big bouquet. Don't know why she cried, carried on so much toward the end. Couldn't understand, no matter how many times I told her, swore to her, it was just a business deal gone bad. A tiny, slight miscalculation I'd made. Could of happen to anyone—it's the American way, that's what I told her—happens all the time to big businessmen. Besides I was gonna take care of it. Just needed some more time, that's all. Had meant to tell her 'bout it when I first started losin', a few years back—just never got 'round to it—wasn't like I was really lyin', just needed more time to win the money back. If she had just given me a little more time. I'll make it up to her, wouldn't be right otherwise. I know that, I ain't no lowlife. I got my pride, if nothin' else, right now. I did some real nice things for her, too.

Always pick the prettiest flowers for her. She called them forgiveness flowers—but only sometimes—not every time. I have this real good taste—everyone always says so—should of been born rich. Man, doan I know that. I gave her some real pretty things, things she would of never bought for herself, even if she did have the money. She must remember that. Nothin' was too good for my babius, that's what I use to tell her all the time. Tried to make her believe it. My babius deserves the very best, not second best, I always said. I thought I could put it all back before she found out how much was missin'. I have every intention of payin' her back for what I took from her—what I borrowed—and I will, I swear on my mother's grave, every last cent, but she must understand that I need to see her, to talk it over, see how we're gonna do it, make the plans, make them right, so they work for real this time. Make her trust me again.

"I don't want you as my enemy," I said. She said, "I don't want to see you again." Won't see me again. Payback is a bitch. If I could just win the lottery I know everything would be okay again between us, just like before. Pay everything back. She'd take me back. Got to get this thing together again. Got to. Best thing that ever happen to me—told her that so many times— she saved my life—can't let it end like this. Locked out. She can't be serious. Never saw her so serious. Got to make her let me back in again. Got to make her laugh, make her laugh again. Don't cry, don't cry, sweet babius. Don't cry, Johnnyolo.

She liked it when I called her babius. She liked it when I made up words like martinizin'. Before dinner I use to say, "Madam, shall we martinize?" and she'd smile her pretty smile—really pretty—and after two or three she'd laugh, all mellow and soft. Bet she still uses some of the funny words we made up together, like the time when we came up with the name Dizzy Daisy for Margarita, my brother's ole lady, perfect for her, 'cause Margarita means Daisy in Spanish and that girl's so out of it dizzy seemed to fit like white on rice—though she wasn't so out of it the night she called at two a.m. scarin' my darlin' half to death, hysterical with her it's time to give you a piece of news that will wake you up, shake your world up voice. Cryin' and tellin' my sweetcakes all in a rush 'bout the fifteen hundred dollars. How it was her whole life savins, tellin' how she had loaned it to me only after I begged her to help me, with tears in my eyes, tellin' how she had believe me when she saw me shakin'. When I told her they was after me. When I cried. When I said it was a matter of life and death. When I promise to pay her back the very next day. Just 'cause I was a coupla weeks late was no reason for D.D. to call in the middle of the night and worry my sweetheart like that. I had meant to double the money and I almost did—I was so close to winnin' I could taste it. It wasn't like I actually stole it—just needed a little more time to get it all back—that's all. After that call things got really bad between me and my babius. It was the last straw, she said. Like she wouldn't take it no more. Like it was the last lie.

But I know it's gonna be okay again, 'cause I still love her. Love her more than me and it just can't be over. Know her too well, gonna win her back. I know she could never, ever really be mean to me, see me cry. If she could just see how I'm sufferin' she would break down, take me back. I know her real good. I feel it in my bones—that special feeling. Like when I'm gonna win. In a little while I'll just call her up, ask can I come over and cook her up a little brunch. I know—I'll make a Spanish omelette. Her favorite.

◻ ◻ ◻

## Home Cookin' (Spanish) Omelette

   1 large onion, sliced thin
   3 large potatoes, peeled and sliced thin
   1/4 cup olive oil
   6 eggs, well beaten
   salt and pepper, to taste

   1. Heat oil in a large, heavy skillet.

   2. Add onion slices and cook over medium flame until soft and taking on a little color.

   3. Add potatoes and distribute evenly in pan. Turn potatoes over and continue cooking until lightly golden brown all over.

4. Pour in well beaten eggs, seasoned to taste with salt and pepper, and let cook for a few minutes until egg mixture appears firm and set.

5. With the aid of a flat plate, turn omelette over and return to pan; cook 2 to 3 more minutes until done.

6. Serve cut into wedges as a main course for 2 or cut into 2 inch squares as hor d'oeuvres for 4.

# Greene

## Leah Ryan

**S**he's back," said Pam. She put up the order slip for eggs over easy, wheat toast, side of bacon. Marty ripped down the ticket beside it and practically threw an order of pancakes at her. "Alright," he said. "Send her in."

Pam's chin dropped. "You're not going to hire her, are you?" Eggs hissed on the grill. Marty pushed the toast down. "That's none of your goddamn business," he said. For years, she'd dreamed of walking out at moments like this, rolling her apron up and throwing it. She had it all planned out. "Deliver that order while it's hot, will you?" Marty said.

Pam shook her head, grabbed the coffee pot off the burner and headed for the corner booth. She wasn't happy at all about what she saw coming. Every now and then Marty did this kind of thing. One time he hired a bum to wash dishes. Not just a bum-type person, like a guy who maybe was out of work for a while or who was between apartments. A real bum that came in from the city somewhere. The guy stank for one thing, and he smoked foul-smelling hand-rolled cigarettes constantly. He would come out from behind the counter with a cigarette hanging out his mouth. For one thing, there was a health department problem with this. You never knew when the health inspector was going to stroll in. Second of all, the customers didn't like it. Even without the cigarette (after Pam had convinced him to leave his cigarette in the back kitchen when he came out to bus the counter) customers didn't like the looks of the guy. He was visibly dirty and he looked crazy, like any minute he might grab a knife and stab somebody. And the person who had to listen to the complaints and worry about this guy most of the time was Pam.

That was the problem. Marty hired these people but then he didn't have to work with them. He was only cooking breakfast this week because Ernie, the regular breakfast cook, was on vacation. Usually, he came and went. Pam worked five, six, seven days a week. It was mostly seven lately because Becky, the other day waitress, had got pregnant, and needed lots of time off. Eventually, she wouldn't be able to work at all. Marty hadn't gotten it together to take out an ad or anything.

Another time, Marty hired a short-order guy who didn't speak English. He just left the guy with Ernie, and Ernie was supposed to train him. He couldn't read the tickets or understand anything that was said. Pam felt bad for the guy. But Ernie couldn't be expected to train him and teach him English at the same time, especially when English is the only language Ernie knows. Pam was pretty sure he was an illegal alien. For one thing, he spoke Spanish and he went by the name of Vladimir.

The good thing was that these guys usually left of their own accord before too long. The bum guy just didn't show up one day after he'd worked there for three weeks. Nobody ever saw him again. Vladimir figured out that it wasn't working out and quit. Pam saw him about a month later working on a painting crew. When she told Ernie, Ernie said he was probably making twice as much money painting anyway.

This girl had been coming in twice a week for three weeks looking for a job. First it was before Becky was pregnant, or before she knew she was pregnant, anyway. So Pam just told her that they weren't hiring. Which was true. She kept coming back anyway. Then it turned out that they did need to hire somebody. But Pam didn't like the looks of the girl so she just gave her an application to fill out. When the girl began to sit down at the counter to fill it out, Pam said, "Why don't you just bring it back later?" and turned her back.

She was surprised when the girl came back in an hour. This time Marty was there. He asked Pam for the girl's completed application. "She's got experience," he told Pam, reading it. "Yeah," Pam said. "I'll bet."

Marty also told her the girl was from Greene, which made sense. Greene was a college town; it was full of rich kids who went there to go to college and then dropped out to become drug addicts. She and Ernie always said they could save their tuition money and just go for the drug addict career right off the bat. Sometimes crowds of them would come in from Greene, which was about forty-five minutes away.

This girl certainly looked like a Greene type. She had about twenty-five earrings in each ear and her hair was dyed flat black. She was wearing beat-up old sneakers with no socks. She was overweight and she wore glasses. They were funny looking glasses, like the ones men wore in the fifties. One thing she had to say was that it didn't look like this girl had spent a lot of money trying to look a wreck. Some of them actually did that. But all the same, she looked like the type that didn't have a clue what work was; the type that would bring two booths full of her weirdo friends in every day to drink coffee, and they'd sit there all afternoon. She might even be the stealing type.

"Go on back and talk to the owner," Pam told the girl with a sweep of her arm indicating the swinging kitchen doors. She shot Marty a warning glance after the girl was out of sight. Marty ignored her, flipped an order of French toast and began scraping the grill. Pam grabbed the coffee pot again, her mood darkening beyond retrieval.

The bell on the door chimed. Jerry walked in and took a seat at the counter. As she was pouring Jerry's coffee and setting up his place with paper placemat, napkin, and silver, she mumbled something under her breath about how there must be a shit storm passing over.

"What?" said Jerry.

"Nothing," Pam said sweetly. "How are you, Jerry?"

"Oh, I'm surviving," he sighed.

"Do you know what you'd like, or . . ." Pam clicked her ball-point pen.

"Well," Jerry took a long breath; too long for Pam. "I really don't know just yet."

"Okay, take your time," Pam said and turned away. It was like this almost every day. Jerry always came in and got the same thing. But he always had the desire, or the intention, to bust out and try something new and different. Invariably, he studied the menu as if he were going to be tested on it. Sometimes he'd ask a question, like did the pancakes come with real syrup? And could he substitute an English muffin for the toast without being charged extra? He would ponder the answers to the questions carefully, and then he would carefully lay down the menu and say, "I'll have two scrambled eggs, white toast, a small OJ, and a side of homefries, please," as if it were the very first time.

Jerry had been married once; he had come in for breakfast with his wife, too, though not as frequently, and they had always seated themselves in a booth, not at the counter, where Jerry always sat now that he was alone. His wife had taken up with some other guy and Jerry pined after her. She had dumped the guy since then, but had made it clear to Jerry that she still wasn't interested. Jerry acted like she was the only good thing that had ever happened to him. He was sure he'd be happy if she'd only take him back. But Pam remembered back when they'd come in together for breakfast and sat in a booth. Jerry was miserable then, too, and he even ate the same thing for breakfast. Pam didn't know what was wrong with him. But whenever he walked in with that miserable look, she felt the energy drain out of her immediately.

"What kinds of toast do you have again?" Jerry asked today.

"White, wheat, rye, pumpernickel, raisin, English muffin," she told him.

"I'll have two scrambled eggs, white toast, a small OJ, and a side of homefries, please," said Jerry.

Pam rang the bell and put the order into the kitchen window. She saw that the girl was still back there talking to Marty. Marty looked at the slip and reached for the cooler door. He looked past the slip and saw that Pam was still standing there.

"Can I help you?" he asked her, snide. Pleasant today, she thought.

"No," said Pam. She poured Jerry's orange juice. She heard the eggs hiss on the grill.

"Did you hear they're reopening the old drive-in movie theater?" Jerry asked when she brought his juice.

"Oh really?" said Pam. Oh, God, she thought. Is he going to ask me out?

"Yes," he said. "It's under new management."

How fascinating, thought Pam. Where is this going, exactly? Just then the girl emerged from the kitchen. This would be the moment of truth.

"My name is Fred," the girl said, moving behind the counter. "I guess I'm going to start work here tomorrow."

"Fred," Pam repeated. That figures, she thought.

"Marty said to introduce myself since you're going to be training me," the girl went on. The bell rang. Jerry's breakfast. Pam turned and picked it up, giving Marty an icy look as she did so. She placed the plate in front of Jerry and tried to read his response. He looked grateful. More grateful than usual? It was hard to say. The girl was still standing there.

"Wear a white blouse and a dark skirt," Pam told her. "Did

he give you that speech?" The girl nodded. Pam wondered if she should tell her to shave. She decided against it.

"See you in the morning," the girl said and turned to leave.

"Who was that?" asked Jerry when she was out of earshot. Pam was certain he had listened to the whole conversation anyway, and wondered if he were just trying to make small talk.

"New waitress," she said shortly.

"So the drive-in," Jerry said, "is going to have all new releases."

"Uh huh," said Pam and refilled his coffee.

"I was just wondering," Jerry began.

"Yes," said Pam. She began totaling his check.

"Are coffee refills still free here?"

"Only if you eat," said Pam, and tore his check off the pad in one clean stroke.

Next morning, Fred tapped on the window at 5:45, fifteen minutes early. Pam, who had arrived at 5:30, turned the lock and let her in.

Fred looked far more respectable than Pam could have imagined the day before. She'd combed her hair back out of her face. She'd lost the Clark Kent look, and Pam even thought she might have ironed her blouse. Pam herself rarely ironed—she was too impatient. She usually just hung things in a hot shower and steamed the wrinkles out. Fred had removed her earrings. Pam could picture her taking them out carefully, one by one, in front of a bathroom mirror, and lining them all up someplace safe.

"Can you see without those glasses?" Pam asked without saying hello.

"Contacts," Fred said, gesturing toward her eyes.

"Good," said Pam. It was the only comment she could make. She had readied a speech on hygiene and appearance. But the speech would go to waste on Fred. "Go easy on her," Marty had said, and Pam had been annoyed. But now Pam admitted to herself silently that she was slightly disappointed at having lost the opportunity to lecture Fred.

"First thing you do when you get here is start coffee," Pam told Fred. But when she turned around, she saw that Fred had already taken two clean pots from the dish drainer and begun filling them with water. Fred grinned shyly as she turned the faucet off and handed the full pots to Pam, who did not smile back. "What kind of places have you worked at?" Pam asked.

"I managed a Chicken Shack," said Fred, a little breathless. "I worked the graveyard shift in an all-night diner for three years." She began filling two more pots. Pam had set up the filter baskets the night before. She began pouring in water and flipping switches.

"Was that in Greene?" Pam asked.

"Yeah," said Fred without apology and handed her the full pots. Pam heard Marty coming in the kitchen door. Last minute, of course. He'd have no time to do his prep work before the first rush, which would mean he'd get behind and be a bastard all morning.

"Morning ladies," Marty called through the order window. Pam cringed. She turned on the local talk radio program. She hated listening to it every day. But the customers liked it, and Marty insisted that they play it. She put Fred to filling the cream and syrup dispensers, and went to open the door. The smell of bacon filled the small restaurant. She heard Marty beating his eggs. There was no one waiting. Maybe he won't get behind after all, Pam thought hopefully.

"I'm not going to give you any tables today," she told Fred when she returned to the counter. "You can shadow me and then maybe later you can work the counter or something."

"Fine," said Fred agreeably.

Jerry walked in, their first customer. He was unusually early.

"Good morning, Jerry," Pam said. She gave him his placemat and silver and the menu. Typically, he began to study the menu as if he had never seen it before.

"He's going to order scrambled eggs, white toast, a small OJ, and a side of homefries," Pam whispered to Fred. Fred smiled.

"Jerry, this is Fred," said Pam. "She'll be working a few mornings a week."

"Pleased to meet you," Jerry said earnestly.

"Fred is from Greene," said Pam.

"Uh huh," Jerry said.

"She managed a Chicken Shack," Pam went on.

"I'm finished with these," said Fred, indicating the cream and syrup dispensers.

"Were you in school there?" Jerry asked Fred.

"No," Fred answered. "I was born there."

"Really?" Pam asked. She was genuinely surprised.

"Some people are, you know," Fred pointed out.

"Is Fred short for something?" Pam asked. She picked up the tray of cream dispensers.

"Yes," said Fred. "Ralph."

Jerry and Pam exchanged a quick look.

"That was a joke," Fred said. "You can laugh if you want." She shrugged.

Jerry closed his menu.

"Winifred," Fred said finally.

"You're not a Winnie," Pam offered.

"Right," said Fred.

"Ready to order, Jerry?" Pam got her order pad ready and winked at Fred.

"Yes. I'll have an order of scrambled eggs, white toast . . ."

"Small OJ?"

"Make it large," said Jerry. "How's the bacon today?"

"Fine," Pam said. "It's good."

"Okay, gimme a side of bacon then."

"Really?" Pam said. "No homefries?"

"Naw," Jerry said, and flipped his menu closed. Pam raised her eyebrows and turned to Marty.

"I've got it all ready," said Marty, holding up a plate. He started to turn away. Pam tapped his shoulder and handed him Jerry's ticket.

"Eat it yourself," she said. "He changed his tune today, for some unknown reason." Fred had found the orange juice and poured a large by the time Pam turned back around. "Why don't you warm up his coffee, too," she suggested, not unkindly. She had three tables waiting. So much for knowing everything, she thought, and braced herself for the first morning rush.

At eleven, Richard the mailman came in for lunch. Though lunch did not officially begin until eleven-thirty, they made special arrangements for Richard, who came in almost every day. Today, he'd brought a postcard from Ernie.

Ernie was on a fishing trip. He was staying at a fishing lodge in the woods. Pam had assumed that it was very remote, but obviously he'd had no trouble sending a postcard. It had a picture of a tranquil lake, and there was a large trout superimposed on top, with the words "Blue Lake Lodge" written across it.

"Dear Pam, Marty, Becky, and all," Ernie wrote, "Weather is here, wish you were beautiful. Ha ha. Having a great time. Been here 5 whole minutes. Don't go changing everything while I'm gone. See you Monday. Peace, Ernie." Pam stuck the postcard up on the milk machine.

Pam sent Fred out on break just as the lunch crowd was starting to pour in. Becky showed up and started taking tables right away.

"How's what's her name doing?" Marty asked. "Frank or whatever."

"Fred," Pam said.

"What's that short for?" he asked.

"Ralph," said Pam. She laughed. It was funny. Marty gave her a steady look.

"Oh, lighten up," she told him.

"Well, how's she doing?" he asked again.

"Fine," Pam told him. "So far, so good."

Through the window, she saw Fred out in the parking lot smoking a cigarette. In the sunlight, Fred didn't look so young. She was maybe thirty, Pam thought. Not that it should matter. But somehow it did. Pam was ready for a smoke break herself. "I'm off," she told Becky.

Outside, Fred was leaned up against Pam's car. Pam pulled her sunglasses and her cigarettes out of her apron pocket.

"So how'm I doing?" Fred asked.

"Hard to tell at this point," said Pam, and lit a cigarette.

"I know," Fred said. "I was sort of kidding."

"Why'd you leave Greene?" asked Pam.

"Sick of it," Fred answered. "How long have you worked here?"

"Too long," Pam said. "Four years."

"That is too long," Fred said. "You remember a guy named Vladimir?"

"Yeah," said Pam. "He worked here for about a month."

"He said it was pretty horrible, but that you and the cook were nice to him."

"He a friend of yours?" Pam asked.

"I'm married to him," said Fred, and she crushed her cigarette. "It's not what you think," she continued, and smiled, smoothing her skirt. "Should I see if she needs help inside?"

"Sure," Pam said, calmly. "I'll be there in a minute."

Pam figured that maybe Fred married Vladimir so that he could stay in the country or something. But how did they know each other? And what if she ever wanted to marry someone else? Maybe she could divorce him after a few years or something.

The day she had seen him working on the painting crew, he was on his lunch break and Pam was walking by the house he was painting. It was her day off. She was on her way to the bank. When she'd seen Vladimir, she'd stopped to say hello. He didn't seem to recognize her at first, without her uniform. But he'd stood up and looked happy to see her. She felt bad—she knew she'd been short with him at times. It had been hard on everybody. "I'm sorry things didn't work out," she'd said to Vladimir. "It was just an impossible situation. It wasn't your fault." For a moment she wasn't sure if he'd understood her. He was shy on top of being foreign, so sometimes it took him a little while to react. His reaction certainly had surprised her. He'd leaned over, kissed her cheek, and said, "Thank you." "For what?" she'd asked, but he waved at her. She'd realized immediately that he was waving goodbye and she'd taken a step back, then walked away. It still surprised her when she thought about it.

Richard the mailman came out of the restaurant and she realized that her break had been excessively long.

"Who's the new waitress?" he asked.

"Did she wait on you?" Pam asked in reply.

"She looks kinda like Natalie Wood," he said.

"Her name is Fred," Pam told him, and squashed her cigarette against the bottom of her shoe. "She's married."

"See you tomorrow," the mailman said, apparently ignoring this information.

Pam pulled the door open and entered. Fred was waiting on a single woman at the counter. They seemed to be sharing a joke. Maybe it was the joke about her name. Fred, Ralph. She watched Fred turn and hand Marty the ticket through the window. She does look kind of like Natalie Wood, Pam thought. Becky squeezed past Fred with a full tray of dirty dishes and Fred, though she had her back turned, moved expertly aside. Pam considered that maybe now she could take a few days off. Maybe she and Ernie both. Let the place run itself.

"I'm back," she told Becky and Fred, squeezing behind the counter. The phone rang. Pam wondered if it was Vladimir.

It was Ernie. It was raining. He was sick of fishing in the rain. He hadn't caught much. "Jerry had bacon today," Pam told Ernie. Marty asked Pam who was on the phone, yelled at her for being on too long. "None of your goddamn business," Pam said, and found herself looking at the other two women. Becky avoided her eyes, but Fred looked right at her, smiled, and shrugged. "I have to go," Pam told Ernie. She thought about his hands, shiny where they'd been burned over and over, but his nails always perfectly trimmed. His cook's hands, holding the phone. She thought about holding his hand. Then she thought about Fred kissing Vladimir. "It isn't what I think," she said to herself. She'd thought she'd just said it inside her head, but Ernie said, "What?" "Just hurry back," she told him, and hung up. It was starting to rain outside. A lone man in a booth raised his coffee cup and looked at her. Against the window, it looked like he was filling his cup with rain. She wanted to grab a coffee pot, but it didn't happen. She stared at the man and his cup. Fred moved past her and toward him with a pot of coffee. "I'll get that," she said. Pam looked down. Her apron was crumpled in her hand. How did that happen, she wondered, and wondered a minute more before she tied it back on.

◻ ◻ ◻

# New Directions from *Wouldn't Take Nothing For My Journey Now*

## Maya Angelou

In 1903 the late Mrs. Annie Johnson of Arkansas found herself with two toddling sons, very little money, a slight ability to read and add simple numbers. To this picture add a disastrous marriage and the burdensome fact that Mrs. Johnson was a Negro.

When she told her husband, Mr. William Johnson, of her dissatisfaction with their marriage, he conceded that he too found it to be less than he expected, and had been secretly hoping to leave and study religion. He added that he thought God was calling him not only to preach but to do so in Enid, Oklahoma. He did not tell her that he knew a minister in Enid with whom he could study and who had a friendly, unmarried daughter. They parted amicably, Annie keeping the one-room house and William taking most of the cash to carry himself to Oklahoma.

Annie, over six feet tall, big-boned, decided that she would not go to work as a domestic and leave her "precious babes" to anyone else's care. There was no possibility of being hired at the town's cotton gin or lumber mill, but maybe there was a way to make the two factories work for her. In her words, "I looked up the road I was going and back the way I come, and since I wasn't satisfied, I decided to step off the road and cut me a new path." She told herself that she wasn't a fancy cook but that she could "mix groceries well enough to scare hungry away and from starving a man."

She made her plans meticulously and in secret. One early evening to see if she was ready, she placed stones in two five-gallon pails and carried them three miles to the cotton gin. She rested a little, and then, discarding some rocks, she walked in the darkness to the saw mill five miles farther along the dirt road. On her way back to her little house and her babies, she dumped the remaining rocks along the path.

That same night she worked into the early hours boiling chicken and frying ham. She made dough and filled the rolled-out pastry with meat. At last she went to sleep.

The next morning she left her house carrying the meat pies, lard, an iron brazier, and coals for a fire. Just before lunch she appeared in an empty lot behind the cotton gin. As the dinner noon bell rang, she dropped the savors into boiling fat and the aroma rose and floated over to the workers who spilled out of the gin, covered with white lint, looking like specters.

Most workers had brought their lunches of pinto beans and biscuits or crackers, onions, and cans of sardines, but they were tempted by the hot meat pies which Annie ladled out of the fat. She wrapped them in newspapers, which soaked up the grease, and offered them for sale at a nickel each. Although business was slow, those first days Annie was determined. She balanced her appearances between the two hours of activity.

So, on Monday, if she offered hot fresh pies at the cotton gin and sold the remaining cooled-down pies at the lumber mill for three cents, then on Tuesday she went first to the lumber mill presenting fresh, just-cooked pies as the lumbermen covered in sawdust emerged from the mill.

For the next few years, on balmy spring days, blistering summer noons, and cold, wet, and wintry middays, Annie never disappointed her customers, who could count on seeing the tall, brown-skin woman bent over her brazier, carefully turning the meat pies. When she felt certain that the workers had become dependent on her, she built a stall between the two hives of industry and let the men run to her for their lunchtime provisions.

She had indeed stepped from the road which seemed to have been chosen for her and cut herself a brand-new path. In years that stall became a store where customers could buy cheese, meal, syrup, cookies, candy, writing tablets, pickles, canned goods, fresh fruit, soft drinks, coal, oil, and leather soles for worn-out shoes.

Each of us has the right and responsibility to assess the roads which lie ahead, and those over which we have traveled, and if the future road looms ominous or unpromising, and the roads back uninviting, then we need to gather our resolve and, carrying only the necessary baggage, step off that road into another direction. If the new choice is also unpalatable, without embarrassment, we must be ready to change that as well.

# Making Do with Food Stamp Dinners

## Trudy Condio

**E**arly in 1995, Massachusetts passed what has been dubbed the most punitive welfare reform package approved in the nation. Here are some of the requirements the legislature passed. Approximately twenty thousand able-bodied recipients with school-age children six and older will be forced into low-wage or community service jobs within sixty days without the support of day care. The state offers an enticement to employers, which I call "state welfare," that includes a payment to the employer of $3.50 per hour for each recipient hired for a nine-month period and $2.50 per hour for three more months. Additionally, an employer who hires a former recipient into nonsubsidized employment receives another "state welfare bennie"; a tax credit of $100 per month for a maximum of twelve months. With both the state and the federal governments clamping down on welfare, the public attitude toward recipients has grown even more hostile.

In response to this hostility, faculty, students, and staff at the University of Massachusetts at Boston, began a project in late January of 1995 that culminated on March 1, 1995, in what came to be known as a Teach-In, modeled after events that occurred during the student movement of the 1960s. In trying to provide a better understanding of the plight of the poor and to protest the recent attacks against them, the Teach-In counterattacked the myths surrounding this volatile subject.

The Teach-In, a day-long event built on the theme "Welfare, It's Not What You Think," included workshops on Changes in the New Welfare Reform Law recently passed by the Massachusetts Legislature, Affordable Housing, Myths and Realities; An Economic Analysis and Dealing with Hostility in the Classroom. A Guerrilla Theater provided an opportunity for recipients to give testimony on video. Using the model of the AIDS quilt and the Domestic Violence Clothesline Project, recipients were given the chance to vent frustrations and feelings on paper through drawings, symbols, and statements and their works were then used to create a paper quilt. The day ended with a forum for faculty, students, and staff to give brief testimony as to what it is or was like to be on welfare.

As a student at U. Mass, a welfare recipient, and an active participant in planning this event, I created a monthly menu to show just how limited your diet is if you are dependent on food stamps. After all, one of the myths about welfare is that an AFDC mom hangs out at the house "eating bonbons and watching soaps." Another myth is that she "regularly eats steak and shrimp." Using my own household information including my food stamp allotment, I created a poster identifying what my daughter and I ate for evening meals for the month of February. I have created a replica that follows this narrative. Please keep in mind several factors when reading the menu. First, it is for dinners only. My seven-year-old daughter is in school and day care, so she is eligible for free breakfast and lunch. I need to provide for my own daily meals during the week. Weekend breakfast and lunch must be included in the food stamp budget. Snacks for my daughter, juice, milk, bread, eggs, and any other staples a family needs are also part of the food stamp expenses. My monthly food stamp allotment for my daughter and myself is $187. This is for FOOD ONLY. Don't forget that every family, including mine, needs soap, shampoo, dish and laundry detergent, toilet paper, toothpaste, and cleaning supplies. Just because we are poor doesn't mean we have to be dirty. All of this takes money. When you live on $466 per month and your bills total about $380, it

# FEBRUARY

| SUNDAY | MONDAY | TUESDAY | WEDNESDAY | THURSDAY | FRIDAY | SATURDAY |
|---|---|---|---|---|---|---|
| | | | 1<br>SOUP<br>PEANUT BUTTER & JELLY | 2<br>HOTDOGS<br>MAC & CHEESE | 3<br>ENGLISH MUFFIN PIZZAS<br>CANNED CORN | 4<br>HAMBURGERS<br>HOMEMADE FRENCH FRIES |
| 5<br>WHOLE CHICKEN ROAST<br>CANNED PEAS<br>RICE | 6<br>AMERICAN CHOP SUEY<br>BREAD & BUTTER | 7<br>SPAM SANDWICHES<br>MAC & CHEESE | 8<br>CHICKEN VEGGIE SOUP (MADE FROM LEFTOVER CHICKEN)<br>BREAD & BUTTER | 9<br>CLEAN-OUT-THE-FRIDGE NIGHT<br>PEANUT BUTTER & JELLY | 10<br>HOTDOGS & BEANS | 11<br>LEFTOVER CHICKEN SOUP |
| 12<br>MEATLOAF<br>NOODLES & BUTTER<br>CANNED PEAS | 13<br>SCRAMBLED EGGS & TOAST | 14<br>FOOD STAMP DAY—GROCERY SHOPPING<br>T.V. DINNERS | 15<br>PORK CHOPS<br>SALAD<br>RICE | 16<br>CHICKEN<br>STUFFING<br>CANNED CORN | 17<br>ENGLISH MUFFIN PIZZAS<br>MIXED VEGGIES | 18<br>CLEAN-OUT-THE-FRIDGE NIGHT |
| 19<br>SPAGHETTI & MEATBALLS<br>HOMEMADE GARLIC BREAD | 20<br>SOUP & GRILLED CHEESE SANDWICHES | 21<br>MEATLOAF<br>BAKED POTATOES | 22<br>CLEAN-OUT-THE-FRIDGE NIGHT | 23<br>PORK CHOPS<br>RICE<br>SALAD | 24<br>HAMBURGER HELPER<br>BREAD & BUTTER<br>CANNED CORN | 25<br>HOTDOGS<br>HOMEMADE FRENCH FRIES |
| 26<br>POT ROAST<br>CARROTS & POTATOES<br>RICE | 27<br>TUNA CASSEROLE | 28<br>CLEAN-OUT-THE-FRIDGE NIGHT | | | | |

doesn't leave you with much left over. To make ends meet, I shop with coupons and compare prices, buying generic as much as possible. A typical monthly "shopping spree" usually takes me about two hours.

Using food stamps becomes a humiliating experience at the checkout line. There is usually one person who scrutinizes my shopping cart and comments as to the contents. It's not enough to be poor, but to have to be accountable to the person behind you because for once you bought a steak that was on sale is a crying shame. I usually exit the store as fast as possible with my head down. So the next time you are at a checkout line and see a mother using food stamps, remember what you've just read. Try and have some compassion, maybe strike up a conversation as to where the "best buys" are, or share a quick recipe. You don't know how grateful that mother might be. Instead of running out of the store like I do, she might just walk with her head a little higher.

❒❖ ❒❖ ❒❖

# PART THREE

# Resolutions

When I consider wrapping grape leaves around various fillings, scooping food up in flatbread, or drying everything from apricots to yogurt under the sun, I revert. I'm back in a time before sitting in a chair at a table, before holding a fork, before ovens in each woman's kitchen. My body wants to squat and reach, along with the rest of my clan. And I remember that Yerevan, the capital of Armenia, was a settled site in 3500 B.C.E.

**Anais Salibian**

Moving from the dorm ... I began to cook Indian food, to invent several recipes, creating from memory, from observing my mother, following the trail of appropriate tastes and smells—add some tumeric, pop the mustard seeds (the black ones) in hot oil (careful not to burn them), add cumin seeds, fry in the basmati rice and add water. Bring to a boil and as the aromas waft in, be transported into other skies.

**Ketu Katrak**


Through deeply imbibing the stories of the lives of slave women I began to see the wisdom, skill, knowledge and love that took the leavings of the Europeans and the denatured foods mandated for them and created the foods that are so good and so nutritious.

**Jennifer Iré**

# Thoughts for Food

## Caroline Urvater

When my last child left home I put flowerpots on the burners on the stove. After twenty years of cooking I was through. My new motto was: any fool can cook, but it takes brains to find a good restaurant.

In the days when the children were small, and my husband and I were young and poor, I knew at least twenty different things to do with a little bit of hamburger, or a piece of chicken, and a lot of potatoes, rice, and vegetables. I was very inventive. The pressure of a phone call saying that several people were coming to dinner was all I needed to spur my creativity. The resulting meal was often much admired. The trouble was that I made things up as I went along, incorporating current leftovers into my meal. Because I could never remember the ingredients which I had used for the previous meal, I never made anything twice.

There were times when I wanted to produce a fancy dessert. My style of cooking precluded following recipes or measuring anything, so I would buy a frozen pie, defrost it, and then pinch its neat edges until they looked really sloppy. After that I baked it according to the instructions on the package and took credit for the tasty, lopsided result.

After my divorce I got a job and returned to college. I would run home from work to cook dinner for the girls and then hurry to my night classes. After a while, the children grew used to a meal which they called "meat loaf'n." They got meat loaf'n potatoes, meat loaf'n rice, meat loaf'n raisins (my version of a Middle Eastern dish), and when I was really pressed for time, meat loaf'n on toast. My children yearned for the gourmet delights of T.V. dinners. I knew that to give the children T.V. dinners was to neglect them. A mother is supposed to cook. Cooking is the natural sequence to breast feeding. So it was rarely, and guiltily, that I allowed the baby-sitter to feed them those neat packages. I hoped that in delegating the betrayal they would remember me for the home cooking, and the baby-sitter for the ersatz stuff.

The low point in my life came when my older child asked me why I could not stay at home and go shopping like other mothers, instead of going to school. After that question I decided to make ice cream for the children. This, I reasoned, would show them how much I loved them. I spent hours beating cream and eggs and vanilla. I had no idea what I was proposing to do to their little arteries. When I presented them with two bowls full of the results of my labors, they complained that this was mush and that they wanted the ice cream on a stick. It was then that I faced my inadequacy as a mother and had to accept it.

Now that my fortunes have improved and I am lucky enough to live in that gustatorial paradise which is New York City, I don't see why I should subject either my friends or my children to the doubtful creations of my limited culinary repertoire when I can more easily take them out to wonderful restaurants. Furthermore, I shall never live long enough to get over the thrill of going out to eat.

When I was a child, in Europe, during the Second World War, we had barely enough to eat, and what we had was British food. I ate my main meal at noon, in school. We were served smelly turnips, watery potatoes, and a wad of dispirited substance called "greens." We rarely had meat. When we did it was a grey stringy mass swimming in fat. Dessert could have been suet pudding, a sticky clump of paste which stuck to the roof of one's mouth, or sometimes an indescribable collection of lumps named "toad in the hole." Worst of all, was tapioca pudding which resembled nothing as much as a collection of frog's eggs swimming in a pale, viscid sauce. Even at home, because of the strict rationing, our food was starchy and dull.

We never went out. It was not until October, 1947, on the way to our new home in the United States, that I experienced the glory of eating out. I shall never forget the scrambled eggs on buttered toast which we ate in a small Newfoundland diner. It was gloriously rich and tasty. The flavor of fresh butter which permeated the crisp toast, mixing with the moist, golden scrambled eggs, was overwhelming. I have often told friends that I am sorry that they have never had the experience of tasting scrambled eggs for the first time, or the thrill of eating their first bag of roasted peanuts while staring incredulously at towering skyscrapers.

After we had been in New York City for a few days, my brother and sister and I realized that our English accents created a stir. We found that if we went into a candy store and loudly admired the enormous array of sweets, sooner or later, someone behind the counter or perhaps a customer, would give us some. We spent a good deal of time going from shop to shop, ruining our appetites. It was only after I was enrolled in P.S. 144 in Queens, where they put me in a remedial speech class to get rid of my English accent, that I started to have to pay for candy.

What I loved above all other foods were egg salad sandwiches on toast, and B.L.T.'s. Whenever I had any money at all, I would rush to the corner candy store to have one or the other sandwich and a milk shake. It seemed to me that nothing I had ever known tasted as good as they did. And today, forty-seven years later, I still feel the same way. Now, however, cowed by the fear of high cholesterol and the specter of clogged arteries, I rarely indulge in my favorite foods. I have managed to convince myself that steamed broccoli and raw carrots are wonderful.

Still, even a sensible meal tastes so much better to me when

I eat it away from home. For that reason, I am happily engaged in researching the hundreds of wonderful restaurants which are available in New York City. And if I feel like a meal at home, I telephone one or another neighborhood restaurant and contentedly eat what they send me. And when the children come over, which they do albeit not often enough to suit me, I offer them my basket full of menus and they choose whatever they would like to eat.

# Boiled Chicken Feet and Hundred-Year-Old Eggs: Poor Chinese Feasting

Shirley Geok-lin Lim

Y ou mustn't eat chicken feet until you are a married woman!" my aunts warned me. "Otherwise you will grow up to run away from your husband."

They sat around the dining table, an unstable jointure of old planks stained by years of soya-sauce drips and scorched by the ashy embers that always fell out of the small coal oven under the metal hot-pot which was fetched out once a year for Chinese New Year family feasts. They chewed on gold-brown chicken feet that had been boiled with ginger, garlic, sugar, and black soy. The feet looked like skinny elegant batons with starred horny toes at one end, their speckled skins glossy with caramelized color, but chicken feet all the same. My aunts and stepmother gnawed at the small bones, grinding the jellied cartilage of the ligaments audibly, and the bone splinters piled up beside their plates.

I would not stay to watch them. I had seen hens and roosters pick their feet through fungal monsoon mud, stepping on duck and dog and their own shit.

My stepmother raised poultry on our leftovers and on chopped swamp vegetation which sprouted lavishly in the greenish slimy wasteland behind our house, and on festival days she slaughtered at least two fat chickens for us—her five step-children, two sons, and cherished husband. Chicken was a luxury we tasted only on these days, on Chinese New Year, Ch'ing Ming, the Mid-Autumn Festival, and the Feast of the Hungry

Ghost. And then, as my aunts told us was the practice even when they were children, the chickens were divided according to gender, the father receiving the white breast meat, the sons the dark drumsticks, and the daughters the skinny backs, while the women ate the feet and wings.

As the only daughter in a family (then) of seven boys, I was excused from such discrimination and took my turn equally with the drumsticks, the favorite meat for all of us. Chicken was always sold whole and freshly slaughtered, and no one imagined then that one could make a dish solely of drumsticks or of chicken breasts. Such mass marketing was possible only with the advent of refrigeration, and although coffee shops in town held large industrial-sized refrigerators for serving shaved iced concoctions and cold sodas, popular refreshments among Malaysians to fend off the humid equatorial temperatures, Chinese Malaysians, like most Asians in the 1950s, would eat only fresh food. We thought of frozen meat as rotten, all firm warm scented goodness of the freshly killed and gathered gone, and in its place the monochromatic bland mush of thawed stuff fit only for the garbage pail.

Still, while no one sold chicken parts separately, fresh chicken feet were always available in the wet market; you could buy them by the kilos, a delicacy to be enjoyed, according to my elders, only by married women. Well, let my aunts and stepmother suck on those splintery bones. I was never comfortable at the table when those feet appeared, when the women waved me away from them. My mother had run away from her husband. A bad woman, a runaway wife, a lost mother. A young girl, I was not to be trusted with those chicken feet, not when I had my mother's history in my blood, my mother's face on my face, still recognizable to my aunts, my father's brothers' wives, good wives and mothers, even though it had been five, six, seven years since she ran away.

I could not face the leathery skin, tightly bound to the long femurs after hours of simmering. And the soft padded soles that my aunts delighted in chewing—it was here that the chicken came closest to the human anatomy: pads like the fat feet of my stepmother's babies. Even now, now that I have grown to become a wife and mother like my aunts and stepmother, like my runaway mother, I will not eat chicken feet, no matter how much wine, cardamom, cumin, honey, or ginger has steeped them. I remember the tiny bones, the crunch of skin and cartilage. I remember my mother.

Almost forty years later, living in the United States, I am constantly reminded of how "Chinese" has become a fetish for Americans looking for a transcending experience of difference and otherness. Ranging from white models with stark black eyeliner and chopsticks in their chignons to "happy" dressing gowns that copy karate-type uniforms, things associated with Chinese culture pervade mainstream American imagination, suggesting, through the fixed acquirement of a traditional middle-class taste—for blue willow-pattern china, for instance, or take-out shrimp in lobster sauce—that Americans are omnivorous consumers rather than Eurocentric ideologues.

Purveyors of such U.S. "multiculturalism," however, usually disguise the material sources of their goods. Difference has to be softened, transformed, before it can be assimilated into Middle America. So also with Chinese food, which, before Nixon's visit to China in 1972, was sold in thousands of small restaurants outside of Chinatowns as egg rolls, egg foo yung, chow mein, and fortune cookies, none of which was recognizable to me who had grown up eating home-cooked Chinese food in Malaysia. Influenced by the increase in Asian immigration to the United States after the 1965 Hart-Celler Act, and thirty years after Mao Tse-tung intoxicated the Nixon presidential party with *maotai* and exotic ten-course banquets, many Americans have learned to dine on "authentic" Chinese food across a number of regional cuisines, from the mild, flavorful fresh steamed dishes of Canton, to the salty fiery peppers of Szechwan and Hunan and the rich elaborate food of the Shanghainese. But mid-Manhattan restaurants and Chinese cookbooks never note the particular dishes peculiar to Old One-Hundred-Name, what the Chinese call the man in the street. These dishes have been the ordinary fare for billions of poor Chinese through the centuries, and for myself as a hungry child in a family of too many children and never enough money.

While the chicken feet my aunts feasted on was forbidden to me, I was repeatedly coaxed to taste *pei ta-an*, the only other dish in my famished childhood that I could not eat. These duck eggs, imported from China, had been selected for their large size, covered with a mix of mud and straw, then stored in a darkened space for at least a month, covered with cloth that had been impregnated with sodium carbonate. You had to knock the dried grey mantle of mud gently off, wash the eggs in cold water, then crack and peel the bluish-white shells. What emerged was a clear glistening gelatinous black oval enclosing a purple-green-black yolk, and a sharp reek of sulfuric vapor, a dense collection of chemicals from decaying things, like the air-borne chemical traces that trigger the salivary glands of scavenging wolves or turkey buzzards.

Father was especially fond of *pei ta-an*, what the expensive restaurants called hundred-year-old eggs, which my stepmother always served sliced thin in sections of eighths accompanied by shredded pinky young ginger pickled in sugared vinegar. He believed it was *poh*, full of medicinal properties that stimulated blood circulation, cleansed the liver and kidneys, sharpened the eyesight and hearing, and elevated the male libido, and my stepmother, a generation younger than he, diligently served it as a cold relish to accompany steaming rice porridge, or alone, as a late-night snack.

Occasionally Father shared this delicacy with us. My brothers hung greedily over him, waiting for their one-eighth sliver of slippery shining jet-black egg, which was served draped with a vinegary-moist ginger shred. Approaching *pei ta-an* for the first time, I thought its glistening black carapace and iridescent green-black yolk beautiful, a magical gem cut open for inspection. But then its acrid stench shot up my olfactory glands, opening passageways more powerfully than a tongueful of green mustard, and I gagged, as close to vomiting over food as I would ever get. Unlike boiled chicken feet which I could ignore by resolutely leaving the table, *pei ta-an* pursued me out of the kitchen, out of the living area, and out of the house, a smell of pollution I feared each time Father called out for us to come and eat some hundred-year-old egg.

At some point in my childhood, however, drawn by my brothers' lust for *pei ta-an*, I pinched my nostrils closed and opened my mouth for the sliver. Its flavor and texture was like nothing I had ever tasted, the combination of the jellied white-turned-to-black and the tightly packed purple-black heart igniting on my taste buds as in intricate instantaneous sensation of bitter and sweet, rawly and densely meaty, yet as delicate as air-spun cotton-candy, primitively chemical and ineffably original. I was hooked. But *pei ta-an*, although not expensive, was what my stepmother bought for Father alone: for his health, his pleasure, his libido. A morsel would always be our share of this pleasure.

Late on the evening that I first tasted *pei ta-an* I walked out to the Chinese grocery store at the corner of the main road and spent some of my cache of coins hoarded from the dollars that my mother far away in another country mailed me once or twice a year. I bought two eggs jacketed in mud and straw. While my brothers were playing Monopoly in the front room, I sneaked into the kitchen, broke open the armor, carefully crazy-cracked the shells, peeled the pair, all the time marveling at the scent that had set my saliva flowing, and ate them slowly, reveling in the gentle chewy texture of the albumin and the heavy metallic yolky overload. My stepmother was right. Eating *pei ta-an* was a libidinous experience.

I have grown accustomed to the absence of strong flavor and scent in food, living in the United States. Many Americans appear to prefer their meals as antiseptic as their bathrooms. The movement toward "health foods" seems to me to be yet another progression toward banning the reek, bloodiness, and decay of our scavenging past and installing a technologically controlled and scientifically scrutinized diet. In some future time, humans may live to a hundred and fifty years, dining on a mass-produced nutritious cuisine of "natural foods" based on grains, vegetables, and roots. Boiled chicken feet and chemically preserved eggs will become gross memories from a horrible history of animal abuse and carcinogenic poisoning. But in the meantime, millions of Asians are still eating these dishes in search of, if not, as my poor father who died young of throat cancer believed, health and longevity, at least a diverse diet that can keep them body and soul.

Thus my eldest brother, by now middle-aged and middle-class prospering, promised me a memorable breakfast when I visited him in Malacca in 1989. It was Sunday, as in the West a day for leisurely gatherings and perhaps some family feasting. We drove to the center of town, up through a narrow side-lane, and parked by an open ditch. Under a galvanized tin roof, crowding with other families, we sat on low stools around a small round wooden table, as scarred and stained as the table around which we ate in our childhood. The hawker, a Chinese

Malaysian, was busy stirring an enormous blackened iron pot from which clouds of steam puffed up. Smaller pots containing various dark and green mashes sat on smaller grills, all fueled by a propane tank. Pouring the boiling liquid from the teapot, Eldest Brother rinsed the bowls, cups, spoons, and chopsticks set before us. Then a woman—the hawker's wife? daughter?—filled our bowls with plain white rice porridge, watery, the grains soft but still separate rather than broken down into a glutinous mass. From the many pots she brought different bowls—salted cabbage cooked to a dark-green slush with slabs of pork fat edged with a little lean; salted pickled cucumber crunchy and sweet; hard-cooked and browned bean curd less chewy than the meat it was processed to imitate; salted dried anchovies smaller than my little finger, fried crisp with their heads on. Nothing was fresh, everything was freshly cooked.

A light in my head flashed and lit something I had always known but never understood. How poor the masses of ordinary Chinese have been for millennia and how inventive hunger has made them. How from the scraps, offal, detritus, and leftovers saved from the imperial maw, from dynastic overlords who taxed away almost everything, peasant Chinese have created a fragrant and mouth-watering survival: dried lily buds and lotus roots, tree cloud fungus and fermented bean mash, dried lichen and salted black beans, pickled leeks and seaweed dessert; fish maw and chicken feet; intestines and preserved eggs. No wonder as a child I was taught to greet my elders politely, "Have you eaten yet, Eldest Auntie? Have you eaten rice, Third Uncle?" Speaking in our dialect, my stepmother still greets me, newly arrived from rich America, thus, "Have you eaten?"

The cook himself approached our table bearing two dishes especially ordered by my brother for me: soy-boiled chicken feet chopped into bite-sized pieces, and *pei ta-an* cut in eighths with a mound of pickled ginger on the side. My eldest brother had figured me out; that, even after decades of American fast foods and the rich diet of the middle class, my deprived childhood had indelibly fixed as gastronomic fantasies those dishes impoverished Chinese had produced out of the paltry ingredients they could afford. This is perhaps the instruction to an increasingly consuming and consumed planet that the cuisine from China offers: to eat is to live. And we multiplicious billions will all have to learn to eat well in poverty, turning scarcity and parsimony to triumphant feasting. Facing my morning's breakfast of preserved vegetables and hundred-year-old eggs, boiled chicken feet, and rice gruel, I knew my brother was offering me the best of our childhood together.

**░ ░ ░**

## Soy-Boiled Chicken Feet*

10 pairs of chicken feet
1 teaspoon salt
1¹/₂ teaspoon pepper
one knob ginger as big as a large walnut
4 cloves garlic
¹/₄ cup sherry
1 tablespoon sesame oil
2 teaspoons sugar
1 cup soy sauce
5 star-anise or 1 teaspoon
     five-spice powder (optional)

*The same recipe can be used or chicken drumsticks, substituting eight drumsticks for the feet, and skipping the initial boiling.

1. Wash chicken feet well, making sure that claws are clipped off and any small feathers plucked with tweezers. Strip the yellow outer epidermis off legs.

2. Fill a large pot with water and set it on high heat. When water boils, place chicken feet in the pot and cook for about 15 minutes, then drain.

3. Peel brown skin off ginger and slice thin in rounds. Peel garlic and crush lightly.

4. Put soy sauce, sherry, ginger, garlic, salt, pepper, sugar, star-anise or five-spice powder, sesame oil, and chicken feet in a large flat saucepan. Bring to a light simmer and leave simmering for about 30 minutes, by which time meat should be falling off the bones.

5. Cool, then chop into bite-sized pieces.

Serves 4 to 6.

# Convalescence

Leah Ryan

Here comes the grocery man with more humble pie; the only thing I've eaten for god knows how long. I was sick, and it was the only thing I could keep down. I had plenty, fresh from my grocer's freezer. Good thing he delivers.

I'm trying to vary my diet now. It isn't easy. The pie still tastes like Home. I've tried fiddleheads, monkfish, cactus leaves. I've had black bell peppers, Jerusalem artichokes, elephant garlic. I keep telling the grocer to hold the pie, but he keeps bringing it anyway. He leaves it at my door when I'm out. He sends me the bill. I've tried nuking it, baking it, braising it, broiling it. It still tastes the same, thick and mealy like sawdust. Sometimes with a warm metallic blood taste.

I go to the store, my empty basket swinging and my damp bills crushed in my hand. The grocer leans against a stack of pies; beige cardboard squares. I get the Japanese eggplants, the tart black olives, the extra vigin olive oil. He rings me up and I glance at his pink-stained apron, but mostly I keep my eyes on my own hands. I hobble out, and look both ways before crossing the street. The grocer's eyes drill into my back.

At home, the pies are waiting in the hall. Now I don't bring them inside. They pile up. The bills keep coming, but I won't pay. The hallway starts to stink. I hang signs on the boxes with scotch tape: "Take Back." "Wrong Address." "No More."

At night I carry the pies to the back fire escape, and I throw them out. They fly like Frisbees and smash on the pavement. I don't care if it's right or good. The grocer and his henchmen are pounding at my door, holding their noses. Around midnight the raccoons come. They bring their friends. No need to fight; there's plenty for everyone. Chattering, they drag the pies away in their deft claws. The raccoons like the taste of pie, and they know nothing of humility.

The grocer, suffering from the delusion that he's going to get paid, continues to deliver the pies. The smell is almost unbearable. I'm still convalescing but I'm feeling stronger every day. Last night at 11:50, the raccoons were snickering outside my window and rubbing their hands together. I went to the hallway and found, instead of the usual ten pies, nine pies. On top of the stack, there was a loaf of Italian bread, a sweet onion, and a chunk of provolone cheese wrapped in white butcher paper. I wrote out a check to the grocer for the amount of these last items, and left it taped to my door.

I carried the nine pies and my own dinner to the fire escape. I flung the pies out one by one and told the raccoons, "You know I think he's starting to get it." The raccoons are unaware of the possible consequences; if the grocer stops bringing pie to me, I stop flinging pie to them. Right now they're happy. They're satisfied, almost. Not grateful. The pie is theirs. They might be rabid. They don't beg. They don't even ask. I feel better today, much.

# Appetite Lost, Appetite Found

## Helen Barolini

**I**taly is as close to me as appetite. My first memory of the country is gastronomic. It's September, 1948. I'm coming into Italy on a train from Cannes, and, at a station stop in Ventimiglia, on the Italian side of the frontier with France, I push down the window in my third-class coach. From among the crowds of milling people and porters on the platform, I unerringly single out the food vendor from whom, with gestures only, I buy my first Italian food, a *panino*, crusty bread around paper-thin slices of smooth white-flecked *mortadella*, a venerable and fragrant sausage of Bologna debased in America as baloney. The good air, the animation of the people, the fact of being in Italy, and the taste of that fundamental food delivered me into the kind of transcendent exaltation I once experienced as a child at the solemn moment of First Communion.

Arrival in Italy was a communion; it was the sense of Italy as the base of my identity and bloodline; the place where all my grandparents, and everyone before them, had been born. My desire for Italy had surfaced on its own thrust, breaking through layers of denial and repression in which Italy and all things Italian were put out of sight and mind, tinged for me with indefinable feelings of shame and embarrassment. Not only was the family fervor centered on being "American," but the surrounding culture instilled in me an image of the demeaned Italian American woman. I felt that in order to be taken seriously as the writer I wanted to be, I had to be other than who I was.

The Anglo-American society of my youth looked at the women of my background and saw only silent, submissive beings stuck in kitchens stirring sauce. The conventional thinking foisted on Italian American women certainly made me feel that to be anyone I had to get out of that kitchen, not be my mother, not be a cook, feign disinterest—even scorn—in food and eating, look on appetite as something nongenteel.

My parents, children of immigrants, had of course been eager to be melted down in the common pot. Still there were exceptions; we ate mostly American, but each night my father brought home from the Columbus Bakery on Syracuse's Italian north side, a long loaf of crusty bread. His allegiance was still intact to the staff of life that in his estimate was insulted by the spongy sliced stuff we called disparagingly "American bread." Pasta, known only as "spaghetti," always the dish spaghetti, we had on Sunday. Christmas meant Grandma's filled cookies, and the strict observance of the fish courses of Christmas Eve.

It was at my grandmother's house in Utica that I had foods that seemed foreign: braciola, ravioli, Italian vegetables from her backyard garden like pole beans, escarole, broccoli, and zucchini that were not known then in American homes. And Grandma herself was foreign, dressed in black with her hair in an old-fashioned knob, and always in the kitchen at her big, black, wood-burning stove. The odors emanating from her kitchen were strikingly different from those in my mother's modern all-white kitchen which had the allure of a hospital. What we ate in the school cafeteria, what I was taught to prepare in my ninth-grade Home Economics class—Welsh rarebit, blancmange, tuna fish casserole—was what being American meant in those days before America discovered the world of food.

Once in a while my mother would have me accompany her on shopping trips to the Italian north side of the city. I was a reluctant tourist. I hated to enter the store where they sold imported cheese because of the smells—strong, pungent Italian aromas that intensified my determination not to be identified with them. I also hated the fish store on the north side because of the revoltingly un-American eels and squid that were on display there. I even hated Josie's pastry shop because Josie, who made all those un-American cookies, was fat and foreign-looking herself, with black circles under her eyes. She was not at all the image of the woman I wanted to be, the women I watched in the movies I saw each Saturday afternoon. American women were independent, snappy talkers with nicknames like Kitty or Patsy, and above all they didn't slave in the kitchen or eat much themselves.

A Latin course at the then Waspy Wells College awakened an unconscious longing for *l'Italia*, and I was ready for the food the moment I leaned out the train window at Ventimiglia and had my first taste of the *panino*. My gastronomic celebration of Italy started there and went on: at Clitunno I had trout just netted from the clear waters, broiled with garlic and sage, and served with liters of Umbrian wine under a leafy arbor; fresh figs with country prosciutto on a Tuscan hillside at the stone house where Leonardo da Vinci was born; the taste of free-ranging, not battery, chicken roasted on the open hearth of a farm in the Appennines; the delectable, woodsy taste of those large, fleshy mushrooms, *funghi porcini*, which appear each fall and can be grilled like steaks; the exquisite aroma of white truffle being thinly grated over fresh, homemade tagliatelli; my first experience, in Taormina at Easter, of true *cassata alla siciliana*, a dessert made with ice cream; the sight, smell, and sound of every marketplace in each Italian town—sensational in the basic meaning of enveloping the senses.

That my memories and ties to Italy are gastronomic seems forecast from the start. The word "recipe" itself is Latin—the imperative form of the verb meaning "procure," commanding the ingredients to be gotten together for whatever dish. In my case, destiny saw to it that I arrived in Italy not knowing anyone

and armed only with the name and address of one Antonio Barolini, a poet and journalist living in Milan. I was in Europe as an
exchange student at the University of London, and having gotten that far, I knew I had to reach Italy. I was writing features for
the Syracuse *Herald-Journal* and was glad when a fellow student
in London provided the name of that journalist contact in Italy.

And so I met signor Barolini. He did not speak English, nor
I Italian. When we first met, we spoke a lingua franca combined
of French, Spanish, and Latin until he found that the true common language between us was food. Antonio courted me with
the efficient stratagem of dining well and often.

That first year of mine in Italy, when Antonio knew I would
be alone in Rome for the holidays, he invited me to spend Christmas at his mother's place in Vicenza where he would join me
from his post in Milan. In 1948 trains were still few. I was lucky
to get a foothold, literally, on one for the trip north; it was so
packed I stood all the way, jammed in the corridor among other
holiday travelers for the long trip. In 1984, I again made a journey to Vicenza, this time comfortably seated in the crack *rapido*
to visit the memorial dedicated by his city to now deceased Antonio. On a June day, I stood in the sunshine in Via Santa Lucia
reading the plaque affixed to the wall of an old palazzo. There the
city fathers recorded that in that building Antonio Barolini had
written his first volumes of poetry and the novel *Giornate di Ste-
fano*, which was the first work of his that I was to read in my
newly acquired Italian.

I recalled the shivery time of Christmas 1948 in the top floor
apartment of the converted palazzo where we sat in the kitchen
around the stove to conserve heat. There signora Lucia, Antonio's mother, had prepared her famous *strudel di gris*, a preparation of spinach and ricotta encased in pastry that looked like a
jelly roll and was served as a first course at Christmas dinner. It
was also in that kitchen that serious deliberations had occurred

concerning where to get the traditional panettone and how large it should be. The purchase was made at the aristocratic Caffè Meneghini on Vicenza's main square, the Piazza dei Signori, a restaurant whose tiny quarters were meant to accommodate only the precious few, while across the way, the hugely democratic Caffè bar della Repubblica had room for all others. I still remember that first Italian Christmas dinner with its (to me) exotic accompaniments of *mostarda*, *cotognata*, *mandorlato*.

The rituals in Italy reminded me of the few remaining rites in my Italian American family at home. I began to sense their beauty and importance and to wish I had paid more attention to them and their celebration through special foods. In Italy I learned not only the ancestral language, but also the traditions of food.

I was enrolled at the University for Foreign Students in Perugia, a hill-town where I found lodgings in the dank medieval building on Via Ulisse Rocchi where Count Lorenzo Beni Fabiani and his florid, ribald wife (who had been elevated from lower class to penniless countess) took in paying guests because they, as everyone in the period following the war, were in straitened circumstances. Again for warmth, in those austere days, we all huddled in the log-filled kitchen under festoons of grapes drying on clotheslines strung criss-cross through a room redolent with the aromas of the count's fabulous cooking. There I learned about *minestrina* and *minestrone*! And wines! I savored the infinite variety of pastas and sauces which made the routine Sunday-spaghetti dinners of Syracuse fade into nothing. For the first time, I began to learn of Italian cheeses—not the strong romano of my childhood, but the fabulous Asiago, fontina, Gorgonzola, cacciotto, and delicate mascarpone. Count Fabiani showed me how perfect an accompaniment a piece of parmesan was for a ripe pear, intoning, *"Al contadino non far sapere / Quanto é buono il formaggio con le pere."* This advice to keep from the peasant (or anyone else) the knowledge of how good cheese and pears are when eaten together, so that, presumably, there will be more for those in the know, was downed with the good wines of the region. And so my education progressed.

In time I learned Italian and then I married Antonio Barolini. Antonio taught me many things, from the poetry and polenta of his Veneto region to the recipe for Horace's classical torte; living in Italy and eating well taught me the rest. My Italian marriage even had a good effect on my mother's cooking. For, won over by Antonio's charm from the moment he first kissed her hand and called her *Mamma*, she resurrected memories of her own mother's southern Italian heritage: hand-made manicotti, stuffed pasta shells, calamari in red sauce, delicious fritters of minced celery leaves, and the wonderful summer vegetable stew known as *giardiniera*.

The first Christmas after my return from Italy, we were photographed for the Syracuse *Herald-Journal* making Italian Christmas sweets—*cannoli*, *cuscinetti*, *amaretti*, *biscotti all'anice*, the whole repertoire! Starting in her kitchen, my mother found her way back to a heritage which, at first, in the throes of Americanizing, she had denied . . . and this, I suspect, happened for many Italian American families who were rescued from lives of denial by the ethnic explosion of the 1970s. As she began remembering the foods, she added stories of her mother, the immigrant from Italy, who hadn't been a simple kitchen slave but the canny entrepreneur who started the family business and made it thrive before finally turning it over to her sons.

I had never, as a child, been able to speak to that strange woman who had been my grandmother; then, when I had her language she was long dead. But I began to see her in a new light—not a silent nobody, but the veritable pillar of the family well-being. She was the prototype of all those strong late-nineteenth-century immigrants who had not only endured the uprooting and transplanting trauma but had used their native intelligence to survive in a radically different environment. I began to see the real strengths of that woman in the kitchen.

*Umbertina*, my first novel, was the fictionalized evocation of my grandmother and an enterprise that had started in her kitchen when she made lunches for millworkers, had developed into a grocery store, and eventually into a successful wholesale food business well known in upstate New York. Later I learned of other stories of Italian American women as I collected their writings for *The Dream Book: An Anthology of Writings by Italian American Women*, the first of its kind. The collection won an American Book Award and then another award as the best anthology for the feminist study of American culture. I had my "credentials." I was an Italian American author, a feminist, and, I could now admit, a cook, as well.

Perhaps more importantly, however, I was introduced to the lives of other Italian American women. Aside from what they did outside the home, I found they were also women who in their kitchens made something of plain food—no matter how simple the ingredients, they elevated them into memorable eating and gave people appetite. I remember my grandmother, long after her corner grocery had grown into a business housed in a huge downtown building, still planting her backyard garden both for frugality and for the pleasure of fresh produce on her table.

I had learned that my grandmother was more than her cooking, and that I was, too, but that we need not excise our pleasure in cooking to prove ourselves. I was no longer willing to be subverted by the imposed stereotype of the Italian American woman as benighted drudge and simple stirrer of sauce.

Growing up I had deliberately stayed as far from my mother's kitchen as I could—I was determined not to be the stock figure Italian American woman. It took years and the women's movement for me to realize that I need not accept the skewed and prejudicial view of myself that came from a biased culture. I could be myself and who that self was had worth from its own tradition even though it was not the dominant one in American culture.

I have since written an autobiographical cookbook: *Festa: Recipes and Reminiscences of Italian Holidays* (1988) from which I've drawn the following two recipes. In putting it together I wanted to defuse the image of the Italian American woman with which I had grown up. I wanted to turn the so-called woman's room (the kitchen) from a holding pen into what it really is—an embassy of cultural tradition. The kitchen is not only the center of food-making—it is the place from which emanate ritual and tradition and family history. From food—both in the making and in the partaking—not only body, but also mind and soul are nourished.

Yes, I believe in good food, and in festivity. I have found my way back as an Italian American, as an Italian American woman who writes *and* cooks.

░ ░ ░

## Horace's Torte

1 cup almonds, blanched and ground fine,
    plus ½ cup whole almonds for decoration
1½ cups unbleached all-purpose flour
1½ cups fine cornmeal
¾ cup sugar
grated rind of 1 lemon
pinch salt
1 egg plus 1 egg yolk, beaten together
2 sticks (16 tablespoons) unsalted butter

1. Put ground almonds, flour, cornmeal, sugar, lemon rind, and salt in a large bowl. Mix well.

2. Add beaten egg mixture; stir vigorously.

3. Cut butter into small pieces. Using a pastry blender or two knives, cut pieces into dry ingredients until mixture resembles coarse crumbs. Work dough as little as possible.

4. Knead dough lightly on a floured work surface, until it just holds together.

5. Wrap dough in a dish towel and chill it in the refrigerator for 20 minutes.

6. Preheat oven to 400° F. Grease and flour a 12-inch round cake pan.

7. Unwrap dough, place it in the prepared pan, and spread it evenly in the pan with your fingertips. Avoid overworking dough, which will be crumbly.

8. Arrange whole almonds on dough in a daisy petal design, or one of your choice.

9. Bake torte until golden, about 40 minutes. If edge of the torte begins to burn, cover edge with aluminum foil.

10. Let torte cool in pan before transferring it to a serving dish. When cool, cut in wedges. Serves 6 to 8.

Note that torte remains flat and will have a grainy texture somewhat like shortbread.

❚❚ ❚❚ ❚❚

## Vegetables Giardiniera

3 tablespoons unsalted butter
3 tablespoons olive oil
2 cups chopped onions
½ cup chopped celery
2 zucchini cut in cubes
1 yellow summer squash cut in cubes
2 green peppers with seeds and membranes
        removed, sliced lengthwise

4 ripe plum tomatoes
4 large fresh basil leaves, torn in pieces
1 sprig fresh marjoram

1. Put butter and oil in a large saucepan over moderate heat and when sizzling, add onions and celery. Cook, stirring occasionally, until they are translucent but not brown.

2. Add zucchini, summer squash, and peppers.

3. Immerse tomatoes in a bowl of boiling water for a minute. Remove from water and remove skins. Quarter tomatoes and add to vegetables in pan.

4. Add basil and marjoram; cover and lower heat. Simmer for about 20 minutes, until vegetables are tender.

Serve with chunks of Italian bread. Serves 6.

**◧ ◧ ◧**

# A Kitchen of One's Own

## Doris Friedensohn

**M**y favorite egg foo yung is the one I ate religiously—in an ammonia-scented Cantonese dive on upper Broadway—every Yom Kippur during my high school years. At Yum Luk, three crunchy "omelettes," neatly stacked and bulging with bean sprouts, onions, and diced roast pork, rose high above a sea of gluey brown sauce. Sweet and salt, crisp and moist, garlic and pungent: the tastes fused in my nose before the first bite reached my mouth. When we initiated the ritual, almost forty years ago, my friend Ruth and I devoured the exotic concoction in a record three and a half minutes. I can still see us, giggling and fussing with our chopsticks, shoveling it in.

The moment and the meal were heavy with meaning. After a morning in the synagogue, dutifully mouthing prayers, we had opted to violate the cardinal rule of the Jewish Day of Atonement: THOU SHALT NOT EAT. It was not mere hunger that impelled us. To appease a growling stomach, a hot fudge sundae or a chocolate malted would have served quite nicely. No. The occasion offered grander possibilities. While the rest of the Jewish community was suffering through the obligatory fast, we would feast on Forbidden Foods.

Of course, we were desperately afraid of being caught. Supposing a friend of our parents'—out for a breath of air between prayers—chanced to pass Yum Luk just as we were emerging from the restaurant? Supposing my chopsticks slipped and some of that sticky sauce stained the pale yellow orlon sweater I was wearing? There would be hell to pay. Not from the all-knowing god of our ancestors, whose being and behavior were matters of indifference to us. But from our parents who would not fail to appreciate the enormity of their daughters' rebellion. God might avert his eyes or remain silent, but we would hear from Them and feel the fullness of Their wrath.

No risk, no gain, the saying goes. In a moment and environment in which so many risks were unthinkable or much too dangerous, food was my frontier of choice. Yom Kippurs at Yum Luk were delicious acts of defiance: the beginning of a long history of infidelities to the culinary tradition in which I was raised.

For the first twenty years of my life, under my parents' roof, I gave little thought to cooking for myself or the family. The ingredients in our refrigerator and pantry were those which my mother selected: fresh, wholesome, and brand-name products from modern, New York Jewish dairies and groceries, bakeries and butcher shops. A healthy culinary canon, but in my mother's hands, narrow and predictable. When I shopped for her, which I often did, I adhered to the list she provided. My occasional deviations—tangy Miracle Whip rather than the canonical Hellman's mayonnaise or a Betty Crocker Angel Food Cake mix in place of our local bakery's famous danish pastry—were greeted with frowns and returned the next day.

The scratch was minor: of course I cared about what I ate at home, but not in the same way that I cared about academic achievement, politics, and athletics. So why wage war with my mother in her kitchen? Besides, in the hierarchy of issues between us, I had more important targets and more urgent conflicts to negotiate.

The first kitchen I could call my own was the one I shared with fifteen other female graduate students on the second floor of Yale University's Helen Hadley Hall. The building was new in 1958, the year I entered graduate school, a characterless, minimal modern box. No matter. The kitchen, with its sparkling, virginal allure, beckoned to me. It was a long, well-lit room with four picture windows and a number of round, blond wood tables catching the afternoon sun. In darker, U-shaped spaces at the "north" and "south" ends were units with a built-in stove, double sink, large fridge, formica counters, and pale wood cabinets above and beneath them. As soon as I unpacked my clothes and books, I rushed out to stock my allotted spaces in "south": a half-shelf in the refrigerator and a half-shelf in the pantry.

For two years, abusing two frying pans and a casserole, I built meals around eggplant and entertained friends with coq au vin and arroz con pollo. I produced omelettes with everything in them, rice dishes with everything in them, and salads with everything in them. But what was everything? And how far had I actually traveled from family traditions on the Upper West Side of Manhattan?

Liberation from family traditions began with the one-dish dinner. At last, I could dispense with the omnipresent tomato juice and grapefruit for openers, the trinity of meat, potatoes, and vegetables, and the trailers of salad (iceberg lettuce and tomatoes with Russian dressing), fruit and danish pastry or pie. Enter frugality. And farewell to the whole marching band of propriety and health!

Casseroles and other one-dish concoctions ran counter to my mother's deepest convictions about good, clean cooking. Beware of dirt you cannot see. When the final product disguises the parts, you eat at risk. The poor depend upon blending to stretch the precious meat or fish; they season elaborately with garlic and spices to cover the inferior quality of ingredients. Blended foods are corrupted by forbidden ingredients which are by definition less well endowed with vitamins and minerals and protein than their sanctified counterparts; they are not simply bad for the body but repulsive, disgusting.

Bad is beautiful, especially when we are young. And the

point of leaving home is to be bad in peace: to pursue proscribed agendas with equanimity and put family traditions—and su- perstitions—quietly behind us. In New Haven, after years of eating forbidden foods at the tables of others—especially in dingy, plate-clanking Chinese joints and in "romantic" Green- wich Village pizzerias with red checkered tablecloths and can- dles in Chianti bottles—I plunged into outlaw cookery.

Shrimp fried rice (years before anyone thought to can it or to serve it up like cheeseburgers in shopping malls) was my first, modest venture. I remember hesitating halfway down the row of canned fish in the supermarket and studying the medium shrimp. Fresh shrimp are too expensive, I rationalized, too hard to find in this strange town, too time consuming and difficult to shell and devein. But I wasn't fooling anybody, lease of all my- self. In buying canned shrimp, I had opted to let someone else do the gritty finger work and inhale the raw sexual perfume; I had opted for a safe, sanitized product which might just as well have been tuna. With time, I vowed, I would do the honest thing.

Cooking meant taking charge of a piece of my life which I had left, until graduate school, largely in my mother's care. It meant claiming control over matters touching on health, sensu- ous pleasure, social relations and—of course—identity. Once the culinary "shoulds" and "should nots" began falling away, a vast playing field appeared before me—in which I could be ath- lete, artist, umpire, and audience: the game of cooking was about imitation, invention, and improvisation; it was about glo- rifying the ordinary and domesticating the exotic.

To cook well I needed to become a more educated eater—not a simple matter during those years at Yale. New Haven in the late fifties and early sixties was a provincial place, sharply divided between Ivy and Other. Those of us who lived near the Univer- sity knew little of the town, and we were busy enough and snobbish enough not to be curious. Without cars, my friends and I did our shopping en route from the library and bookstore—at a market of such unalloyed WASPness that even Italian sausages were *hors de combat*.

In the Other New Haven, however, Italian products were readily available. Vast sections of the town, beginning a mile or so from the University, were Italian; and New Haven's pizzerias—large, boisterous places, with oversized booths for six and eight—were among the city's most renowned institutions. The trip to Wooster Street for Pepe's or Sal's thin crusted, aromatic cheese and sausage pizzas was a gustatory event: no shortcuts, no tricks, just the mouth-scorching mozzarella and the olive oil dripping down our chins, the delicate tomato sauce and the pile of filthy napkins on worn formica tables. These pizzas were the stuff of legends then; today they are enshrined on the food pages of the *New York Times*.

Competition with Wooster Street came, not from my still immature skillet and saucepan, but from the soirees hosted by my friends Mary Ellen and Burhan. In Mary Ellen's tiny apartment opposite Helen Hadley Hall, her Louisiana hospitality set the stage for his Middle Eastern kitchen savvy. Both were lawyers, in their mid-thirties, pursuing graduate law degrees and reshaping their careers. Mary Ellen was the intellectual and the charmer: a tall, strikingly handsome, and utterly undomestic woman. When they entertained together, Burhan was the cook. Long before any of us could possibly imagine pita as a household word, Burhan fed us the eggplant dip *babaganoush*, falafel, and hummus. A short man with a round face and thinning hair, he would wait for us to gather around—in our roles of audience, support staff, and clack—as he stirred extra virgin olive oil into ground chickpeas and tahini, added just the right dash of lemon and fresh garlic, and swirled the mixture with Syrian bread brought directly from Atlantic Avenue in Brooklyn. He would amuse us, in his heavy Jordanian accent, with tales of high living and petty politics as a junior diplomat at the U.N.—while supervising the transfer of marinated lamb, onions, and peppers from bowl to skewers to oven. Yes, Burhan was a bright spot on our culinary scene—at least when he wasn't moping about his difficulties with English or flirting outrageously with Mary Ellen's female guests. In provincial New Haven, what is a New Yorker to do but be grateful for the generosity of friends.

In addition: a New Yorker can do herself a favor by choosing the right non–New Yorkers for housemates and cooking partners. After two years of nervously guarding our private stocks of coffee, eggs, butter, and beer, three of us moved across the street from Helen Hadley Hall to a fourth floor walk-up with an old-fashioned yellow kitchen and plenty of storage. There, Ruth Ann from upstate New York and Isabel from southern California—both Protestant and distinctly nonethnic—introduced me to "real" American food: breakfast sausages and baked pork chops, Indian pudding and buttermilk biscuits, fresh corn (count on three ears apiece) and artichokes a la greque; and they nurtured my hankering for real American booze: bourbon on the rocks, bourbon old-fashioneds, manhattans, mint juleps, and Almaden by the jug.

In the realm of food Isabel, Ruth Ann, and I were at our most relaxed and playful; when we cooked—with amateurish abandon—we were more venturesome than in our scholarship and more self-preserving than in our sexual and amorous lives. In our eclectic, improvisatory style, we developed a predictable pattern: French food for birthdays, chili for crowds, paella for small parties and pasta when the budget was blown. We all leaned on James Beard for basics, Julia Child for sophistication, and *Marion Tracy's Casserole Cookery Complete* for one-dish curried lamb chops, chicken stewed in sherry, and shrimp more or less New-berg. It was a rich and generous diet for graduate students without family money.

Actually, the late fifties and early sixties at Yale were good years for graduate study, even for women. Generous government grants and Yale University fellowships covered our tuition and expenses, and the future seemed promising. Each of us had been admitted to a relatively small graduate program with the expectation that we would complete our Ph.D.s and find good jobs. Unless, of course, we married and dropped out to support or follow our spouses (or heaven forbid, became pregnant) before the process was finished. So we put in long hours and ploughed away under only our own personal clouds.

Like our course work and qualifying exams, skills at the stove helped form our professional self-images. Nourishment apart, our forays into continental cuisine seemed a necessary foundation for three not yet worldly American women who would be Yale Ph.D.s in European History (Isabel), Russian Literature (Ruth Ann), and American Studies (me). In 1960, we certainly envisioned cooking for husbands, lovers, and friends—for other, more worldly academics, male and female, who would take our culinary accomplishments as a measure of our sophistication. The meals we planned and the dishes we perfected were preparation for the social side of world-class, fast-track academic life—as we imagined it from our peripheral, graduate student outpost.

Of course, we never uttered such notions to one another in any but the wryest of terms; we were too self-consciously intellectual and too self-aware to fantasize even for a moment about enhancing our social mobility or viability through food. But what woman doesn't think such thoughts? And what aspiring female academic—especially at a chauvinist Ivy League University where we were few in number, sexually visible in our short skirts and high heels, and second class—did not wonder about whether she would make it alone or coupled and what tradeoffs might await her in the role of faculty wife?

In the kitchen, we tested ourselves in utter safety. Failure was possible and friendship was not at stake: the few fights we had were not about food. We could give vent to ambition and "waste" a Friday afternoon and all day Saturday preparing a twelve-hour cassoulet; and we could just as easily drift into down-home, no-fuss franks, beans, and packaged biscuits. Food work was communal, creative, and comforting. Cooking and eating together, we supported one another on the strenuous road ahead.

# Getting Hungry

## Leah Ryan

Recently I spent some time with an old friend, a friend of fifteen years. That's about as long as my friendships last. For one thing, I'm only thirty. For another, I have spent a number of years in a prickly, antisocial state that defies name or description. To say that the awkwardness of adolescence began before my fifth birthday and did not loosen its grip until I was twenty-seven would be one way of explaining it. In any case, I'm amazed that I have fifteen-year-old friendships, few as they may be.

I'm slightly less amazed that during a rare visit with one of these precious few old friends, I find myself in a discussion of leeks.

Understand that in the earlier incarnation of our relationship, we were not eaters. Rather, we were drinkers, smokers. Party was a verb. We partied, I suppose, though it was rarely festive. We spent a lot of time outside, avoiding home, school, whatever. In winter, my friends and I nursed cups of coffee in diners. I nibbled countless orders of pallid french fries, which could be rendered palatable only with a generous dousing of hot sauce. Not exactly what I would (now) call eating.

I recall just one meal that this friend and I cooked together, in the home of a vacationing parent. Homemade linguine, red sauce with mushrooms. Add one quart wine to cook. No boys, formal attire. I believe there were eight of us at table, gotten up in crushed velvet tuxedo jackets, top hats, terrible thrift store dresses. I don't remember much else about the evening. I remember feeding the pasta endlessly through the hand-cranked machine, and stirring the sauce. We all got plastered.

After going our separate ways while we were still in our teens (I left town—she came out and found a new crowd) we both turned out to be professional cooks. Thus, we find ourselves in a discussion of leeks a decade and a half later.

When I was growing up, food was the closest thing our household had to a religion. Unearthly devotion, personal sacrifice, occasional ecstatic experiences, you name it. Also, strict codes of conduct in regard to what was fit for consumption and what was not. My mother's mother had a specific list. My mother has her own list. I, coming of age, find tenets of my own beginning to form. I hear myself saying things like, "Raisins in salad can never be a good thing," with such finality that it leaves me a little stunned.

As a child I was immensely fond of sardines and pickled herring. I was quick to volunteer that artichokes and mushrooms were my favorite vegetables, and that I didn't like peanut butter. I never got used to the shocked responses to this last statement; after a while I started telling people that I was allergic to peanut butter. I was intrigued by Wonder Bread, however; I had a friend in elementary school who brought four Bologna-with-Miracle-Whip-on-Wonder Bread sandwiches for lunch every day. It was way too much for her (I have no idea why her parents packed her such a lunch) and she would always give me one. This was exotic. I also recall being shocked to visit a school friend's kitchen and find that there were Hostess Cup Cakes in the cupboard. In my understanding, not only were such things contraband, but they were not classed with other things edible. The idea that they could share a shelf with tuna fish or rice seemed terribly dangerous to me.

I'm half Armenian, but I didn't grow up in an Armenian community (or in any particular ethnic community at all). I knew that there was something different about dinner at our house. It was too much, too wonderful, too big a deal. It was too good. We talked about it too much, and too loud. We marked occasions with memories of what was cooked and what we ate, while others recalled blizzards and the heat waves and the religious holidays. This was only one of many reasons why I felt different from other kids. What made it worse, however, is that I was even an outcast at home, at my own family's table. I didn't have much of an appetite.

As an adult, I have learned some simple truths about my stomach. If ever I am angry or afraid, I will lose my appetite completely. Today, I can sort this out with some ease. But for much of my life, I was so full of rage and anxiety that I knew only this: I wasn't happy and I wasn't hungry. And I was very thin.

I got older, I learned to cook (when my parents divorced and my mother returned to school, my brother and I began officially to share in the cooking and cleaning), but as I approached puberty I ate less and less. I got a job working in a restaurant kitchen at sixteen. During this time I ate so little that I sometimes passed out in the middle of the day. I drank like a fish, though, and (with the help of my friends) tried to convince myself that there was real nutrition available in cheap American beer.

It took only a few years to learn the many sad ironies of being female in the restaurant business; that while I came from a long line of female kitchen geniuses, if I stayed in the business I would likely always work for men who would fail to promote me, and from whom I would have to beg for tiny raises. In my grandmother's house, men didn't go into the kitchen. Their food was brought to them and their soiled plates removed by women. I have rarely seen any of my male relatives standing at the stove or washing a dish. As a little girl, I was expected to help in my grandmother's kitchen while my brother was not. I didn't really resent this because I wanted to be there anyway, but it drove my mother insane. Little did I know that I would grow up to work in a kitchen and be treated like an amateur by men who had quite possibly never washed a dish until they were twenty.

When I was twenty-two, I began a process of elimination. It is perfectly logical in retrospect, but it was utterly bewildering at the time. Mentally, physically, and emotionally sick from years of alcohol and drug abuse and the degrading, dangerous lifestyle that goes with it, I was clearly at an impasse. Something had to change, or I was going to die. First, and rightly so, I gave up alcohol and drugs. I didn't know that I would spend the rest of my twenties giving things up in order to live, but that is exactly what I did. Shortly after drugs and alcohol, I gave up all contact with my natural father. It took a little while longer to give up abusive men in general, but within a few years, they went too.

At twenty-three, I got my GED and went to community college. I hadn't given up coffee, cigarettes, or chaos. And I still didn't eat. I smoked two packs of Camels a day. I got accepted to a four-year college. I began to have some successes as a playwright.

I went to Chicago in 1993 to see a production of one of my plays, and nearly passed out on the street several times. The director of the play, with whom I was staying, is also a professional cook and never eats anything either (he grew up in a catering business; I did not know this about him until we had been friends for some time). After my fainting episodes, we resolved to do things differently, and went to the grocery store at three in the morning, on day three of my four-day stay in Chicago. Being people who don't eat, we might have gotten something drab and simple for sustenance. But no. It was July, there were some nice tomatoes. We got some kind of imported cheese and some Italian bread and some tomatoes and avocados and some nice pickles and olives and some Bermuda onion. He says he never eats anything because he can't decide what to have, which may be partially true. As I recall, we circled the store several times before we even narrowed it down.

After mean men, cigarettes were the next thing I gave up. When you imagine this, you must see that I was a chain-smoker, a heavy smoker, a smoker who loved to smoke. I look like a smoker. Strangers still approach me on the street and ask for a smoke, or a light. When I took English 101 in community college and had to write an essay about a "coming of age" experience, I wrote about the day I bought my first pack of cigarettes, a very happy memory. My nicotine withdrawal was typically awful, fraught with rage and despair and extreme irritability. But there was something else. I was hungry.

I couldn't remember ever feeling so ravenous. I'd been hungry before, but in a different way. I'd stood in parking lots of convenience stores and wolfed down horrible sandwiches at five in the morning, having had nothing for days. This wasn't like that. Further, when I felt hungry, I could actually eat. Sometimes I could eat quite a bit. I had always cooked for economy. Because I lived on about $10,000 a year, cooking was necessary. Fortunately, I knew how. Eating out was rarely an option, and quick foods prohibitively expensive. But now, I began to cook with relish.

By this time, I was involved with a very nice man named Dan, who was a food person waiting to happen. We didn't plan this, but right after I quit smoking, he quit smoking. Right after that, we moved in together. Predictably, we fought a lot. But also, we ate. We grazed. We took everything out of the refrigerator and piled it onto my small kitchen table. It was my mother's table; chances are I ate my first sardines and artichokes at that table. I cooked things I didn't know I could make, things I didn't know I liked. The apartment's refrigerator, which seemed perfectly roomy at first, eventually proved to be inadequate. We cursed at it daily.

I graduated from college and put on about ten pounds, which to me seemed an enormous amount. Over and over I tried my jeans on, refusing to believe that they didn't fit. I had been the same size since adolescence. No one noticed that I had put on weight specifically. Rather, they noticed that there was something "different" about me. I began to panic about weight gain. I didn't know how much I was supposed to eat, what, how often. Now, I thrill at the novelty of getting hungry three or four times a day.

The novelty still hadn't worn off when I was discussing leeks with my friend of fifteen years. The discussion went something like this: she said she didn't like them and I was surprised. How can you not like them, I said. I just made some potato and leek soup a few weeks ago, I told her, that was great. Dan volunteered his agreement. My friend confessed that she understood what we were saying in theory, but couldn't grasp it completely because she didn't really like soup that much. At this a small silence fell. We moved on to talk about something else.

Later that night Dan and I sat in a low-budget Italian restaurant. I had a feeling that the food would be dull, but all the same, I was excited about ordering (manicotti) and about eatng. My thoughts drifted back to the leeks. There were so many things about this friend of fifteen years that I had never known. Not like soup? It seemed impossible. I recalled the leek soup, how good it was, how we'd both eaten so much of it. How I'd scraped my bowl and decided to have more. Maybe that soup would make a believer out of her, I considered. But maybe not. In any case, she'd just started a catering business, and I fantasized that I would go there and make soup for her customers. That I'd sit in her kitchen and eat.

When my manicotti arrived, it was nothing special, but I ate it and enjoyed it and we had a great meal together. Dan and I are becoming old friends now. I still live on about $10,000 a year. Neither of us really has any money, but we eat very well at our house. I haven't given up coffee. We get beans in bulk from a local roaster.

Two apartments later, the fridge seems big enough. I don't know if it's much bigger than the old one, the one I cursed at. It seemed too small, but maybe my food and my hunger were too big for any refrigerator, and table, any kitchen in the world. I was making up for all those lost, lean years when my back was up against the wall and I watched the food wither on my plate. I've leveled off now. I'm hungry. I eat. The novelty hasn't worn off yet.

▯▮ ▯▮ ▯▮

## Spicy Greens with Hot Vinegar

Note: The vinegar for this recipe must be prepared at least a week ahead.

Greens:

> 1 pound fresh spinach, chard, broccoli rabe,
>> or other tender green (kale and heartier
>> greens can be used if they are steamed first)
> 1 clove garlic, peeled and sliced
> 1 fresh or dried chili pepper, chopped or crushed
> 1 tablespoon olive oil

1. Sauté garlic and pepper in oil in a large frying pan. Cook gently; do not brown the garlic.

2. Add greens. Stir until greens are thoroughly wilted, adding a little water to the pan if necessary. Serve hot with Hot Vinegar. Serves 2.

Hot Vinegar:

> 1 pint-sized glass bottle with cork top
> 1 clove garlic, peeled
> 1 fresh or dried chili pepper
> white vinegar

Place pepper and garlic in bottle, cover with vinegar. Cork and let stand for at least 1 week.

▯ ▯ ▯

## Pasta Salad

> 1 pound pasta shells, elbows, bowties,
>    corkscrews, etc.
> 2 carrots, cut into matchsticks
> 1 bunch scallions, chopped
> 1 bunch Italian parsley, chopped
> 1 green pepper, diced
> 2 sticks celery, diced
> 1 fresh tomato (in season), chopped and drained
> 2 tablespoons mayonnaise
> 1/4 cup vinegar (an herb-flavored vinegar is ideal)
> 2 tablespoons olive oil
> salt and freshly ground pepper to taste
> 1 teaspoon dried or fresh tarragon
> 1 teaspoon dried or fresh dill

1. Cook pasta according to package directions, careful not to over-cook. Chill with cold water.

2. Beat mayonnaise while slowly adding oil and vinegar. To this dressing, add seasonings and vegetables.

3. Mix into cold pasta. Correct seasonings. Best if chilled for a few hours or overnight. Serves 4.

❏❏ ❏❏ ❏❏

## Garlic and Olive Spaghetti

I pound spaghetti
6 cloves garlic, peeled and sliced once lengthwise
½ cup Calamata olives, pitted (squeeze the olive
    until it bursts)
2 tablespoons olive oil
crushed red pepper to taste
grated Parmesan cheese

1. Cook spaghetti according to package directions.

2. Heat olive oil in a small, heavy saucepan. Add garlic when oil is hot. Simmer the garlic very carefully; do not brown. It will take a little while to cook the garlic this way, but resist the temptation to turn up the heat. The garlic will not taste right if it is cooked too quickly.

3. When garlic is tender, add olives and pepper. Heat thoroughly.

4. Serve over spaghetti with Parmesan cheese. Add salt if desired. Serves 3 to 4.

❏❏ ❏❏ ❏❏

# The Power of the Pepper:
# From Slave Food to Spirit Food

## Jennifer Iré

**W**hen I was growing up in Trinidad, West Indies, I never questioned why, in a land surrounded by water and abounding with fish, we ate saltfish. Saltfish was a staple, cooked in so many different ways. We ate it in *buljol*, a Trinidad and To-bago heritage dish made from a mixture of shredded, de-salted codfish, oil, onions, tomatoes, and green pepper, which was deli-cious especially when it was accompanied by roasted coconut bake. We ate it in stew. We ate it in *accra*, a variation of West Af-rican fritters, accompanied by floats. I never questioned why "salt meat" which is pig parts, mostly tails and feet, flavored al-most everything—soups, stews, peas, beans. Why we used con-densed milk. I just knew those were some of the foods I ate and loved. Our women made magic with them.

It was only when I began to teach myself about the history of slavery in the West Indies that I found out some of the favorite foods of my people came from the creation of the "slave diet" by Europeans and are therefore an artifice of slavery. The people who needed and deserved nourishment, the people who per-formed the backbreaking labor on the slave plantations, were de-nied the wholesome foods Europeans ate and were forced to sub-sist on the tail, feet, and ribs of animals, the parts Europeans didn't want. My ancestors were fed denatured food, salted meat and fish and condensed sweetened milk, and we came to treasure these foods as our heritage.

On first learning this history of the foods I loved I was angry and for months I could not look at, far less eat those foods. I was sickened to my stomach at the thought that even the food I loved was shaped by Europeans and by slavery. I thought of the women having to cook for these colonials and then for their own families knowing the vast difference in the fare they were forced to serve each group and I cried for them. I cried for myself and the generations who lived before me.

I had a dilemma. I could not stomach the food and yet I craved the food. After all, I was raised on the stuff; it is part of my heritage, part of who I am, part of my ancestry. What to do? I read more of the history and thought more of what it took for those women to bear, birth, and raise children who survived to produce the generations that allowed me to come forth. Through deeply imbibing the stories of the lives of slave women I began to see the wisdom, skill, knowledge, and love that took the leavings of the Europeans and the denatured foods mandated for them and created the foods that are so good and so nutritious. I imagined the women knowing that the green leaves of root crops were spirit food, that would nourish the body. I imagined the collaboration among women, slave and native who survived, to use the roots that looked and tasted like the foods of Africa, the foods used to produce meals that kept them alive, like the hot pepper. I came to understand that they had to have a relationship with all the ingredients in order to take the little that was given and produce nourishment for abused bodies.

I thought about my food in this new way, rejoicing and feeling profound respect and gratitude for the women's ability to ensure survival. Food was a part of slavery and I was raised on slave food. I had to accept that fact. I had to be able to acknowledge my African ancestors and their relationship with plants. I imagined them making a relationship with the hot, hot pepper which I have always loved. In Trinidad, like in the other islands, we have hot peppers. In cooking with our pepper, the proper, respectful and loving handling of the pepper gives food flavor that is exquisite. But you must be mindful in your relationship with this pepper to be rewarded with its sweetness. In Trinidad our women are sometimes described as being "hot like a pepper." A proper respectful and loving relationship with us provides life a flavor that is exquisite. On the other hand, improper, disrespectful, or loveless relating produces the sharp hot edge, just as with the pepper. I formed a relationship with the pepper and she infused flavor and spared the sting. Hot pepper helped me to recover my relationship to slave food. I began to use more hot pepper, making pepper sauce to baptize the food before eating it, to infuse the food with the love that flows from the generation who began in the West as slave women. As I drink the pepper, I honor the women, the strong women who endured, who created, whose knowledge has kept us alive.

◻️ ◻️ ◻️

## Jennifer's Trinidadian Curry Chicken

> 2 whole chicken breasts, with or without bones
> 2 large limes
> 1 bunch scallions
> 1 head garlic
> 2 medium onions
> 2 to 3 sprigs thyme
> 3 to 4 stalks cilantro
> salt
> ¾ cup apple cider vinegar
> 2 tablespoons curry powder
> 3 tablespoons peanut oil
> ¼ inch piece ginger

1. To prepare the marinade for the chicken, put in food processor or blender scallions, all but 2 cloves garlic, onions, thyme, cilantro, vinegar,

and about 1 tablespoon salt. Bottle and set aside. Leftover marinade may be kept in the refrigerator.

2. Remove skin and fat from chicken breasts. Split whole raw breasts and cut each half into thirds. Wash well and place in a bowl in enough water to cover the chicken. Squeeze juice of limes into water; add limes and 2 tablespoons salt. Stir to dissolve the salt. Set aside for 1 hour.

3. Rinse chicken thoroughly and pat dry. Thoroughly rub 3 to 4 tablespoons of marinade into the meat. Refrigerate for 2 to 3 days, turning chicken occasionally to make sure it is evenly marinated.

4. Remove chicken from refrigerator about an hour before cooking. Pour 3 tablespoons peanut oil in large skillet. Crush remaining 1 or 2 cloves garlic. Slice piece of ginger and pound it in mortar. Add garlic and ginger to oil and cook over medium heat to lightly brown garlic.

5. When garlic is lightly brown add 2 tablespoons curry powder and stir. Add more oil if needed to prevent the curry from burning. Add chicken a couple pieces at a time, stirring each in the mixture to ensure the chicken is immersed in the curry.

6. Reduce heat to simmer, cover skillet, and let chicken cook quietly for a few minutes, stirring as needed to prevent sticking. After about 5 minutes, add some additional marinade and sliced onion. Tightly cover skillet and continue simmering for about 15 minutes, adding remaining marinade and water as needed. Test chicken to see if it is cooked.

7. You can also add a Habañero chile to the pot as you begin to simmer chicken pieces. Wash and place whole pepper including stem into pot. As you stir ingredients be careful not to break the pepper since all you want is what flavor she holds. If you can find West Indian hot pepper, use this instead of Habañero because the flavor is "sweeter." Serves 4.

0: 0: 0:

# Jennifer's Trinidadian Pepper Sauce

Hot peppers (about a dozen)
2 medium tart/acid or semisweet fruit in season,
    like green mangoes or sour green apples
approximately $1/4$ small green pawpaw
    (papaya), optional
2 cloves garlic
1 small onion
$1/2$ cup apple cider vinegar
salt to taste

1. Wash, seed, and cut up peppers and fruit. (Remember the peppers are HOT, so use a knife and fork. If it gets on your hands, then wash your hands with sugar to cut the pepper. You may want to wear rubber gloves. Be very careful not to rub your eyes with hands.)

2. Cut up onion and garlic.

3. Mix peppers, onion, garlic, and fruit with $1/4$ to $1/2$ cup water. Add salt to taste and bottle.

4. Hot sauce can be used sparingly on any dish that needs spicing and lasts indefinitely if refrigerated. Experiment with the taste of different fruits that you like, using tart fruits more than semisweet. For variation chop ingredients into about half-inch bits, add vinegar and salt, and bottle sauce ensuring that the vinegar covers ingredients in the bottle. Store in the sun for about 2 weeks before using. Think of the creativity of the slave women and create you own sauce in their honor.

❏: ❏: ❏:

# Hunger

## Jyl Lynn Felman

**B**efore I am born I float in my mother's yolk and I am never hungry. Soon after I am born the hunger begins. By seventeen I am so hungry I do not know what to do with myself. All I can think about is food and how I cannot get enough.

At seventeen I leave the States for Israel. I have to leave. When I arrive *b'eretz* (in Israel) I cannot stop eating. I stuff myself the way my mother stuffs her kosher Shabbas chicken breasts. I stuff myself with grilled lamb shaved right off a hot, rotating skewer and stuffed into warm, fresh pita filled with sautéed onions and lemon juice. In Jerusalem I cannot stop eating waiting for the bus to take me to the Turkish Bath House where I crouch in the corner on a low stool, sip steaming Turkish coffee, suck on floating orange peels, and stare at all the naked bodies.

I cannot stop eating halvah laced with green pistachios while Mizrachi women, Jews from North East Africa and the Middle East, with olive skin soak in pools of turquoise water. Slowly as though praying, they unbraid each other's long thick dark hair. Standing in water up to their waists, they comb out the knots. They knead their scalps and foreheads gently, washing their hair in the juice of fresh squeezed lemons. The women soak in silence. Large round bodies move from pool to sacred pool; hot then cold, tepid and cool. Back and forth. Tall and thin. Brown skin. Torsos dip and soak in swirls of foaming water. Surrounded by the scent of eucalyptus they soak their feet in burning crystals. Bodies in water float through steam.

I want to take my clothes off but I cannot stop eating whole figs with date jam spread on fresh Syrian bread while Sephardic women lie on heated marble slabs and close their eyes. Their breasts sag; sunlight doesn't filter in. Bodies in steam float through air. But I am never full. They drink chilled yellow papaya juice from thin paper cups while cooling their sweating foreheads. I want to take my clothes off but I cannot stop eating. Wings and thighs. Breasts and legs. They soak and they salt in pools of blue water. With avocado soap they wash each other's spines and massage their aching muscles. Jewish women bathe in ancient cleansing waters. Wrapped in soft terry cloth they climb the steps to the roof and begin to eat: plates of hummus lined with purple olives, smooth *babaganoush*, and almond macaroons. I can almost touch the sky, sitting on the roof; the Jerusalem sun is hot and strong.

Down below I see the streets of *Meah Shearim*. Narrow sidewalks and small shops. Women concealed within their bodies. Safely covered from head to toe. Orthodox men in black. Praying as they walk. Their eyes never meet. On the street. Their hands never touch. On the street. Women are covered from head to toe.

On the rooftop women eat, naked in the sun; mothers and daughters; sisters. They lounge on cement slabs, laugh among themselves, and feed each other grape leaves. But I cannot stop eating staring at the street below. Women with children; live chickens squawking. Preparing for Shabbat. Men in black hats. Long beards. Everything ordered and prearranged. *Ani Adoni Elochechah*. I am the Lord thy God. The Torah is absolute. I love my People Israel. (I loathe my female self.) I cannot stop eating caught between the roof and the street below. I dream that I am falling, falling to the ground. But I never land. I stay caught forever hanging limb by limb. Caught forever limb by limb. The Jerusalem sun is hot and strong. Burning me at seventeen. Suspended as I am. Between my people and myself.

The suspension makes me crazy as I wander the biblical streets. Where do I belong? The suspension is intolerable. I have no place to go. Every week I visit *Meah Shearim*. Searching not just for my head but my body too. Every Friday I stay with an Orthodox family and light Shabbas candles as the sun sets. When I'm in my head my body disappears and then I cannot find my Jewish female self. At night I wander back alone from the center of the city, to where I live on *Har Hatzofim*. I search as I walk, staring in the dark, peering into windows looking for my soul.

In the States, I'm in my body, but I cannot find my head. At home *b'eretz* I eat my way through the city longing to be whole. With my bus fare I buy a kilo of jelly cookies. I eat as I walk in the dark through villages and urban streets. All I do in Israel at seventeen is eat. I tap a hunger so wide that I do not know what to do. I know that I will have to leave the country. There is no one to tell how hungry I have become because a hunger like this is forbidden.

I have no place to go. I do not know it yet completely. But I fall in love with Israel the way I will fall in love with a woman for the first time. With all my heart and with all my soul. I want to return to the land forever. To live in *Meah Shearim*. That will save me from my hunger, or so I think and pray. At seventeen, I wander the streets of Jerusalem, terrified at what I know I will grow up to be. But there is no one to tell how hungry I have become because a hunger like this is forbidden. I swallow my passion whole; my body swells until I am so enormous that I have to leave the land I love.

□: □: □:

# Food and Belonging:
## At "Home" and in "Alien-Kitchens"

Ketu H. Katrak

Aromas at Amy Villa, 675 Parsi Colony (near Vadala Market), Dadar, Bombay 14. India. Dawn. The sun's first rays kiss the Arabian Sea. *Om jaye jagdish hare* . . . Clanging sounds from the kitchen enter my waking body as mouth-watering aromas waft in—moist *chapatis, kando-papeto, kheechree-kadhi, papeta ma gosh*. These word-sounds in Gujarati, my mother tongue, carry the tastes and aromas that are lost in their English translations: *chappatis*, round flat wheat bread roasted on an iron griddle; *kando-papeto*, onions and potatoes spiced with pepper and ginger; *kheechree-kadhi*, spiced yoghurt sauce eaten with rice; *papeta ma gosh*, meat and potato stew. And their tastes and aromas are as different from English food as the sound of their names. Even after two hundred years in India, the British did not improve their cuisine.

*Om jaye jagdish hare* . . . is playing loudly in the living room, on Vividhbharati, our local Bombay radio station. *Om jaye jagdish hare*, Vividhbharati's signature tune is a popular hymn, a Sanskrit *bhajan* whose rounded notes mingle with the Avesta prayers being recited devoutly by my father. *Om jaye jagdish . . . yatha ahu vahiro, om jaye jagdish . . . kemna mazada, moveyte payum dada, yethma dregava*. Our Zoroastrian prayers are in the ancient Avesta and Pahlavi languages. Our mother tongue is Gujarati, adopted a long time ago when the Zoroastrians fled Persia and came to India around 1350.

All these sounds mingle with the aromatic spices wafting over my waking body. The sounds of prayer and the smells of *chappatis* and vegetables weave into a pattern of belonging, of home-sounds and home-aromas. In Bombay, certain foods, such as bread and milk, are delivered to our door: TRING TRING: *pao-walla* (fresh bread delivered to the door); TRING TRING: *dooth-walla* (milkman); TRING TRING: *kerawalla* (banana-seller); TRING TRING: *tarkariwalli* (vegetable seller). Lots of traffic. No chance of lying quietly in bed! These words that simultaneously convey the food and a particular food-seller in a single musical sound lose their power when split into their English units. But worse even, *paowalla, doothwalla, kerawalla*, so familiar to me in India, sound exotic in this, my American-alien-home context. How does one create the truth of one's life without slipping into outsiderness?

I love to shake out my half-sleep with a cup of hot tea, prepared with lemon grass and mint leaves, and it tastes even better when made by my mother. I keep lingering in that safe space of being held in unspoken love. Waking up would be to leave it. Softly, like childhood.

As a child, I remember that the kitchen was expected to be my mother's domain though she was not happy inhabiting that space. She is a very fine and intuitive cook, but her spirit of accomplishment was often snuffed out by my father's critical palate. He was a Victorian man, born in 1902, authoritarian and domineering, certainly with a rigid sense of male and female roles and the sexual division of labor: he went to the office, and my mother cooked and took care of us at home. My father, the only son who lost his father when he was barely fourteen, was thrust into adult male responsibility, looking after his mother and two sisters. A highly motivated person, he put himself through school, determined to get an education and to raise his family's economic status. In the 1920s, his patriarchal status within his own family was never challenged, and with a college degree and an income his male status was strengthened further.

His doting mother spoiled him in terms of his expectations of food. Her identity and love were focused on making my father happy with varieties of homemade pickles, elaborate delicacies, and snacks. He began to regard such labor and such love as normative roles for women, especially within the parameters of home.

When my father got married, he expected the same kind of culinary performances from his wife. He expected my mother to embrace this role wholeheartedly. My mother, newly married, had to find a way to negotiate her own identity between the demanding personalities of a strong husband and a domineering mother-in-law who still wanted to play a role in her son's happiness at home. The classic scenario of an older woman oppressing her younger daughter-in-law was true in my family. Women in this patriarchal power structure gain power as mothers of sons; their seniority accords them the dubious privilege of dominating their young daughters-in-law in the joint family.

By the time I was growing up, being the last of five siblings, my parents had lived through two world wars, had moved from Calcutta to Nagpur, and finally had settled in Bombay. My memories of food as a child are filled with not tasting the food, feeling tense and fearful about the conflicts between my parents that erupted inevitably around the dining table. My father, a fastidious connoisseur of food, often found something missing and would be vocal about it. He craved a delicate, subtle blending of flavors; he envisioned every meal as a work of art. So, with *kheechree-kadhi*, he had to have a *papad*, with *dhan-shak* (a heavily spiced Zoroastrian dish that combines five varieties of dals, or lentils, with vegetables), he had to have a particular kind of *kachumber* (a salad made of onions, tomatoes, fresh coriander leaves, and green chilies) and lime, and on and on. If some condiment, pickle, or appropriate chutney were missing, he would vent his distress, would enjoin my mother to leave the table, and gratify his needs. The table was the place where he expressed whatever frustrations he dealt with at work. He never talked about work at home, not that my mother was much interested.

My father's work—as chartered accountant for the Tata Steel Company—earned him considerable respect. The Tata, a multi-faceted industrialist company, played a key role in developing India's industrial base prior to and after independence from the British in 1947. The Tata companies shared a certain nationalist spirit that my father imbibed and practised in his activist work during India's independence struggle. My father was a Gandhian and was so convinced of the Gandhian philosophy of supporting Indian-made versus European goods that he ran a modest Sarvodaya (homemade, indigenous goods) store in Bombay. The centerpiece of Gandhian philosophy was *khadi* (home-spun cotton), and my father imbibed the politics of *khadi* so integrally and devoutly that from the 1930s until his death in 1992, he wore *khadi*. This often distressed relatives abroad who were used to bringing back "phoren-made" clothes. I remember my father's stories about his involvement with Gandhi's Quit India movement in the 1940s, and the sheer exuberance of that midnight hour on August 15, 1947, when the country became independent.

As a child, I knew very little about my father's political activism as a Gandhian nationalist, nor did I understand his forthright manner, and at times stark honesty in abiding by his convictions until I was much older. My father was a distant and powerful influence whose impact I realized only later in life, and I still retain some perhaps unfair memories of my father, all centered around the dining table, the site of conflicts between my parents.

Food was not pleasurable to me as a child. Thinking about this now as an adult, I can say that food was an overdetermined category for me in my childhood years; it tasted of the conflictual relationship my parents shared, it smelt of the heady tropical environment, it delineated who was in and out of favor with my father. I tasted anxiety in the onions fried a bit too brown and tension in the too many dark burned spots on the roasted *papads*. One never knew what would be considered faulty at a particular meal, and the uncertainty overwhelmed any pleasure in what was eaten. The walls around our dining table must hold those memories of silent anxiety, of quiet fear, retaining those emotions even after the white-washing given them by painters every two years. My parents wanted that newness and freshness on the walls, but underneath the layers of paint, long memories still throb.

As a child, I used to think that all this trouble of cooking was for naught, a waste of time, hours of chopping, grinding spices, stirring, sautéeing, frying, boiling, and all consumed so quickly and without any appreciation or acknowledgement of the hard work. It was not customary for that generation to compliment the cook as it is common nowadays among my peers and with my sisters and their husbands. Perhaps because my mother's work was rendered so invisible and unrewarded, I did not want any part of it. It took me many years, and a long journey halfway around the world, from Bombay to the United States, before I understood the reasons behind my resistance. As a child and later as an adolescent, I had observed (though I can only now articulate this) that cooking did not give my mother any authority within the family hierarchy. I recall a deep sense of her powerlessness and invisibility—so much effort and so little acknowledgement. I was stopped short in my sadness for her. I could not enjoy the food, and I could not articulate why I felt distressed. Looking back now, her situation and my response seems to be dictated by the power structure within a joint family's hierarchy. Since the greatest authority was enjoyed by my father, I identified with him rather than with my mother.

The conflicts that seeped into our meals around the dining table filled me as a child with unexpressed rage against my father. At that age, I did not have the vocabulary or the intellectual tools to speak up for my mother. Usually, she acquiesced quietly. That was her role. No argument. Period. Later in her own life, in her seventies, I have been fascinated at my mother's own growing feminism. She began to resist by simply refusing to comply with certain demands. Although she never abandoned her responsibilities, she began to express the limits of what she would do.

My mother cooked because she had to. That was not her passion. But she handled this chore so efficiently, and despite the invisibility of her labor, with love. She would rise very early and labor to complete the cooking for the entire day. At home, the afternoon meal is a hot cooked meal quite unlike the cold sandwich that is so common in Western cultures. (When my mother visited me in the States, and when she spent time with my brothers in Australia, she said that she'd take a serious break from sandwiches when she returned to India!) At home, we had a large, cylindrical cooker, about three feet tall with a coal *sagdi* (heater). The coals would be lit and crackling very early in the morning, and the *sagdi*'s smoky smell mingled with the spices as they were fried in order to be added to the vegetables, the rice, and on certain days, the meat before all the various pots were placed into the cooker. All the aluminum pots were stacked up—beginning with meat at the bottom, closest to the highest heat—and four to five different dishes cooked at once.

Most of our cooking began with chopping and frying onions. As my father remarked jokingly to me, "However much you study, and however highly educated you are, ultimately you will always have to chop onions." He did not mean to be unsupportive about my education and career; in fact, he encouraged and provided emotional and material support for not only my brothers' but also my sisters' higher studies. It is thanks to him that I am in the United States today. Nonetheless, for him, all such intellectual labor had to be balanced for women by our culinary abilities.

My mother had help in chopping the onion, garlic, ginger, often the staples for most of our cooking. At times, our *bai* would grind the spices such as cumin, coriander, roasted peanuts, and many other varieties of spices in seed form that I am unable to translate, on a grindstone with a heavy grinder that looked like a thick, stone rolling pin. This was in the days before grinders became common. And I recall our *bai* being very upset when my sister returned from her studies in France with a mixer/blender. My sister thought that it would ease the hard work; our *bai* was worried that this gadget would make her dispensable.

As a young girl, I helped my mother—chopping onions, observing, and soaking the flavors almost through the pores of my skin where those memories were held intact. Years later, I tapped into those early remembrances that seem to be held as lovingly in my body as in my mind.

My mother longed to complete her cooking chores and would prepare all the food in the morning for the entire day. In some other communities in India women are enjoined to prepare each meal just before it is eaten, and as a result spend most of their day inside the kitchen walls, but my mother was always very clear about not doing that. She'd often complete all the cooking by the time my father left for his office, around 8:30 A.M. Then she would be free for the rest of the day to spend time with her most beloved activity—painting on fabric, on sarees, scarves, and runners, creating magic in color, an activity that she enjoys to this day in her eighty-fifth year. I remember my mother most at peace with herself when engrossed at her painting table. My mother painted forget-me-nots, daffodils, poppies, flowers that I had never seen in Bombay. I wonder now why my mother always painted foreign flowers, not our own bougainvilleas, shoeflowers, *gulmohur*. She used to go to an art class at the J. J. Institute of Art in Bombay during the thirties and forties where, I guess, they taught her as part of our colonial heritage that foreign flowers were better. Ironically, they became more real to her than the ones in our own backyard.

Growing up in an atmosphere of unspoken love, I never recognized my mother's incredible creativity, not just in her obvious talents as a painter, but in her artistry in the activities of daily living, particularly in her inventiveness in creating new recipes without taking any credit; her practical creativity in creating my lunch-packets to take to college. Putting together meals from minimal ingredients, knowing how to replace one missing ingredient with another, not complaining, and accomplishing delightful feasts.

My own memorybanks about food overflowed only after I left India to come to the United States as a graduate student. The disinterest in food that I had felt during my childhood years was transformed into a new kind of need for that food as an essential connection with home. I longed for my native food as I dealt with my dislocation from the throbbing Bombay metropolis with its dust, crowded public buses and trains, the prevalence of so many languages on the street, Hindi, Gujarati, Marathi, and strange new world in the quiet insularity of Bryn Mawr College with its academic-towerish atmosphere, where I was one of few foreigners, exotic and exoticized. English language only. American food only. Language, languish, anguish of belonging. Institutional cafeteria food in the graduate dorm. As cafeteria food goes, I suppose that it was decent, but suddenly, I was so bereft, longing for those early morning aromas of spices mingling with the igniting coals. I kept a packet of garam masala in my dorm room and would often close my eyes and take a long whiff in order to be transported to my tropical home in Bombay.

Cafeteria food and a new geography mingled in alienness. There were new trees and flowers, new and shiny trains, and everything was so orderly and quiet that the silence rang out to my ears that were used to the bustle of crowds, the chaos and shouting of the Bombay locals. My spirit inhabited a new sky, and new air getting crisper as fall slid into winter and I encountered snow for the first time in my life. The alienness deepened as a white landscape replaced a perpetually green one at home.

Moving from the dorm into apartment living—and learning an American-style independence—I began to cook Indian food, to invent several recipes, creating from memory, from observing my mother, following the trail of appropriate tastes and smells—add some turmeric, pop the mustard seeds (the black ones) in hot oil (careful not to burn them), add cumin seeds, fry in the basmati rice and add water. Bring to a boil and as the aromas waft in, be transported into other skies. My Amherst friends call this "Yellow rice."

A recipe has so many different hands and minds in its history—I cannot recall who taught me what, and what parts I invented. That is the boundaryless pleasure of cooking; no one authorship. What counts is the final taste. *Rye na Papeta*, which my friends call "Ketu's potatoes." Yes, today, I cook this dish, but many hands and minds are part of its history and its success.

Today, homesickness often drives me (sometimes for miles depending on where I am) in search of a samosa, or *masala chai*, a spiced tea, or *masala dosa*, the paper-thin pancakes made of different dals and filled with spiced potatoes, or sweet *lassi*, a sweetened yoghurt drink. The fullness and varied nature of Indian cuisine, so regionally diverse, was very much a part of my life in Bombay, a cosmopolitan community of Gujaratis, Tamilians, Maharashtrians, and Zoroastrians among other communities, each with its own special flavors in spicing and cooking. Luckily, even in the United States, I've never had to live in a place where I would panic about running out of coriander or cumin and not being able to find these in a specialty store. It's part of a pilgrimage "home" for me to visit the Indian grocery stores wherever there is a sizeable South Asian presence—as India Food and Spices, in Cambridge, Massachusetts, my savior when I'm in Amherst; or Bharat Bazar in Los Angeles.

Food and home. Returning home through the tastebuds, through the aromas. Now, having homes in so many locations, different foods also provide a kind of anchor for my wandering spirit—the reliable predictability of eating at our corner Greek restaurant after sharing a yoga class with my close friends in Northampton, breathing in unison, and eating in unity, falafel, souvlakia, salad and tzaziki sauce. Breathing consciously for our hour-and-a-half yoga class connects us with our bodies, renews our bodily location, connects mind and body, integrates body, soul, and spirit. Here, accepting this body as home, I often try to rest and stop my frantic search for home. From that space of belonging, touched at times fleetingly, at other times deeply as in intense meditation, I can touch the limits of my being often in turmoil in alien-homes.

Sitting cross-legged in lotus position, eyes closed, breathing in and breathing out—yogic practice brings me home to myself, takes me home to India, brings me home into my body. My body. As a child, I used to observe my father practising yoga—he usually did the headstand. I was too fearful then. Now as an adult, and living in this foreign home, I discover the ancient principles of yoga, simple and profound. Yoga in Northampton—a sort of West meets East, the United States and India, at times a polarity, at other times a harmonious weaving together of many colored strands of values, music, languages, rhythms. Chanting Sanskrit *slokas* (religious words and syllables) with many-flavored accents in America; relaxing to the sounds of New Age rhythms. Mind and body integrating, the many public and private selves weaving together in a harmonious tapestry. Like a vast ocean, joyously exuberant and incredibly calming. Yoga's symmetry and asanas center my wandering spirit.

This body is home. This writing is home. The body into which we put food is our first and most inescapable home. As basic as breathing in and breathing out, as the breath consciously washes over the body, it calls up the mind, finding that space of rich silence, a kind of emptiness that is very full with a vibrant peacefulness. From that space of wholeness there is a language that is similar to the language of food—the tongue that speaks and the tongue that tastes. This is the speaking of my mother tongue Gujarati, but I also claim this alien English tongue that speaks and tastes. As the poet Kamala Das puts it, "I speak three languages, write in / Two, dream in one. / Don't write in English, they said, / English is not your mother-tongue. Why not leave / Me alone, critics, friends . . . The language I speak / Becomes mine." This body that breathes, that craves breath, water, and food is home. And this body finds new language-homes and new food-homes sharing and mingling spices and friendships. This body is home. This writing is home. Its labyrinthine journeys weave soul, sinew, and mind into union.

⬚ ⬚ ⬚

## Ketu's Rice

I cup rice, preferably basmati
2 cups water
I tablespoon vegetable oil

½ teaspoon each black mustard seeds, turmeric,
    and cumin seeds
¼ teaspoon salt (an important ingredient, use unless
    you have a dietary restriction)

1. Wash rice and soak in cold water for at least 10 minutes.

2. Heat oil in heavy bottom pot with tight fitting lid. Add mustard seeds when oil is hot enough to pop seeds. When you think it has reached the right temperature, drop in one seed. If it pops immediately, the oil is ready. Cover pot immediately, reduce heat, and shake pot as if making popcorn until you no longer hear the seeds popping.

3. Lower heat and add turmeric, cumin seeds, and salt. Cook for a minute or two, stirring at all times.

4. Add thoroughly drained rice and stir until grains are well coated with oil and spices.

5. Add water, raise heat to high, and bring to a boil. Reduce heat to low, cover pot, and cook for 25 minutes. Rice will be fragrant and a beautiful yellow color. Serves 4.

❒ ❒ ❒

## Yellow Potatoes

4 white potatoes
¼ cup vegetable oil
1 green chili (or to taste), finely diced
1 teaspoon each mustard seeds, turmeric,
    and chopped ginger
juice of one lime
a few strings of cilantro, chopped
salt to taste

1. Peel and cut potatoes into small (¼ inch) dice.

2. Heat oil in heavy bottom pot with lid and add mustard seeds when oil is hot enough to pop them. When you think the oil has reached the

right temperature, drop in one seed. If it pops immediately, the oil is ready. Cover pot immediately, reduce heat, and shake pot as if making popcorn until you no longer hear the seeds popping.

3. Lower heat and add the potatoes, stir well. Cover pot and cook for about 10 minutes, until the potatoes are half-cooked.

4. Add chopped chili, ginger, turmeric, and salt, stirring until potatoes are coated with spices. Cover and cook for about 15 minutes or until potatoes are cooked, stirring often and adding more oil if potatoes stick to pan.

5. When potatoes are done add lime juice and cilantro. Serves 4.

❊ ❊ ❊

# A Lesbian Appetite from *Trash: Stories by Dorothy Allison*

## Dorothy Allison

**B**iscuits. I dream about baking biscuits, sifting flour, baking powder, and salt together, measuring out shortening and buttermilk by eye, and rolling it all out with flour-dusted fingers. Beans. I dream about picking over beans, soaking them overnight, chopping pork fat, slicing onions, putting it all in a great iron pot to bubble for hour after hour until all the world smells of salt and heat and the sweat that used to pool on my mama's neck. Greens. Mustard greens, collards, turnip greens, and poke—can't find them anywhere in the shops up North. In the middle of the night I wake up desperate for the taste of greens, get up and find a twenty-four hour deli that still has a can of spinach and half a pound of bacon. I fry the bacon, dump it in the spinach, bring the whole mess to a boil and eat it with tears in my eyes. It doesn't taste like anything I really wanted to have. When I find frozen collards in the Safeway, I buy five bags and store them away. Then all I have to do is persuade the butcher to let me have a pack of neck bones. Having those wrapped packages in the freezer reassures me almost as much as money in the bank. If I wake up with bad dreams there will at least be something I want to eat.

Red beans and rice, chicken necks and dumplings, pot roast with vinegar and cloves stuck in the onions, salmon patties with white sauce, refried beans on warm tortillas, sweet duck with scallions and pancakes, lamb cooked with olive oil and lemon slices, pan-fried pork chops and redeye gravy, potato pancakes with applesauce, polenta with spaghetti sauce floating on top—

food is more than sustenance; it is history. I remember women by what we ate together, what they dug out of the freezer after we'd made love for hours. I've only had one lover who didn't want to eat at all. We didn't last long. The sex was good, but I couldn't think what to do with her when the sex was finished. We drank spring water together and fought a lot.

I grew an ulcer in my belly once I was out in the world on my own. I think of it as an always angry place inside me, a tyranny that takes good food and turns it like a blade scraping at the hard place where I try to hide my temper. Some days I think it is the rightful reward for my childhood. If I had eaten right, Lee used to tell me, there would never have been any trouble.

"Rickets, poor eyesight, appendicitis, warts, and bad skin," she insisted, "they're all caused by bad eating habits, poor diet."

It's true. The diet of poor Southerners is among the worst in the world, though it's tasty, very tasty. There's pork fat or chicken grease in every dish, white sugar in the cobblers, pralines, and fudge, and flour, fat, and salt in the gravies—lots of salt in everything. The vegetables get cooked to limp strands with no fiber left at all. Mothers give sidemeat to their toddlers as pacifiers and slip them whisky with honey at the first sign of teething, a cold, or a fever. Most of my cousins lost their teeth in their twenties and took up drinking as easily as they put sugar in their iced tea. I try not to eat so much sugar, try not to drink, try to limit pork and salt and white flour, but the truth is I am always hungry for it—the smell and taste of the food my mama fed me.

Poor white trash I am for sure. I eat shit food and am not worthy. My family starts with good teeth but loses them early. Five of my cousins bled to death before thirty-five, their stomachs finally surrendering to sugar and whiskey and fat and salt. I've given it up. If I cannot eat what I want, then I'll eat what I must, but my dreams will always be flooded with salt and grease, crisp fried stuff that sweetens my mouth and feeds my soul. I would rather starve death than myself.

In college it was seven cups of coffee a day after a breakfast of dry-roasted nuts and Coca-Cola. Too much grey meat and reheated potatoes led me to develop a taste for peanut butter with honey, coleslaw with raisins, and pale, sad vegetables that never disturbed anything at all. When I started throwing up before classes, my roommate fed me fat pink pills her doctor had given her. My stomach shrank to a stone in my belly. I lived on pink pills, coffee, and Dexedrine until I could go home and use hot biscuits to scoop up cold tomato soup at my mama's table. The biscuits dripped memories as well as butter: Uncle Lucius rolling in at dawn, eating a big breakfast with us all, and stealing mama's tools when he left; or Aunt Panama at the door with her six daughters, screaming, *That bastard's made me pregnant again just to get a son*, and wanting butter beans with sliced tomatoes before she would calm down. Cold chicken in a towel meant Aunt Alma was staying over, cooking her usual six birds at a time. *Raising eleven kids I never learned how to cook for less than fifteen.* Red dye stains on the sink was a sure sign Reese was dating some new boy, baking him a red velvet cake my stepfather would want for himself.

"It's good to watch you eat," my mama smiled at me, around her loose teeth. "It's just so good to watch you eat." She packed up a batch of her biscuits when I got ready to leave, stuffed them with cheese and fatback. On the bus going back to school I'd hung them to my belly, using their bulk to remind me who I was.

When the government hired me to be a clerk for the Social Security Administration, I was sent to Miami Beach where they put me up in a crumbling old hotel right on the water while teaching me all the regulations. The instructors took turns taking us out to dinner. Mr. McCullum took an interest in me, told me Miami Beach had the best food in the world, bought me an order of Oysters Rockefeller one night, and medallions of veal with wine sauce the next. If he was gonna pay for it, I would eat it, but it was all like food seen on a movie screen. It had the shape and shine of luxury but tasted like nothing at all. But I fell in love with Wolfe's Cafeteria and got up early every morning to walk there and eat their danish stuffed with cream cheese and raisins.

"The best sweet biscuit in Miami," I told the counter man.

"*Nu?*" he grinned at the women beside me, her face wrinkling up as she blushed and smiled at me.

"*Nischt*," she laughed. I didn't understand a word but I nodded anyway. They were probably talking about food.

When I couldn't sleep, I read Franz Kafka in my hotel room, thinking about him working for the social security administration in Prague. Kafka would work late and eat polish sausage for dinner, sitting over a notebook in which he would write all night. I wrote letters like novels that I never mailed. When the chairman of the local office promised us all a real treat, I finally rebelled and refused to eat the raw clams Mr. McCullum said were "the best in the world." While everyone around me sliced lemons and slurped up pink and grey morsels, I filled myself up with little white oyster crackers and tried not to look at the lobsters waiting to die, thrashing around in their plastic tanks.

"It's good to watch you eat," Mona told me, serving me dill bread, sour cream, and fresh tomatoes. "You do it with such obvious enjoyment." She drove us up to visit her family in Georgia, talking about what a great cook her mama was. My mouth watered, and we stopped three times for boiled peanuts. I wanted to make love in the back seat of her old DeSoto but she was saving it up to do it in her own bed at home. When we arrived her mama came out to the car and said, "You girls must be hungry," and took us in to the lunch table.

There was three-bean salad from cans packed with vinaigrette, pickle loaf on thin sliced white bread, American and Swiss cheese in slices, and antipasto from a jar sent directly from an uncle still living in New York City. "Deli food," her mama kept saying, "is the best food in the world." I nodded, chewing white bread and a slice of American cheese, the peanuts in my belly weighing me down like a mess of little stones. Mona picked at the pickle loaf and pushed her ankle up into my lap where her mother couldn't see. I choked on the white bread and broke out in a sweat.

Lee wore her hair pushed up like the whorls on scallop shells. She toasted mushrooms instead of marshmallows, and tried to persuade me of the value of cabbage and eggplant, but she cooked with no fat; everything tasted of safflower oil. I loved Lee but hated the cabbage—it seemed an anemic cousin of real greens—and I only got into the eggplant after Lee brought home a basketful insisting I help her cook it up for freezing.

"You got to get it to sweat out the poisons." She sliced the big purple fruits as she talked. "Salt it up so the bitter stuff will come off." She layered the salted slices between paper towels, changing the towels on the ones she'd cut up earlier. Some of her hair came loose and hung down past one ear. She looked like a mother in a Mary Cassatt painting, standing in her sunlit kitchen, sprinkling raw seasalt with one hand and pushing her hair back with the other.

I picked up an unsalted wedge of eggplant and sniffed it, rubbing the spongy mass between my thumbs. "Makes me think of what breadfruit must be like." I squeezed it down, and the flesh slowly shaped up again. "Smells like bread and feels like it's been baked. But after you salt it down, it's more like fried okra, all soft and sharp-smelling."

"Well, you like okra, don't you?" Lee wiped her grill with peanut oil and started dusting the drained eggplant slices with flour. Sweat shone on her neck under the scarf that tied up her hair in back.

"Oh yeah. You put enough cornmeal on it and fry it in bacon fat and I'll probably like most anything." I took the wedge of eggplant and rubbed it on the back of her neck.

"What are you doing?"

"Salting the eggplant." I followed the eggplant with my tongue, pulled up her T-shirt, and slowly ran the tough purple rind up to her small bare breasts. Lee started giggling, wiggling her ass, but not taking her hands out of the flour to stop me. I pulled down her shorts, picked up another dry slice and planted it against her navel, pressed with my fingers and slipped it down her pubic mound.

"Oh! Don't do that. Don't do that." She was breathing through her open mouth and her right hand was a knotted fist in the flour bowl. I laughed softly into her ear, and rocked her back so that she was leaning against me, her ass pressing into my cunt.

"Oh. Oh!" Lee shuddered and reached with her right hand to turn of the grill. With her left she reached behind and pulled up my shirt. Flour smeared over my sweaty midriff and sifted down on the floor. "You. You!" She was tugging at my jeans, a couple of slices of eggplant in one hand.

"I'll show you. Oh you!" We wrestled, eggplant breaking up between our navels. I got her shorts off, she got my jeans down. I dumped a whole plate of eggplant on her belly.

"You are just running salt, girl," I teased, and pushed slices up between her legs, while I licked one of her nipples and pinched the other between a folded slice of eggplant. She was laughing, her belly bouncing under me.

"I'm gonna make you eat all of this," she yelled.

"Of course." I pushed eggplant out of the way and slipped two fingers between her labia. She was slicker than peanut oil. "But first we got to get the poison out."

"Oh you!" Her hips rose up into my hand. All her hair had come loose and was trailing in the flour. She wrapped one hand in my hair, the other around my left breast. "I'll cook you . . . just you wait. I'll cook you a meal to drive you crazy."

"Oh, honey." She tasted like frybread—thick, smoked, and fat-rich on my tongue. We ran sweat in puddles, while above us the salted eggplant pearled up in great clear drops of poison. When we finished, we gathered up all the eggplant on the floor and fried it in flour and crushed garlic. Lee poured canned tomatoes with basil and lemon on the hot slices and then pushed big bites onto my tongue with her fingers. It was delicious. I licked her fingers and fed her with my own hands. We never did get our clothes back on.

In South Carolina, in the seventh grade, we had studied nutrition. "Vitamin D," the teacher told us, "is paramount. Deny it to a young child and the result is the brain never develops properly." She had a twangy midwestern accent, grey hair, and a small brown mole on her left cheek. Everybody knew she hated teaching, hated her students, especially those of us in badly fitting worn-out dresses sucking bacon rinds and cutting our names in the desks with our uncle's old pocketknives. She would stand with a fingertip on her left ear, her thumb stroking that mole, while she looked at us with disgust she didn't bother to conceal.

"The children of the poor," she told us, "the children of the poor have a lack of brain tissue simply because they don't get the necessary vitamins at the proper age. It is a deficiency that cannot be made up when they are older." A stroke of her thumb and she turned her back.

I stood in the back of the room, my fingers wrapping my skull in horror. I imagined my soft brain slipping loosely in its cranial cavity shrunk by a lack of the necessary vitamins. How could I know if it wasn't too late? Mama always said that smart was the only way out. I thought of my cousins, big-headed, watery-eyed, and stupid. VITAMIN D! I became a compulsive consumer of vitamin D. Is it milk? We will drink milk, steal it if we must. *Mama, make salmon stew. It's cheap and full of vitamin D.* If we can't afford cream, then evaporated milk will do. One is as thick as the other. Sweet is expensive, but thick builds muscles in the brain. Feed me milk, feed me cream, feed me what I need to fight them.

Twenty years later the doctor sat me down to tell me the secrets of my body. He had, oddly, that identical gesture, one finger on the ear and the others curled to the cheek as if he were thinking all the time.

"Milk," he announced, "that's the problem, a mild allergy. Nothing to worry about. You'll take calcium and vitamin D supplements and stay away from milk products. No cream, no butterfat, stay away from cheese."

I started to grin, but he didn't notice. The finger on his ear was pointing to the brain. He had no sense of irony, and I didn't tell him why I laughed so much. I should have known. Milk or cornbread or black-eyed peas, there had to be a secret, something we would never understand until it was too late. My brain is fat and strong, ripe with years of vitamin D, but my belly is tender and hurts me in the night. I grinned into his confusion and chewed the pink and grey pills he gave me to help me recover from the damage milk had done me. What would I have to do, I wondered, to be able to eat pan gravy again?

When my stomach began to turn on me the last time, I made desperate attempts to compromise—wheat germ, brown rice, fresh vegetables, and tamari. Whole wheat became a symbol for purity of intent, but hard brown bread does not pass easily. It sat in my stomach and clung to the honey deposits that seemed to be collecting between my tongue and breastbone. Lee told me I could be healthy if I drank a glass of hot water and lemon juice every morning. She chewed sunflower seeds and sesame seed candy made with molasses. I drank the hot water, but then I went up on the roof of the apartment building to read Carson McCullers, to eat Snickers bars and drink Dr. Pepper, imagining myself back in Uncle Lucius's Pontiac inhaling Moon Pies and R.C. Cola.

"Swallow it," Jay said. Her fingers were in my mouth, thick with the juice from between her legs. She was leaning forward, her full weight pressing me down. I swallowed, sucked between each knuckle, and swallowed again. Her other hand worked between us, pinching me but forcing the thick cream out of my cunt. She brought it up and pushed it into my mouth, took the hand I'd cleaned and smeared it again with her own musky gravy.

"Swallow it," she kept saying. "Swallow it all, suck my fingers, lick my palm." Her hips ground into me. She smeared it on my face until I closed my eyes under the sticky, strong-smelling mixture of her juice and mine. With my eyes closed, I licked and sucked until I was drunk on it, gasping until my lungs hurt with my hands digging into the muscles of her back. I was moaning and whining, shaking like a newborn puppy trying to get to its mama's tit.

Jay lifted a little off me. I opened stinging eyes to see her face, her intent and startling expression. I held my breath, waiting. I felt it before I understood it, and when I did understand I went on lying still under her, barely breathing. It burned me, ran all over my belly and legs. She put both hands down, brought them up, poured bitter yellow piss into my eyes, my ears, my shuddering mouth.

"Swallow it," she said again, but I held it in my mouth, pushed up against her and clawed her back with my nails. She whistled between her teeth. My hips jerked and rocked against her, making a wet sucking sound. I pushed my face to hers, my lips to hers, and forced my tongue into her mouth. I gripped her hard and rolled her over, my tongue sliding across her teeth, the taste of all her juices between us. I bit her lips and shoved her legs apart with my knee.

"Taste it," I hissed at her. "Swallow it." I ran my hands over her body. My skin burned. She licked my face, growling deep in her throat. I pushed both hands between her legs, my fingertips opened her and my thumbs caught her clit under the soft sheath of its hood.

"Go on, go on," I insisted. Tears were running down her face. I licked them. Her mouth was at my ear, her tongue trailing through the sweat at my hairline. When she came her teeth clamped down on my earlobe. I pulled but could not free myself. She was a thousand miles away, rocking back and forth on my hand, the stink of her all over us both. When her teeth freed my ear, I slumped. It felt as if I had come with her. My thighs shook and my teeth ached. She was mumbling with her eyes closed.

"Gonna bathe you," she whispered, "put you in a tub of hot lemonade. Drink it off you. Eat you for dinner." Her hands dug into my shoulders, rolled me onto my back. She drew a long, deep breath with her head back and then looked down at me, put one hand into my cunt, and brought it up slick with my juice.

"Swallow it," Jay said. "Swallow it."

The year we held the great Southeastern Feminist Conference, I was still following around behind Lee. She volunteered us to handle the food for the two hundred women that were expected. Lee wanted us to serve "healthy food"—her vegetarian spaghetti sauce, whole wheat pasta, and salad with cold fresh vegetables. Snacks would be granola, fresh fruit, and peanut butter on seven-grain bread. For breakfast she wanted me to cook grits in a twenty-quart pan, though she wasn't sure margarine wouldn't be healthier than butter, and maybe most people would just like granola anyway.

"They'll want donuts and coffee," I told her matter-of-factly. I had a vision of myself standing in front of a hundred angry lesbians crying out for coffee and white sugar. Lee soothed me with kisses and poppyseed cake made with gluten flour, assured me that it would be fun to run the kitchen with her.

The week before the conference, Lee went from church to campus borrowing enormous pots, colanders, and baking trays. Ten flat baking trays convinced her that the second dinner we had to cook could be tofu lasagna with skim milk mozzarella and lots of chopped carrots. I spent the week sitting in front of the pool table in Jay's apartment, peeling and slicing carrots, potatoes, onions, green and red peppers, leeks, tomatoes, and squash. The slices were dumped in ten-gallon garbage bags and stored in Jay's handy floor-model freezer. I put a tablecloth down on the pool table to protect the green felt and made mounds of vegetables over each pocket corner. Every mound cut down and transferred to a garbage bag was a victory. I was winning the war on vegetables until the committee Lee had scared up delivered another load.

I drank coffee and chopped carrots, ate a chicken pot pie and peeled potatoes, drank iced tea and sliced peppers. I peeled the onions but didn't slice them, dropped them into a big vat of cold water to keep. I found a meat cleaver on the back porch and used it to chop the zucchini and squash, pretending I was doing karate and breaking boards.

"Bite-sized," Lee told me as she ran through, "it should all be bite-sized." I wanted to bite her. I drank cold coffee and dropped tomatoes one at a time into boiling water to loosen their skins. There were supposed to be other women helping me, but only one showed up, and she went home after she got a rash from the tomatoes. I got out a beer, put the radio on loud, switching it back and forth from rock-and-roll to the country-and-western station and sang along as I chopped.

I kept working. The only food left in the apartment was vegetables. I wanted to have a pizza delivered but had no money. When I got hungry, I ate carrots on white bread with mayonnaise, slices of tomatoes between slices of raw squash, and leeks I dipped in a jar of low-sodium peanut butter. I threw up three times but kept working. Four hours before the first women were to arrive I took the last bushel basket of carrots out in the backyard and hid it under a tarp with the lawn mower. I laughed to myself as I did, swaying on rubbery legs. Lee drove up in a borrowed pickup truck with two women who'd come in from Atlanta and volunteered to help. One of them kept talking about the no-mucus diet as she loaded the truck. I went in the bathroom, threw up again, and then just sat on the tailgate in the sun while they finished up.

"You getting lazy, girl?" Lee teased me. "Better rev it up, we got cooking to do." I wiped my mouth and imagined burying her under a truckload of carrots. I felt like I had been drinking whiskey, but my stomach was empty and flat. The blacktop on the way out to the Girl Scout camp seemed to ripple and sway in the sunlight. Lee kept talking about the camp kitchen, the big black gas stove and the walk-in freezer.

"This is going to be fun." I didn't think so. The onions still had to be sliced. I got hysterical when someone picked up my knife. Lee was giggling with a woman I'd never seen before, the two of them talking about macrobiotic cooking while rinsing brown noodles. I got the meat cleaver and started chopping onions in big raw chunks. "Bite-sized," Lee called to me, in a cheerful voice.

"You want 'em bite-sized, you cut 'em," I told her, and went on chopping furiously.

It was late when we finally cleaned up. I hadn't been able to eat anything. The smell of the sauce had made me dizzy, and the scum that rinsed off the noodles looked iridescent and dangerous. My stomach curled up into a knot inside me, and I glowered at the women who came in and wanted hot water for tea. There were women sitting on the steps out on the deck, women around a campfire over near the water pump, naked women swimming out to the raft in the lake, and skinny, muscled women dancing continuously in the rec room. Lee had gone off with her new friend, the macrobiotic cook. I found a loaf of Wonderbread someone had left on the snack table, pulled out a slice and ate it in tiny bites.

"Want some?" It was one of the women from Atlanta. She held out a brown bag from which a bottle top protruded.

"It would make me sick."

"Naw," she grinned. "It's just a Yoo-hoo. I got a stash of them in a cooler. Got a bad stomach myself. Only thing it likes is chocolate soda and barbecue."

"Barbecue," I sighed. My mouth flooded with saliva. "I haven't made barbecue in years."

"You make beef ribs?" She sipped at her Yoo-hoo and sat down beside me.

"I have, but if you got the time to do slow pit cooking, pork's better." My stomach suddenly growled loudly, a grating, angry noise in the night.

"Girl," she laughed. "You still hungry?"

"Well, to tell you the truth, I couldn't eat any of that stuff." I was embarrassed.

My new friend giggled. "Neither did I. I had peanuts and Yoo-hoo for dinner myself." I laughed with her. "My name's Marty. You come up to Atlanta sometime, and we'll drive over to Marietta and get some of the best barbecue they make in the world."

"The best barbecue in the world?"

"Bar none." She handed me the bottle of Yoo-hoo.

"Can't be." I sipped a little. It was sweet and almost warm.

"You don't trust my judgment?" Someone opened the porch door, and I saw in the light that her face was relaxed, her blue eyes twinkling.

"I trust you. You didn't eat any of those damn noodles, did you? You're trustworthy, but you can't have the best barbecue in the world up near Atlanta, 'cause the best barbecue in the world is just a couple of miles down the Perry Highway."

"You say!"

"I do!"

We both laughed, and she slid her hip over close to mine. I shivered, and she put her arm around me. We talked, and I told her my name. It turned out we knew some of the same people. She had even been involved with a woman I hadn't seen since college. I was so tired I leaned my head on her shoulder. Marty rubbed my neck and told me a series of terribly dirty jokes until I started shaking more from giggling.

"Got to get you to bed," she started to pull me up. I took hold of her belt, leaned over, and kissed her. She kissed me. We sat back down and just kissed for a while. Her mouth was soft and tasted of sweet, watery chocolate.

"Uh huh," she said a few times, "uh huh."

"Uh huh," I giggled back.

"Oh yes, think we gonna have to check out this barbecue." Marty's hands were as soft as her mouth, and they slipped under the waistband of my jeans and hugged my belly. "You weren't fixed on having tofu lasagna tomorrow, were you?"

"Gonna break my heart to miss it, I can tell you." It was hard to talk with my lips pressed to hers. She licked my lips, the sides of my mouth, my cheek, my eyelids, and then put her lips up close to my ears.

"Oh, but think . . ." Her hands didn't stop moving, and I had to push myself back from her to keep from wetting my pants. ". . . Think about tomorrow afternoon when we come back from our little road trip hauling in all that barbecue, coleslaw, and hush puppies. We gonna make so many friends around here." She paused. "They do make hush puppies at this place, don't they?"

"Of course. If we get there early enough, we might even pick up some blackberry cobbler at this truck stop I know." My stomach rumbled again loudly.

"I don't think you been eating right," Marty giggled. "Gonna have to feed you some healthy food, girl, some *healthy* food."

Jay does karate, does it religiously, going to class four days in a week and working out at the gym every other day. Her muscles are hard and long. She is so tall people are always making jokes about "the weather up there." I call her "Shorty" or "Tall" to tease her, and "Sugar Hips" when I want to make her mad. Her hips are wide and full, though her legs are long and stringy.

"Lucky I got big feet," she jokes sometimes, "or I'd fall over every time I stopped to stand still."

Jay is always hungry, always. She keeps a bag of nuts in her backpack, dried fruit sealed in cellophane in a bowl on her dresser, snackpacks of crackers and cheese in her locker at the gym. When we go out to the women's bar, she drinks one beer in three hours but eats half a dozen packages of smoked almonds. Her last girlfriend was Italian. She used to serve Jay big batches of pasta with homemade sausage marinara.

"I need carbohydrates," Jay insists, eating slices of potato bread smeared with sweet butter. I cook grits for her, with melted butter and cheese, fry slabs of cured ham I get from a butcher who swears it has no nitrates. She won't eat eggs, won't eat shrimp or oysters, but she loves catfish pan-fried in a batter of cornmeal and finely chopped onions. Coffee makes her irritable. Chocolate makes her horny. When my period is coming and I get that flushed heat feeling in my insides, I bake her Toll House cookies, serve them with a cup of coffee, and blush. She looks at me over the rim of the cup, sips slowly, and eats her cookies with one hand, the other hooked in her jeans by her thumb. A muscle jumps in her cheek, and her eyes are full of tiny lights.

"You hungry, honey?" she purrs. She stretches like a big cat, puts her bare foot up, and uses her toes to lift my blouse. "You want something sweet?" Her toes are cold. I shiver and keep my gaze on her eyes. She leans forward and cups her hands around my face. "What you hungry for, girl, huh? You tell me. You tell mama exactly what you want."

Her name was Victoria, and she lived alone. She cut her hair into a soft cloud of curls and wore white blouses with buttoned-down collars. I saw her all the time at the bookstore, climbing out of her baby blue VW with a big leather book bag and a cane in her left hand. There were pictures up on the wall at the back of the store. Every one of them showed her sitting on or standing by a horse, the reins loose in her hand and her eyes focused far off. The riding hat hid her curls. The jacket pushed her breasts down but emphasized her hips. She had a ribbon pinned to the coat. A little card beneath the pictures identified her as the steeplechase champion of the southern division. In one picture she was jumping. Her hat was gone, her hair blown back, and the horse's legs stretched high above the ground. Her teeth shone white and perfect, and she looked as fierce as a bobcat going for prey. Looking at the pictures made me hurt. She came in once while I was standing in front of them and gave me a quick, wry grin.

"You ride?" Her cane made a hollow thumping sound on the floor. I didn't look at it.

"For fun, once or twice with a girlfriend." Her eyes were enormous and as black as her hair. Her face looked thinner than it had in the pictures, her neck longer. She grimaced and leaned on the cane. Under her tan she looked pale. She shrugged.

"I miss it myself." She said it in a matter-of-fact tone, but her eyes glittered. I looked up at the pictures again.

"I'll bet," I blushed, and looked back at her uncomfortably.

"Odds are I'll ride again." Her jeans bulged around the knee brace. "But not jump, and I did love jumping. Always felt like I was at war with the ground, allied with the sky, trying to stay up in the air." She grinned wide, and a faint white scar showed at the corner of her mouth.

"Where you from?" I could feel the heat in my face but ignored it.

"Virginia." Her eyes focused on my jacket, the backpack hanging from my arm, and down to where I had my left hip pushed out, my weight on my right food. "Haven't been there for a while, though." She looked away, looked tired and sad. What I wanted in that moment I will never be able to explain—to feed her or make love to her or just lighten the shadows under her eyes—all that, all that and more.

"You ever eat any red velvet cake?" I licked my lips and shifted my weight so that I wasn't leaning to the side. I looked into her eyes.

"Red velvet cakes?" Her eyes were friendly, soft, black as the deepest part of the night.

"It's a dessert my sister and I used to bake, unhealthy as sin and twice as delicious. Made up with chocolate, buttermilk, vinegar, and baking soda, and a little bottle of that poisonous red dye number two. Tastes like nothing you've ever had."

"You got to put the dye in it?"

"Uh huh," I nodded, "wouldn't be right without it."

"Must look deadly."

"But tastes good. It's about time I baked one. You come to dinner at my place, tell me about riding, and I'll cook you up one."

She shifted, leaned back, and half-sat on a table full of magazines. She looked me up and down again, her grin coming and going with her glance.

"What else would you cook?"

"Fried okra maybe, fried crisp, breaded with cornmeal. Those big beefsteak tomatoes are at their peak right now. Could just serve them in slices with pepper, but I've seen some green ones, too, and those I could fry in flour with the okra. Have to have white corn, of course, this time of the year. Pinto beans would be too heavy, but snap beans would be nice. A little milk gravy to go with it all. You like fried chicken?"

"Where you from?"

"South Carolina, a long time ago."

"You mama teach you to cook?"

"My mama and my aunts." I put my thumbs in my belt and tried to look sure of myself. Would she like biscuits or cornbread, pork or beef or chicken?

"I'm kind of a vegetarian." She sighed when she said it, and her eyes looked sad.

"Eat fish?" I was thinking quickly. She nodded. I smiled wide.

"Ever eat any crawfish pan-fried in salt and Louisiana hot sauce?"

"You got to boil them first." Her face was shining and she was bouncing her cane on the hardwood floor.

"Oh yeah, 'course, with the right spices."

"Sweet Bleeding Jesus," her face was flushed. She licked her lips. "I haven't eaten anything like that in, oh, so long."

"Oh." My thighs felt hot, rubbing on the seams of my jeans. She was beautiful, Victoria in her black cloud of curls. "Oh, girl," I whispered. I leaned toward her. I put my hand on her wrist above the cane, squeezed.

"Let me feed you," I told her. "Girl . . . girl, you should just let me feed you what you really need."

I've been dreaming lately that I throw a dinner party, inviting all the women in my life. They come in with their own dishes. Marty brings barbecue carried all the way from Marietta. Jay drags in a whole side of beef and gets a bunch of swaggering whiskey-sipping butch types to help her dig a hole in the backyard. They show off for each other, breaking up stones to line the firepit. Lee watches them from the porch, giggling at me and punching down a great mound of dough for the oatmeal wheat bread she'd promised to bake. Women whose names I can't remember bring in bowls of pasta salad, smoked salmon, and jello with tangerine slices. Everybody is feeding each other, exclaiming over recipes and gravies, introducing themselves and telling stories about great meals they've eaten. My mama is in the kitchen salting a vat of greens. Two of my aunts are arguing over whether to make little baking powder biscuits or big buttermilk hogsheads. Another steps around them to slide an iron skillet full of cornbread in the oven. Pinto beans with onions are bubbling on the stove. Children run through sucking fatback rinds. My uncles are on the porch telling stories and knocking glass bottles together when they laugh.

I walk back and forth from the porch to the kitchen, being hugged and kissed and stroked by everyone I pass. For the first time in my life I am not hungry, but everybody insists I have a little taste. I burp like a baby on her mama's shoulder. My stomach is full, relaxed, happy, and the taste of pan gravy is in my mouth. I can't stop grinning. The dream goes on and on, and through it all I hug myself and smile.

❙❘ ❙❘ ❙❘

*A Lesbian Appetite* / **295**

# Kitchens from *Getting Home Alive*

## Aurora Levins Morales

I went into the kitchen just now to stir the black beans and rice, the shiny black beans floating over the smooth brown grains of rice and the zucchini turning black, too, in the ink of the beans. Mine is a California kitchen, full of fresh vegetables and whole grains, bottled spring water and yoghurt in plastic pints, but when I lift the lid from that big black pot, my kitchen fills with the hands of women who came before me, washing rice, washing beans, picking through them so deftly, so swiftly, that I could never see what the defects were in the beans they threw quickly over one shoulder out the window. Some instinct of the finger-tips after years of sorting to feel the rottenness of the bean with a worm in it or a chewed-out side. Standing here, I see the smooth red and brown and white and speckled beans sliding through their fingers into bowls of water, the gentle clicking rush of them being poured into the pot, hear the hiss of escaping steam, smell the bean scum floating on the surface under the lid. I see grains of rice settling in a basin on the counter, turning the water milky with rice polish and the talc they use to make the grains so smooth; fingers dipping, swimming through the murky white water, feeling for the grain with the blackened tip, the brown stain.

From the corner of my eye, I see the knife blade flashing, re-ducing mounds of onions, garlic, cilantro, and green peppers into *sofrito* to be fried up and stored, and the best of all is the pound and circular grind of the *pilón: pound, pound, thump, grind, pound, pound, thump, grind. Pound, pound* (the garlic and oregano mashed together), *THUMP!* (the mortar lifted and slammed down to loosen the crushed herbs and spices from the wooden bowl), *grind* (the slow rotation of the pestle smashing the oozing mash around and around, blending the juices, the green stain of cilantro and oregano, the sticky yellowing garlic, the grit of black pepper).

> It's the dance of the cocinera: to step outside
> fetch the bucket of water, turn,
> all muscular grace and striving,
> pour the water, light dancing in the pot,
> and set the pail down on the blackened wood.
> The blue flame glitters in its dark corner,
> and coffee steams in the small white pan.
> Gnarled fingers, mondando ajo,
> picando cebolla, cortando pan,
> colando café,
> stirring the rice with a big long spoon
> filling ten bellies
> out of one soot-black pot.

It's a magic, a power, a ritual of love and work that rises up in my kitchen, thousands of miles from those women in cotton dresses who twenty years ago taught the rules of its observance to me, the apprentice, the novice, the girl-child: "Don't go out without wrapping your head, child, you've been roasting coffee, *y te va' a pa'mar!*" "This much coffee in the *colador*, girl, or you'll be serving brown water." "Dip the basin in the river, so, to leave the mud behind." "Always peel the green bananas under cold water, *mijita*, or you'll cut your fingers and get *mancha* on yourself and the stain never comes out: that black sap stain of *guineo verde* and *plátano*, the stain that marks you forever."

So I peel my bananas under running water from the faucet, but the stain won't come out, and the subtle earthy green smell of that sap follows me, down from the mountains, into the cities, to places where banana groves are like a green dream, unimaginable by daylight: Chicago, New Hampshire, Oakland. So I travel miles on the bus to the immigrant markets of other people, coming home laden with bundles, and even, now and then, on the plastic frilled tables of the supermarket, I find a small curved green bunch to rush home, quick, before it ripens, to peel and boil, bathing in the scent of its cooking, bringing the river to flow through my own kitchen now, the river of my place on earth, the green and musty river of my grandmothers, dripping, trickling, tumbling down from the mountain kitchens of my people.

❙❙ ❙❙ ❙❙

# Sacred Food

## Anais Salibian

There are places on earth that are not subtle, where creation has thundered forth and left behind its image to shape your psyche. For millennia, my people have lived in the shadow of such a place—Mount Ararat. Picture a high, flat plateau out of which a twin-peaked volcanic mountain suddenly rises for two miles into the sky.

In its shadow two thousand years ago, a woman prepared for the New Year, which was then celebrated in the spring, by gathering the fruits of the four seasons: wheat, which she boiled in plenty of water; apricots and raisins, which she added toward the end of the long hours of preparation; and finally almonds or pomegranates, with which she made a mandala over the surface of her sweet, thick pudding. This she took, along with the other women who had all made the same *anoushabour*, to the great communal feast. She taught her daughter how to make the pudding, who taught her daughter, who taught hers, and so on down the ages until my mother taught me.

This image of a direct, abiding lineage experienced through food obsesses me. *Anoushabour* is not the only Armenian food that makes me feel something ancient in my gestures when I make or eat it, in the tastes and textures on my tongue. When I consider wrapping grape leaves around various fillings, scooping food up in flatbread, or drying everything from apricots to yoghurt under the sun, I revert. I'm back in a time before sitting in a chair at a table, before holding a fork, before ovens in each woman's kitchen. My body wants to squat and reach, along with the rest of my clan. And I remember that Yerevan, the capital of Armenia, was a settled site in 3500 B.C.E.

I sense a connection to something ancient, something which goes even beyond culture and history. When I open a package of my mother's braided *choeregs* and bite into an untranslatable pastry, I fall into the grip of something primordial. I am eating my mother. It's the closest I'll get to remembering breast feeding, understanding the Christian eucharist, or experiencing the world-view of Paleolithic cave-painters, who lived in the fertile and nourishing body of the Great Mother.

Experiencing food this way puts me in touch with something sacred, and with what it means to be a woman. These two turn out to be the same thing. For I feel and see how women moved in their bodies when they knew they were world creators, culture creators, and feeders of their people. The past is not quite vanished when I eat *anoushabour*, and so it returns to me and brings this power: to remember who we are as women. Once, when women looked at Ararat, we saw a feminine creative force and named the mountain after Her. (This is true of other magnificent mountains running with the milk of glacier-fed streams; Mt. Everest was originally "Goddess Mother of the Universe," Annapurna translates as "Great Breast Full of Nourishment.") Once, women knew themselves to be the center around which they organized their culture.

And so I think of how these women walked, with an easy grace and inherent pride. I think of their awareness of the connections between the cycles of their bodies and those of the earth and sky, and how they created calendars, mathematics, astronomy out of these. I think of their roles as food gatherers, and how they invented container-making, horticulture, pottery, writing, and medicine out of these. Once women were priestesses, shamans, midwives, yes, but also lawmakers, artists, ship captains, merchants, and craftsmakers of every sort. No one had ever conceived of the idea that women were inferior in any way, for the evidence was around them that women were the creators and sustainers of life and culture.

One Armenian friend told me that in her family, they sprinkle pomegranate seeds on *anoushabour*. Since pomegranates have a long history as symbols of female sexuality and fertility, I think this is a perfect touch. The seeds are like drops of menstrual blood, which was once the most sacred of all substances, for its life-giving abilities. In more than one story, pomegranate seeds are what a soul eats in the underworld to bring about rebirth.

*Anoushabour* becomes a symbol of all this for me. When I eat it, I ingest the aura of free women. Their bodies become mine, and I want to share the bounty. I'm obsessed with making *anoushabour*. This year, I made it for holiday potlucks, solstice rituals, and Christmas gifts to friends. I've experimented with barley (reduce water and/or increase cooking time; perhaps use a little cornstarch to thicken), red spring wheat (don't bother), cardamom and pistachio nuts (tastes Indian). I come up with new designs with the almonds: mandalas, spirals, flowers. I tell my women's group it's Goddess food.

I give you *anoushabour*. Take and eat.

○: ○: ○:

## Anoushabour
### (Armenian Christmas Pudding)

3 quarts (12 cups) water
1 cup white winter wheat berries
1½ cups (packed) chopped dried apricots
1½ cups (packed) chopped golden raisins
2 tablespoons rosewater

cinnamon
blanched almonds (approximately 1 cup) for garnish
pomegranate seeds (optional)

1. Bring wheat to a boil in water and set aside to soak overnight. Next day, bring it to a boil again, lower heat, and simmer for 1½ hours.

2. Add apricots and raisins and cook another half hour, stirring occasionally to make sure it doesn't stick. The pudding should be thickening by now; it's done when it's not runny anymore.

3. Add the rosewater, stir, and pour into serving dish or bowl. Sprinkle with cinnamon and garnish with almonds in a beautiful pattern. You may also sprinkle pomegranate seeds over the pudding. Serves 15 to 20.

Variations: For a wheat-free pudding, reduce water to 9 cups and use 1 cup barley instead of wheat. If you can't find rosewater (in Armenian, Middle Eastern, or Indian groceries or even drug stores), or if you want a different and wonderfully refreshing taste, use grated rind of 1 lemon and 1 orange for flavoring. If you like your desserts *really* sweet, add sugar to taste. (The recipe in one cookbook suggests 2 cups, but I find no sugar necessary at all. Unsulphured apricots tend to be sweeter than packaged apricots.)

# Corn-Grinding Song

*from* The Half-Breed Chronicles and Other Poems

## Wendy Rose

1.
My heart is asleep
in the peace of pollen,
        in a wide purity,
        in the yellow squash.
My hands dream
of gathering honey
        from heavy-breasted women
        going into the mountain
        with Hoonaw* dreams.
My hips, butterfly-lifted,
crowd with children,
        dip and flow with the sun,
        roll from the granite like salt.
My lips bleed,
continue to sing,
beat the hand drum quick
        relax and flex within the earth.
        Be a bridge, be a path, be tomorrow.

2.
Sprouts
rise
pollinate
blow away
lodge
on badger
drop
from birds

*Hoonaw: Bear (Hopi).

change
the sky
sing us
to completion
burrow
keep
the seeds
within.

䷗ ䷗ ䷗

# Credits

Grateful acknowledgment is made for permission to reprint the following:

"A Lesbian Appetite" from *Trash: Stories by Dorothy Allison*, by Dorothy Allison (Ithaca: Firebrand Books), copyright 1988 by Dorothy Allison, reprinted by permission of Firebrand Books.

"New Directions" from *Wouldn't Take Nothing for My Journey Now*, by Maya Angelou (New York: Random House, Inc.), copyright 1993 by Maya Angelou, reprinted by permission of Random House, Inc.

"Gravy" by Sally Bellerose, previously appearing in *Cachet* (August 1991), edited by Beth Maurer and in *Women's Glibber*, edited by Roz Warren (Trumansburg: The Crossing Press), copyright 1992 by Sally Bellerose, reprinted by permission of the author.

"A Kitchen of One's Own" by Doris Friedensohn, originally appearing in *13th Moon: A Feminist Literary Magazine* 12, no. 1 (1983–84), copyright 1983–84 by Doris Friedensohn, reprinted by permission of the author.

"Family Liked 1956" by Sharon L. Jansen, originally appearing in *Frontiers* 13, no. 2 (1992), copyright 1992 by Sharon L. Jansen, reprinted by permission of the author.

"Kitchens" from *Getting Home Alive*, by Aurora Levins Morales and Rosario Morales (Ithaca: Firebrand Books), copyright 1986 by Aurora Levins Morales and Rosario Morales, reprinted by permission of Firebrand Books.

# Contributors

Writer and feminist activist **Dorothy Allison** is author of the best-selling *Bastard Out of Carolina* (1992), a finalist for the National Book Award; *Trash* (1988), the collection of short stories and winner of two Lambda Literary Awards; and *Skin: Talking about Sex, Class, and Literature* (1994). The first in her family to graduate from high school, she earned a bachelor's degree from Florida Presbyterian College and a master's degree from New York's New School of Social Research. She lives in California.

**Maya Angelou's** autobiographical novel *I Know Why the Caged Bird Sings* (1969) is the first in a series of five books which chronicle her life within its historical and social context. Angelou has also published many books of poetry including *Just Give Me a Cool Drink of Water 'fore I Diiie* (1971) which was nominated for a Pulitzer Prize. Also writing for television beginning in the 1960s, Angelou's credits include the ten-part series for PBS, *Black, Blues, Blacks* and an adaption of *Caged Bird*. Angelou is also an actress, nominated for a Tony Award for best supporting actress for her role in *Roots*.

**Arlene Voski Avakian** is an associate professor of women's studies at the University of Massachusetts/Amherst. Her autobiography, *Lion Woman's Legacy: An Armenian American Memoir*, was published in 1992. She has also coedited *African American Women and the Vote, 1837–1965* (forthcoming 1997).

**Martha A. Ayres** was born in 1940 in West Virginia. In 1969 she immigrated to western Massachusetts where she established a private practice with a specialty in feminist therapy and Jungian dream analysis. She has led groups in dream work both in the United States and in Northern Ireland. She also met her soul mate and helped raise two wonderful children who are now wonderful adults. She has one published poem and many unpublished poems and stories in a manila folder.

**Caroline Babayan** was born in Tehran in 1958 into an eccentric Armenian family. She studied in England and now lives in Norway with her fourteen-year-old son. She works as a filmmaker anywhere she can raise finances. Some of the films she has been involved in as writer or director are: *A Life Before Death, South Africa — My Home, Bohemian Rhapsody, Condemn Condome Condone, Old Habits Die Hard*.

**Helen Barolini** was born as raised in Syracuse, New York. She earned her M.A. from Columbia. She has worked as a translator, librarian, oral historian, and magazine editor, and taught for Trinity College's, Westchester Community College's, and Pace University's programs in Italy. Her first book-length work was the novel *Umbertina* (1979), followed by *The Dream Book: An Anthology of Writings by Italian American Women* which received an American Book Award in 1986. Barolini is the author of four other books of fiction and nonfiction and over fifty published short stories and essays.

**Sally Bellerose** writes fiction and poetry. Her chapbook of poetry, *Sex Crimes*, was published in 1995. She has been published in numerous anthologies and small press publications and is a 1995 recipient of a National Endowment for the Arts Creative Writer's Fellowship Grant.

**Trudy Condio** is a single parent of one child and was on welfare for seven years. After being out of school for fifteen years, she enrolled in a degree program at the University of Massachusetts/Boston where she marched, demonstrated, spoke, and wrote about the challenges she faced as a woman on welfare. She is currently a law student and intends to use her degree to represent those who need it most—women on welfare.

**Karen Coody Cooper** is a Cherokee from Oklahoma. Her favorite childhood times were spent on her grandparents' farm where much time was spent harvesting nature's gifts of grapes, nuts, pokeweed, and sand plums (quarter-sized, yellow-pink fruit from short, wild trees). She manages the American Indian Museum Studies program at the Smithsonian Institution and lives in Maryland. Besides taking pleasure in writing poetry, she also enjoys an old craft called fingerweaving.

**EL. Cortés** has been writing since she was seven years old, but has only been committing the writing to paper within the last five years. She was born to Puerto Rican parents and raised in Brooklyn. She works with the Division of Bilingual Education of the New York City Board of Education. Currently, EL. Cortés is at work on a collection of short stories about a Puerto Rican girl growing up in Williamsburg, Brooklyn, during the 1950s, tentatively titled, "A Boricua Grows in Brooklyn."

**Clare Coss** is a playwright, psychotherapist, and activist who lives and works in New York City. Her plays include *The Blessing* (American Place Theatre); *Growing Up Gothic* (Theatre for the New City and Interart Theatre); and *Lillian Wald: At Home on Henry Street* (New Federal Theatre), which was included in her book, *Lillian Wald: Progressive Activist*. She edited with an introduction *The Arc of Love: An Anthology of Lesbian Love Poems* (1996).

**Julie Dash** is a filmmaker whose critically acclaimed work *Daughters of the Dust* is regarded as the first feature-length film by an African American woman. An early film, *Four Women*, won the Golden Medal for Women in Film at the Miami International Film Festival in 1977. In the same year she won the Director's Guild Award for *Diary of an African Nun*, and in 1983 her film *Illusions* was nominated for a Cable ACE Award in art direction. She is currently working on a series of films on Black women.

**Jyl Lynn Felman** is the author of *Hot Chicken Wings* (1992), a Lambda Literary Award Finalist. Her work has been widely anthologized and appears in a wide variety of journals including, *Tikkun*, *The National Women's Studies Journal*, *Lambda Book Report*, *Lilith*, *Bridges*, *Sojourner*, and *The Forward*. Ms. Felman is an attorney who lectures in the United States and England on racism, homophobia, and anti-Semitism. She also has an M.F.A. and teaches in the women's studies program at Brandies University.

**Doris Friedensohn** is a professor of women's studies and American studies at Jersey City State College. She has written and lectured widely on diversity in America, new approaches to teaching about immigration, women's oral and photo history, and eating in contemporary America. In recent years, as a consultant for USIA in Turkey, Mozambique, the Czech Republic, Nepal, and Japan, she has stolen time from curriculum development projects to fatten her repertoire of ethnic and transnational food anecdotes; she is incorporating these into a collection of autobiographical essays on eating and everyday life.

**Barbara Haber** is the curator of books at Radcliffe's Schlesinger Library where she oversees the development of the book collection. Cookbooks have always been part of the collection, for they are recognized as legitimate documents that reveal the daily lives of women.

Haber is the author of *Women in America: A Guide to Books* and many articles on women's history. Her recent articles and speeches focus on the social history of food, especially as it relates to the lives of women and their families. As both a committed feminist and a devoted cook, she has never experienced conflict between these two passions, but instead sees them as the ideal blending of her public and private lives.

**Ruth Hubbard** is a professor *emerita* of biology at Harvard University. She was the first woman to hold a tenured professorship in her department. She was a founding member of the Council for Responsible Genetics and has written and lectured extensively on scientific representations of women and on women and health, focusing most recently on the impact of reproductive and genetic technologies on women and society. She is the author of many books, including: *The Politics of Women's Biology* (1990), *Profitable Promises: Essays on Women, Science, and Health* (1995), and with her son Elijah Wald, *Exploding the Gene Myth* (1993).

**Jennifer Iré** was born in Trinidad and Tobago, West Indies, and immigrated to the United States eighteen years ago. She currently lives in Massachusetts where she is completing a Ph.D. in counseling. Her interest in cooking is matched by her love of growing food crops.

**Sharon L. Jansen** is a professor of English at Pacific Lutheran University. Her previous work includes articles published in *The Shakespeare Quarterly*, *The Sixteenth-Century Journal*, and *English Literary Renaissance*, among others, as well as three books, *Dangerous Talk and Strange Behavior: Women and Popular Resistance to the Reforms of Henry VIII* (forthcoming), *Protest and Prophecy under Henry VIII* (1991), and with Kathleen Jordan *The Welles Anthology (Ms. Rawlinson C.813): A Critical Edition* (1991). As this essay suggests, she loves to cook. She lives in Steilacoom, Washington.

**Ketu H. Katrak,** born in Bombay, India, is the director of Asian American studies and professor of English and comparative literature at the University of California, Irvine. Katrak specializes in Asian American and postcolonial literatures in English from Africa, India, and the Caribbean, Third World women writers, and feminist theory. She is the author of *Wole Soyinka and Modern Tragedy: A Study in Dramatic Theory and Practice* (1986), and coeditor of *Antifeminism in the Academy* (1996) and "Desh-Videsh: South Asian Expatriate Writing and Art," a special issue of the *Massachusetts Review* (1988/89). Her essays on Third World literature and culture have appeared in a wide variety of publications. Katrak is also a published poet.

**E. Barrie Kavasch** is an ethnobotanist, herbalist, and food historian who teaches and writes extensively about Native Americans. Her books include *Native Harvests: Recipes and Botanicals of the American Indians* (1979) and *Enduring Harvests: Native American Foods and Festivals for Every Season* (1995), and she is editor of the award-winning anthology *Earthmaker's Lodge: Native American Folklore, Activities, and Foods* (1994). Barrie is an expert on wild mushrooms, healing plants, and natural remedies and healing—continuing generations of these interests in her heritage. Her sense of family and foods are abiding passions.

**Shirley Geok-lin Lim**, an award-winning short-story writer and editor, received the Commonwealth Poetry Prize for her first book of poems, *Crossing the Peninsula*. Her memoir *Among the White Moon Faces: An Asian American Memoir of Homelands*, appeared in 1996. Her most recent critical study is *Writing South/East Asian in English* (1994). She is a professor of English and women's studies at the University of California, Santa Barbara.

**Paula Martinac** is a writer, editor, and activist. Her published novels include *Home Movies* (1993) and *Out of Time* (1990), winner of the Lambda Literary Award for best lesbian fiction. She is also author of *k.d. lang* (1996), a young adult biography, and is currently working on a popular history book called "The Queerest Places: A Guide to Gay and Lesbian Historic Sites and Landmarks in the United States" (1997). Since writing "Fast, Free Delivery," she quit her day job to become a full-time writer and now eats dinner at home much more often.

**Elizabeth Kamarck Minnich** is a professor of philosophy and women's studies at the graduate school of the Union Institute. She has also held the Hartley Burr Alexander Chair at Scripps College and served as an administrator and faculty member at Barnard, Sarah Lawrence, Hollins, and the New School. Minnich also studied classical Indian dance in India on a Fulbright. Her books include *Transforming Knowledge* (1990) and *Reconstructing the Academy: Women's Education and Women's Studies* (1988), which she coedited. In North Carolina, where she lives with her life partner, she writes columns for the "Charlotte Observer" and has worked with grassroots leadership on issues of community organizing theory and practice.

A recipient of the National Endowment for the Arts Fellowship, a

Kellogg National Fellowship, and three Southwest Book Awards, **Pat Mora** is the author of numerous books, including the family memoir *House of Houses* (1997), the poetry collection *Agua Santa: Holy Water* (1995), and the essay collection *Nepantla: Essays from the Land in the Middle* (1993). Pat is also a well-known author of children's books, the most recent of which is *Confetti: Poems for Children* (1996). The mother of three children and a woman who enjoys kitchens and gardens, she's presently living in Santa Fe, writing new books.

**Aurora Levins Morales** was born in Indiera Baja, Puerto Rico, of Jewish and Puerto Rican parents, and grew up eating fried plantain and blintzes. She has recently completed a doctorate in women's studies and cultural activism and is at work on "Remedios," a prose poetry retelling of the history of Caribbean women. She lives in Berkeley, California.

Originally from Pakistan, **Tahira Naqvi** is now settled in the United States with her husband and three sons. She teaches English at Western Connecticut State University and is a translator of Ismat Chughtai, an Indian woman writer. Her translation of Chughtai's novel *Tehri Lakir* was published in 1995. Naqvi's own fiction has been published in a wide variety of journals. Her first collection, *Attar of Roses and Other Stories from Pakistan*, is forthcoming. "Song of My Mother" is dedicated to her mother.

**Joan Ormondroyd** has worked as a teacher and librarian most of her adult life, while raising four children and helping to put several husbands through graduate school. When her second marriage broke up she decided to put herself through graduate school. She completed her M.L.S. just as her oldest son finished high school. Joan retired six years ago from Cornell University where she was the women's studies bibliographer and the head reference librarian in the undergraduate library. Cooking and gardening are her favorite pastimes. Although she has been published extensively in her professional field, this story is her first "creative" endeavor.

**Marge Piercy** writes poetry, novels, and essays and has published more than twenty books including: *Dance the Eagle to Sleep* (1970), *Small Changes* (1974), *Gone to Soldiers* (1987), *Woman on the Edge of Time* (1983), *Mars and Her Children* (1992), and *The Longings of Women* (1994). She is also the recipient of the May Sarton Award, the Arthur C. Clarke Award, the Borenstone Mountain Poetry Award, the National Endowment for the Arts Award, and the Shaeffer-Eaton-PEN New England Award among many others.

**Letty Cottin Pogrebin** is a writer, activist, and nationally known lecturer with a special interest in women's and family issues, Jewish renewal, and Mideast peace. A founding editor of *Ms.* magazine, she is the author of eight books, most recently, *Getting Over Getting Older* (1996) and *Deborah, Golda and Me* (1992). Pogrebin also serves on the boards of many social change organizations. Among her honors and awards are a Poynter Fellowship in Journalism and an Emmy Award for her work on "Free to Be, You and Me."

**Margaret Randall** is a writer who cooks and a chef who loves to eat. Her most recent titles include *Sandino's Daughters Revisited: Feminism in Nicaragua* (1994) and *The Price You Pay: The Hidden Cost of Women's Relationship to Money* (1996). A new collection of poems, some which double as recipes and all having to do with food, will be out in 1997. "The Staff of Life" is from that book. Randall lives in New Mexico, but travels widely to read and lecture.

**Janet Dike Rood** has spent most of her adult life involved in the arts communities of Vermont, founding the Vermont Youth Orchestra and working as a development consultant and fund-raiser for many organizations. She developed her administrative skills working in the businesses she and her husband started while she was bringing up five children. She has spent more than a dozen years marketing and distributing a classic fifty-six-year-old church cookbook and is spearheading the making of another. When this latest project has been completed to her satisfaction, she will get back to the one she started five years ago for her children—the writing of her life story.

**Wendy Rose** has published eight books of poetry, and her work has been widely anthologized. She was nominated twice for the Pulitzer Prize in poetry. She is the coordinator and an instructor of American Indian studies at Fresno City College. Her tribal affiliations are Hopi and Mohawk.

**Leah Ryan** is an M.F.A. student at the Iowa Playwrights workshop. Her plays have won numerous prizes and have been produced in many cities including New York, Chicago, and London. In addition to being a tablewear sanitation engineer, Ms. Ryan has also worked as a short-order cook, nose-ring salesperson, angst-ridden telemarketer, and sandblaster. Her fiction and poetry have appeared in numerous publications. She writes a regular column for *Punk Planet* and edits her own 'zine, *Violation Fez*.

**Anais Salibian,** M.A., L.M.T., has a private practice in therapeutic bodywork in Rochester, New York. She also teaches writing at Nazareth College and at Writers and Books, a community literary organization. Her special interest is in how bodywork, writing, and expressive arts work together to nurture the emergence of the authentic self.

**Cheryl Savageau's** second book of poetry, *Dirt Road Home* (1995), was a finalist for the Paterson Prize and was nominated for a Pushcart Prize. She has received fellowships in poetry from the National Endowment for the Arts and the Massachusetts Artists Foundation. Her poems have been widely anthologized in books and literary journals. She is also the author of a children's book, *Muskrat Will Be Swimming*. She lives in Worcester, Massachusetts, with her husband where she teaches at Holy Cross College. She is also doing doctoral work at the University of Massachusetts/Amherst. She is of Abenaki and French Canadian heritage.

**Ester Rebeca Shapiro** is an associate professor of psychology at the University of Massachusetts/Boston and the director of health research at the Mauricio Gaston Institute for Latino Research, Public Policy, and Community Development. She is the author of *Grief as a Family Process: A Developmental Approach to Clinical Practice* (1994) and coeditor with Murray Meisels of *Tradition and Innovation in Psychoanalytic Education* (1990). An avid cook, she specializes in food which promotes creative transculturation of disasporic cuisines.

**Beheroze Shroff** is a documentary filmmaker who lives in India and the United States. Her films include *Sweet Jail: The Sikhs of Yuba City* and *Reaching for Half the Sky*. Most recently she codirected *A Life Before Death* with Caroline Babayan for Norwegian television. Shroff teaches Third World film at various institutions in the United States and is a published poet.

**Marie Smyth** was born in the early fifties into a rural Catholic family in the North of Ireland. She has worked in community development, psychotherapy, and university teaching. She is on the faculty of the University of Ulster and is currently completing a two-year full-time research project on segregation and sectarian division in Derry/Londonderry. Her forthcoming research project will examine the effects of the "troubles" on the population of Northern Ireland. Marie returns each summer to Massachusetts, where she teaches as summer faculty at Smith College. She is also a published poet.

Born in London, **Caroline Urvater** moved with her family to Amsterdam, but was forced to leave the city when the Nazis entered. Transported to England in the care of strangers, by means of a straw-lined cattle transport, she was reunited with her family and moved to the United States after the war. She has an M.A. in comparative literature and an unfinished Ph.D. in the same area. She currently directs a privately endowed scholarship program, based at the CUNY graduate school. She loves music, people, books, food, and politics, but not necessarily in that order. She writes poetry, short stories, and essays. She rarely finishes anything, except what is on her plate.

Described as "one of our foremost spiritual authors," **Gloria Wade-Gayles** has written two personal essay collections, *Rooted Against the Wind: Personal Essays* (1996) and *Pushed Back to Strength: A Black Woman's Journey Home* (1993); a critical essay collection, *No Crystal Stair: Race and Sex in Selected Black Women's Novels, 1946–1976* (1984) and is editor of *Father Songs: Testimonies by African-American Sons and Daughters* and *My Soul Is a Witness: African-American Women's Spirituality* (1995). A recipient of the Kellogg National Fellowship and a DuBois Fellowship, she is a professor of English and women's studies at Spelman College in Atlanta.